Advanced Praise

You are about to take a journey that will spark your heart and soul, and most likely leave you speechless. After reading 2200 nonfiction books and working behind the scenes in the personal development industry for twenty-five years for Tony Robbins, Ginny & Jean Brown's, This Sweet Life is far beyond a must read.

~Gary King, author of *The Happiness Formula*

A beautiful, heart-breaking book that exposes the dangerous side of the self-help industry. It tells the story of Kirby Brown who died after being deprived of water, food and sleep and then put in a sweat lodge by James Arthur Ray, a man who was not qualified to run a sweat lodge, ignored pleas for help once participants were inside the lodge and left the scene immediately afterwards. I was shocked to read that he is still working in the self-help industry. This book poses important questions about how the $10 billion industry should be regulated and paints a picture of how charismatic figures can manipulate innocent people. Thought provoking and rage-inducing in parts, it's also a tribute to Kirby, written with the love of a mother and sister.

~Marianne Power, author *Help Me!... One Woman's Quest to Find Out if Self-Help Really Can Change Her Life*

This Sweet Life: How We Lived After Kirby Died, is of extreme value to anyone recovering from a great loss. It is two books in one since it alternates between a parent's and a sibling's perspective of their experiences and recovery process after the tragic loss of a family member. It also describes how they molded their grief into something positive, forming the Seek Safely Foundation to aid the public with informa-

tion so as to avoid having this heartbreak happen to them, or their loved ones. Both Ginny and George Brown had extensive experience as counselors before their daughter was killed, and they let you in on how they applied that education and knowledge to helping their own family work through their grief. I strongly recommend this book.

~Connie Joy, author of *Tragedy in Sedona: My Life in James Arthur Ray's Inner Circle*

In describing what they went through with the death of Kirby, Ginny and Jean Brown have told a story that is heartbreaking-- but it's so much more. It's not just a description of a tragedy and its aftermath. It's also the story of a family, and the powerful, intensely personal, and intimate bonds that tie families together. James Arthur Ray wrote his own memoir of what happened in Sedona, and it reads like a marketing tool— which is exactly what he intended. Ginny and Jean's book is vastly different from James's account, not just in perspective, but in the depth of its authenticity. In the end, this is not a book about blame. It's a book about responsibility. Their story is raw, honest...and, like Kirby, hopeful.

~Dr. Glenn Doyle, psychologist, author *Wish I'd Known That*

While the Sedona sweat lodge deaths have received extensive media coverage over the years, *This Sweet Life* shows for the first time what the tragedy was like for family members of the victims. It offers a moving tribute to the radiant spirit of Kirby Brown as well as a chilling example of how a woman's admirable determination to better herself was fatefully exploited. There is a dark side to the quest for enlightenment that few books dare to explore but the curtain is finally pulled back here as the authors courageously chronicle how an unregulated self-improvement industry can have deadly consequences.

~ Annette McGivney, author *Pure Land: A True Story of Three Lives, Three Cultures,* and *The Search for Heaven on Earth*

This Sweet Life is a captivating account of seeking and finding truth amid grief and loss. Kirby Brown's death in a sweat lodge organized by self-help guru James Arthur Ray — and his subsequent conviction on three counts of manslaughter — made headlines, but this first-person narrative by Kirby Brown's mother and sister brings the events to life. It's a beautiful memorial to a life of seeking — and leaves us with the deeply important message of the SEEK Safely mission: If a program or advice is powerful enough to transform our lives for the better, it is powerful enough to harm us as well, so we must empower consumers and promote professional standards within this psychologically powerful, financially lucrative and legally unregulated self-help industry.

~Christine B. Whelan, Ph.D., Clinical Professor, University of Wisconsin - Madison

This Sweet Life speaks to three distinct audiences: grievers, seekers and self-help professionals. The Brown family shines a powerful light into the emotional abyss of grief, validating the fits of sadness and rage, powerlessness yet determination for others to understand their pain that accompanies inexplicable loss. Their unique story offers grievers a path forward, not to "get over" their loss but to learn how to live with it. By sharing her story, readers get to experience Kirby's presence and energy. We are inspired to live large as she did, with an open mind and heart to seek new ways to become the best-version-of-ourselves. Finally, This Sweet Life reminds self-help professionals of what a privilege it is to aid seekers in their journey and the responsibility to know our own limits. Every self-proclaimed self-help professional should make a SEEK-Safely promise...starting with James Ray.

~ Kathleen Brady, PCC, Career/Life Wellness Coach

Ginny and Jean Brown have crafted a detailed and deeply affecting chronicle of death at the hands of a movement that is often played for laughs but is seldom considered a source of real danger. In painstaking step-by-step fashion, they reconstruct the hopeful life of Ginny's daughter, Kirby, and the tragic ending of that life and two others amid the suffocating mind-control climate created by messianic New Age guru James Arthur Ray. Ray ultimately went to prison for negligent homicide. A must-read at a time when people are again made vulnerable by their desperate thirst for inspiration.

~Steve Salerno, author *Sham: How the Self-Help Movement Made America Helpless*

Ginny and Jean Brown have written an important book that allows us to better understand the inner world of seminar-selling gurus, who often offer what seems like a panacea. Ginny and Jean show us that there is a dark side of the self-help industry, which includes deceptive, manipulative, and ultimately destructive gurus, who have quite literally controlled people to death. This is at times a sad, but inspiring book about surviving tragedy and ultimately using such an experience to help others. We must be vigilant in scrutinizing leaders who tell us they supposedly have all the answers. If you are considering enrolling in a self-help seminar of some sort this book is must read, before you pay a deposit and/or sign any paperwork.

~Rick Alan Ross, author of *Cults Inside Out: How People Get in and Can Get Out*; fact witness in the trial of NXIVM leader Keith Raniere.

THIS

how we lived

SWEET

after

LIFE

Kirby died

GINNY BROWN | JEAN BROWN

the three
tomatoes

The Three Tomatoes Book Publishing

Published June 2020
Printed in the United States of America
ISBN: 978-0-578-70879-9
Library of Congress Control Number:
2020910633

For information address:
The Three Tomatoes Book Publishing
6 Soundview Rd.
Glen Cove, NY 11542

Interior design: Tony Iatridis

Cover design: Susan Herbst

Dedication

To all who considered themselves Kirby's best friend, as well
as those who were traumatized by the events in Sedona.
(Ginny)

and

To Kirby's nieces and nephews–Angus, Lyle, George,
McCloy, Quinn, Linden, and Machrie–who will meet
their amazing Aunt Kirby in the telling of her story.
(Jean)

THIS

how we lived

SWEET

after

LIFE

Kirby died

GINNY BROWN | JEAN BROWN

Introduction

" I have an unbending commitment to do what is necessary.

I am willing to give up all that does not serve me... experiences, people, places.

I take greater responsibility for my existence... loving within and externally.

I am opening my heart to all that is righteous and true... to the universe and understand we are all connected energies. "

—*Kirby's Vision Quest Journal*

"It begins..." These are the words written on the evening of October 9, 2009, in my date book. I knew something momentous and life-changing was beginning on that day. I knew, in the future, I would always divide the moments in our lives by this date.

On October 8, 2009, Kirby Brown, the oldest of our four children, died in a sweat lodge conducted by James Arthur Ray, an internationally known motivational speaker. The next day, a New York state trooper informed us of Kirby's death. After being featured in *The Secret* book and DVD in 2006, Ray became a rising star in the self-help industry. He was interviewed on national television numerous times and was twice a guest on

The Oprah Winfrey Show. One of his books made *The New York Times* bestseller list. Without much training or any professional credentials, he had spun his natural charisma and speaking ability into a lucrative self-improvement brand.

My husband, George, and I had attended Ray's events with Kirby—tame, introductory sorts of events. I was impressed by his ability to put together interesting concepts from different sources and explain them in an accessible and engaging way. Ray was certainly charismatic but did not seem dangerous.

The sweat lodge was the culminating activity of a five-day retreat Ray called "Spiritual Warrior." A sweat lodge is a sacred Native American tradition. The lodge is a low-lying tent with a pit in the center for steaming hot rocks to create a sauna-like environment, intended to be a meditative, spiritual experience that brings healing and clarity.

The time of death noted for Kirby at the hospital was October 8, 2009, 6:21 pm, but we are sure she died earlier at the Angel Valley Ranch in Sedona, Arizona. James Shore, another participant who lay next to Kirby, also died that afternoon. Liz Neuman, a woman who had worked as a volunteer for Ray, died in the hospital nine days later. Numerous others suffered injury and a least twenty of the sixty participants were taken to area hospitals on that fateful night. James Arthur Ray was found guilty of negligent homicide in June 2011, in the deaths of Kirby Brown, James Shore, and Liz Neuman. He was sentenced in November 2011 and served twenty months in prison.

Kirby had lived in Baja, Mexico, after growing up first in Brooklyn until age ten, and then in Westtown, New York— a small rural town about seventy-five miles northwest of Manhattan—where we still live. She was thirty-eight years old when she died. She was a typical oldest child, with a take-charge (sometimes bossy) attitude, who often set the agenda of family activities and gatherings. Her siblings are Kate, who lives in the Dominican Republic with her two sons; Bobby, who lives in Connecticut with his family; and Jean, who lives in Toronto with her family and who co-wrote this book with me. Despite our distances, we've always been a supportive and tight-knit bunch, who enjoy big family parties, travel adventures, and surprises—often orchestrated by Kirby.

With an inexhaustible thirst for life, Kirby was an adventurer, who was always looking to grow, improve herself, expand her life. She had seen Ray, a self-proclaimed millionaire guru, in the Baja in the fall of 2008. I have often been asked, "Why was Kirby there? What was she looking for? She seemed to have it all together." What others may see when assessing another person is rarely what that person may see in themselves. I know the teachings of James Ray resonated with her. Live impeccably. Be fully responsible for all your actions, intended or unintended. Visualize what you desire and set your attention on your intentions. I believe Kirby trusted that James Ray held all the answers she needed to break through any doubts, insecurities, or anxieties in order to reach new heights of success, professionally and personally. Unfortunately, she gave Ray all her savings, all her trust, and her very life.

Kirby's death was sudden, untimely, tragic, criminal, and public. This story traveled internationally, was covered on all the major stations in the US, was written about in countless articles, a number of books, on *20/20*, *Dateline*, and on an Investigation Discovery TV reenactment that is still airing across the globe. Her brother, Bobby, noted in his eulogy, "Kirby, you never did anything small!" She died as she had lived.

After Kirby's death, we started looking into the self-help/self-improvement world. We have learned that there are many charismatic charlatans dispensing advice without proper training or knowledge in this unregulated industry. While there may be wonderful, inspirational teachers, people are routinely scammed and hurt financially, emotionally, and physically. Often, stories of abuse are not reported because victims are embarrassed and ashamed or have been paid off. Our family started SEEK Safely, a 501(c)(3) charity, to educate the public and consumers about this industry.

Jean, the youngest in our family, and I thought that telling our story together would be an interesting exploration of how tragedy affects an entire family. Giving these two perspectives offers a more complete picture of the complex tragedy we experienced. We traveled this journey with faith, and we hope that sharing our story will be helpful to others who are also negotiating the turbulent waters of grief and loss.

I kept a journal during the first two years and during the trial. Dialogue shared in these pages is taken from my notes of numerous conversations I had with others affected by this tragedy. The quotes represent what I heard during that tumultuous time and are my own interpretation. Some names have been changed at the request of the individuals. We—Jean and I—have tried to be totally honest and respectful of others in sharing our experience. Kirby is also a voice in this book. We use quotes from the journals she kept at Spiritual Warrior, including one she wrote on her vision quest, just days before she died.

The story of the Sedona sweat lodge was, and still is, a compelling, curious tale for many people. Our story, as presented in this book, will move through the time period when we first learned of what happened to Kirby in that sweat lodge—a period of frenetic discovery that nevertheless still left us with many questions and feelings of confusion. Next, we will lay bare our experience with grief and how we managed the intense despair that comes with a loss like this. As a therapist, I hope my insights will be helpful to others who have experienced a difficult loss. Finally, we detail our experience of James Ray's criminal trial in 2011 and some of the events that followed. We do not go into every detail of what happened in Sedona or during Ray's criminal trial. Instead, this is the story of how we experienced these events and how they became part of our own stories.

In telling Kirby's story, our hope is that her life will inspire others to live fully and her death will serve as a cautionary tale—a warning to those seeking growth to pay close attention to their teachers and surroundings. We hope telling her story will also influence those in the self-help industry. Consumers deserve self-help providers who operate in an ethical and safe manner.

But, ultimately, this book is our story. When Kirby died, the details of her death were for public consumption and so much of what happened—the criminal investigation, the media and public interest—was beyond us and out of our control. The public story was incomplete. Now, ten years later, we are reclaiming this story for ourselves, showing how it has impacted and changed us. We are taking this story back, to complete the picture of what we really lost in that deadly sweat lodge in October 2009 and who we are today.

Virginia (Ginny) Brown
Jean Brown

Table Of Contents

Eulogy

Eulogy by Bob Brown,
brother of Kirby Brown

October 17, 2009

Well Kirby, you did it again, didn't you? You just can't do anything quietly!

Before I begin, I need to ask you all a question. Can I please see a show of hands of all those present who at one time in their life considered Kirby Brown their best friend?

And I assure you, you were all her best friend too.

Downtown Kirby Brown, Derby-Dan, Hurricane Kirby, The Kirby, Action Figure cousin, Our Supernova... A free spirit, a woman of constant action, a force of energy, a truly passionate soul, the love of our life. You taught us so much about how to live life and how to love one another. Your spirit lives on in each of us... we will never forget you. You won't let us, by the way. I'm pretty sure in this past week you've already told Mom how to rearrange the kitchen twice and told Dad he needs to buy a new phone. (Jean, Kate, and I can probably help you out with that one). I think you've also told everyone in Cabo exactly how to plan the next party. And by the way, Cabo, the Brown family expects a HUGE one the next time we're in town. Kirby won't be there to plan it all, so it better be a rager.

I know I can stand here for days telling all of the beautiful and inspirational stories about how Kirby lived her life, and how she touched us all so deeply. How she literally saved a friend's life in Cabo when he was hit by a car, how she taught children to ride horses in such a special way, or how her love of music was so incredibly contagious. But the thing is, we all lived these stories with Kirby in our own special way, and my words just cannot give them justice.

Instead, today I will be Kirby's voice, I simply need to speak for Kirby to all of you…

To all my dear friends and family:

Do not cry for me. I am here with you today and I will always remain a special part of each and every one of you. You speak of the magic and me, but it is I who experienced the magic in all of you. I love you all for who you are, and I love you all for what you taught me and what you've all done for me… But today, there are a few things I need you to do for me.

LAUGH. I need you to laugh for me. Laugh with each other every day. Tell my story and laugh out loud. Take time from your busy life, think about me, and laugh. Sing out loud, dance with an unending joy and passion, and laugh as hard as you can for me… but do not cry for me.

LEARN. I need you to learn for me, and never stop. Learn about yourself, learn about one another; learn about everything you possibly can. Learn how to climb your mountain and learn how to surf your wave. Open yourself up to new possibilities and learn for me… but do not cry for me.

LOVE. I need you to love for me. Continue to love me as I will always love you. Tell people you love them as I have told you. And show each other how to love as I have shown you. Live your life as an example of my love and exude that love. Do this for me… but do not cry for me.

LIVE. I need you to live for me. Really and truly live your life each and every day. Take a moment, think about what it means to live… take this thought and make it a part of your every moment of every day. Live your life with a fierce energy that penetrates those around you. Focus on what it means for YOU to live… then think about me and live some more. Live for me…but do not cry for me.

Now To my beautiful sister Kate,

Please stay true to yourself. Take care of yourself and your Mighty-mighty Angus first. Use the example that our Mom and Dad created for our family and make it your own. You have become such a beautiful, loving mother and wife. Please know that I will always be there for you to help and guide you along the way. We may have battled at times, but I am certain that these times only made our bond stronger. You are my beautiful friend, and I love you.

To my special little sister Jean,

Jean-the-Bean The Dancin' Machine! I give to you my joyous spirit and my boundless energy, so you can carry it on. Please continue to travel for me, and see as much as you can, meet new faces, and explore exciting new worlds. Every time I saw you, I was more impressed by the incredible woman you've become. My little sister - now a model of grace and beauty for us all. Your intelligence and your thirst for knowledge and what is right will lead people for years to come. Your future is an amazing place. I love you, my shining star.

And finally, to my beautiful Mom and Dad,

The two people I admire the most, and whose mere presence offers us all hope in this world. Please celebrate for me, celebrate all that is good, and celebrate together. Hold each other close and feel my arms around you. Feel my spirit, my energy, and my passion within you. People talk about my strength, but the source of this strength was always the two of you. Your wisdom, love, loyalty, and strength are what guided me my whole life.

To my sweet Papa G,

Please focus on keeping our family together. Take my energy and focus it on one another but take care of yourself first. You do so much for so many. Now, let me be a source of motivation for you, so you can take care of yourself. Do this, so you can keep us all together… and as you love to say, 'Be excellent to one another.'

To my inspirational Mom,

I know you will stay strong for me. I love you with all of my heart and soul. Please know that you did more for me than I ever could've imagined. You guided me through so many tough times, even when I wouldn't listen. But I always heard your voice… your tender, steady, loving and true voice. Thank you for teaching me how to see God in everything, everyone, and every beautiful place. I now just have one request of you…

Please speak for me.

My Kirby Brown… Our loving sister, daughter, cousin, aunt, best friend, our Supernova…

Your force will be missed, but it will live on in us all. Your radiant glow will shine bright through all of us for as long as we all shall live.

And now, we will stand up together and we will celebrate. We will sing and dance, and we will shout to the ends of the earth and we will celebrate! We will celebrate Kirby Brown!

Part I:
Finding Out

Chapter 1

" I must absolutely change all of these limiting beliefs because I can, and I deserve it. Life goes too fast to wait. I must learn to set my boundaries with my relationships to protect myself. I must practice being true and honest with myself of exactly what I want. Give exactly what feels good to give with no conditions."

> — *Kirby's Harmonic Wealth Journal,*
> *March 2009*

Ginny

When our children were young, we took a number of cross-country camping trips. On one such trip while driving through the Midwest, through golden fields of corn and dancing grasses, open plains that stretch as far as the eye can see, George abruptly stopped the van. He told everyone to get out of the car. I remember looking at him quizzically and, then, he said, "Look around you. Now scream as hard as you can." Everyone started yelling, trying to outdo each other, only to realize that there was no lingering sound; our voices were swallowed up, snuffed out, disappearing into the air. There was nothing to hold, receive, or reverberate the sound—nothing: silence, just silence. Since October 8, 2009, dealing with Kirby's death and all that came with it—the trial, the media, legislators, lawyers, judges, participants, and self-help providers—I have often been screaming only to have my voice disappear.

FRIDAY MORNING, OCTOBER 9

At 8:15 in the morning, an incredibly young and tall state trooper stands at my door, hat in hand, asking: "Do you know Kirby Brown?" His eyes are full of concern and kindness.

In 1971, natural childbirth and nursing were not the norm. But I was determined to birth my babies naturally and that is how Kirby entered the world, a textbook birthing experience. It was love at first sight: total, unconditional, tender, teary, protective, gentle, fierce, all-consuming love wrapped around one pink almost seven-pound infant. I was also determined to nurse, despite the unpopular, negative perception many held toward breastfeeding at that time. She latched onto my breast and we began.

I would often joke that there are four years between Kirby and her sister, Katie, because I wasn't sure I could handle more than one Kirby. She was so... herself. Determined, strong-willed, vibrant, perpetually curious, physically adroit, always challenging. We lived in Bay Ridge, Brooklyn, in a basement apartment that we called the "mole hole." Because there was little light and low ceilings, going to the park on Shore Drive was a necessary daily outing. At the end of our street, the East River and the Hudson River joined up to flow under the Verrazano-Narrows Bridge which connects Brooklyn to Staten Island. I loved walking along the drive next to the river, the sparkle of the water playing in the morning sunlight. The park was a few short blocks from our apartment. However, I soon discovered that, for Kirby, climbing up the steps on every front stoop on our way to the park was more important than getting to the swings.

I do not recall her ever napping after she started walking at nine months; there was too much to see and do.

Do I know Kirby Brown? Why is he asking this? I'm confused—is she in some kind of trouble?

Growing up in Brooklyn until the age of ten, Kirby challenged the criteria for the "gifted and talented" program at the local public school. Her younger sister had been admitted to a preschool spot based on IQ. The fourth grade teacher interviewed Kirby and fought for her admittance into the program based on the strength of her desire to learn, her curious nature and vibrant spirit. She was considered an "experiment" and graduated at the top of the class, proving her teacher's assessment to be correct: a thirst for knowledge is often more important than raw IQ.

Ours was an ethnically changing neighborhood; when a young African American girl was bullied, I remember how proud I was that Kirby stood up for her, to the point of being harassed herself. She was angry that those kids were so stupid. Her sense of justice was strong. I have often witnessed her standing up for the one being marginalized, left out, forgotten.

Adolescence was a challenging time. She was an adventurer, a risk-taker, an adrenaline junkie. She owned a motorcycle for a while. She got caught up in the party scene in college and had to spend a year in the local community college to get refocused. I found out she dove from the cliffs near Port Jervis into the Delaware River (a teenage daredevil feat, one all local parents warned their children never to try). She would dance all night if the music was right.

However, she is an adult—mature, responsible for her own life—living in the Baja in Mexico.

"Do you know Kirby Brown?"

Kirby was an incredible life force. I always describe her to people as someone "drunk on life." She mountain-biked, hiked, rappelled, rode horses, kite-boarded, surfed the big waves on the East Cape in the Baja. She loved to entertain friends, cook fabulous meals, tend a garden, celebrate any and every occasion. A lover of blues and jazz, musicians and any kind of music, she danced till dawn. Kirby was a movable party.

When she came home to Westtown, where we lived after leaving Brooklyn, it was like a tornado hit the house. The phone began ringing, music would be blaring, and friends and family would clamor to spend time with their favorite cousin and friend. When she would visit in the summer, I had to schedule a lunch date so we could spend time together because her "dance card" was always so full.

She had lived in New York after college. She managed an Arabian horse farm for a year and then drove limousines in Manhattan, before moving to Lake Tahoe to be with friends and work in a restaurant. It was at Lake Tahoe that she met a woman who asked her to assist with some decorative painting jobs in the area. The colors and techniques appealed to her creative nature. When this friend moved to San Jose to open a jazz club which needed to be decorated, she happily followed, a new adventure on the horizon. Once in the Baja, Kirby met Nancy, an accomplished artist who would become her partner in a decorative painting business. They worked in high-end homes on the Sea of Cortez, "antiquing" new mansions, painting in shadows, cracks, and water marks. They painted walls to look like stone, leather, parchment, metals, or marble. Kirby and Nancy had worked together for ten years and it was this business that Kirby wanted to find the courage and motivation to expand and grow.

"Yes, I know Kirby…"

She is in Sedona at a Spiritual Warrior Retreat. She has been so excited about these five days. She has been preparing all summer—meditating, journaling, reading. Why is he asking if I know her?

Kirby had signed up for this retreat in May and started preparing for it with reading, breathing exercises, and meditation. She read *The Alchemist* by Paulo Coelho and had underlined these words:

> When a person really wants something, all the universe conspires to help that person realize his dream. ...There is only one way to learn. It's through action. Everything you need to know you have learned through your journey. ... Listen to your heart... because wherever your heart is, there you will find your treasure." (pp.120–135)

I believe she was in search of her treasure, some answers and directions to transform her experience, ratchet it up another notch, to "self-actualize," as Abraham Maslow would define it. She was always looking to expand, see more, experience more. When I taught parenting programs for the Archdiocese of New York, I created a slideshow for a prayer service. It included pictures, many of Kirby growing up, which were accompanied by *I Want to Live*, a song written by John Denver. The inspirational words epitomize Kirby's irrepressible spirit, her desire to live life to the fullest, to grow, to seek knowledge, to become her best self and share that self in service to others.

I know she wanted to expand the decorative painting business but had doubts about her business and technical capabilities. She told me, "I need to confront any self-limiting beliefs."

She also wanted to find her "soulmate" and understand why she had experienced disappointing personal relationships.

She witnessed both her sisters getting married in the summer of 2009. "I need to find out why I am attracting the wrong men."

A bit baffled and tongue-tied: "Yes, yes... I'm her mother."

The trooper lowers his head and says, "Ma'am, I am so sorry. She passed in a sweat lodge in Sedona, Arizona."

Passed? What did that mean? Passed? Did he mean, died? Dead? At 8:15 in the morning, his words initially confounded, shocked, and then hit with a horrific impact, like a physical blow to the gut. Our daughter Kirby was dead in Sedona, Arizona, at a self-help retreat?

As I screamed, my husband, George, rushed forward and led the trooper and myself into the house where the officer confessed he had no other details but gave us the name of the detective in Sedona to get more information about the particular circumstances.

Disbelief. Shock. How could this be? Kirby had gone to the Spiritual Warrior retreat the Sunday before. It concluded on Thursday, October 8, and we had been expecting her to call to tell us all about it. She had been so psyched and sure that this experience would obliterate personal doubts and provide her with the motivation and tools she needed to catapult her business and her life to great success.

The trooper handed me the paper with the Arizona police investigator's number. I kept thinking, "Maybe there has been a mistake. If I call, maybe we'll discover Kirby is really okay. She can't be dead. I don't want to know that she is dead."

It felt like we were in a car wreck. Could I reverse that moment of impact, that split second before the sickening crunch of metal and screech of tires, the knowing that there is no turning back, the car is wrecked? After he left, we both hesitated to pick up the phone, not wanting confirmation, yet instinctively knowing that we were being propelled headlong into the wreckage.

The police in Arizona told us another person had died and multiple people had been taken to the hospital, but they could give us no real information about what had gone wrong. Oh my God! How could this have happened? They promised to stay in touch and share whatever they learned as it became available.

We began making phone calls. Who to call first? What to say? "Your sister, died, is dead?" "Kirby died in a sweat lodge in Arizona?" Horror and shock greeted us as we called our other children. The complete unreality of the moment enveloped me as I called my daughter's mother-in-law in Montréal to make sure someone was with Jean when she heard the news. Next, our extended family and closest friends were contacted, and with this news their lives were forever altered. Friends and family cut vacation plans short, booked emergency flights to New York. A birthday spa weekend cancelled. When my closest friend, Liz Holst, arrived, I handed her my phone book and she began making phone calls for me. I had to notify my job, not knowing when I would be able to return to the mediation center where I ran psycho-educational programs for parolees, teens on probation, and their families, and a program for parents whose children had been removed by Child Protective Services.

As our home filled with family, friends, and food, I needed information. I was desperate to reach people who might know about the event or people who were there. When I spoke to the investigating police in Arizona, we were told that James Ray was not cooperating with their inquiries. He had left the scene hours after the tragedy, in the middle of the night, on the advice of his lawyers, never addressing his traumatized participants or checking the hospitals where the injured were sent. Those who were unconscious were unidentified.

Kirby dead. How could this have happened? She was so

strong; her decorative painting work was physically demanding. She fell in love with the Baja when she learned how to surf; she surfed the big waves on the East Cape with world class surfers. She was a horsewoman.

When we moved to Westtown, a small rural town seventy-five miles northwest of New York City, the kind of place we always made fun of when we were city dwellers, we were able to get Kirby her own horse, fulfilling a dream she had had for many years. A beautiful but skittish Arabian, Happy Dot was Kirby's. She brushed her and turned her out in the field behind our home each morning before school, carrying the water and hay down to the pasture. After getting some initial riding lessons, she fearlessly rode the local roads and woods around our home.

By high school, she was teaching riding and training horses. One day, she asked me to pick her up from work. I watched from the fence as she led the horse on a long lunge rope, snapping it to keep the animal in line. When this huge stallion reared up, she jumped on his back and brought him down and under control. Watching, I had been clearly terrified; I asked her later if she was scared. Unfazed, she explained, "He needed me to be in control." I told her I would no longer pick her up from work; she'd have to ride her bike home. This was too scary for me.

Now, the news was simply too unreal to take in. I had to find out how this could have happened. I tried to think of anyone I could call who might know what had happened. Kirby and I had attended James Ray's two-day Harmonic Wealth seminar in Jersey City earlier in March. In the Baja, at a free James Ray presentation, Kirby signed up for this introductory event and received a complimentary ticket. When she asked me to join her, I rearranged work commitments, thinking it would be a great opportunity to spend quality time with my daughter. I had emails and phone numbers for a few people I had met there, so I began calling. One man told me his son Connor was also at the retreat in Sedona with Kirby but had been taken to the hospital. He was unclear about his son's condition but thought he would be released within a day or two. I asked him to have his son call us.

More family and friends were filling our home with their loving concern, their tears, long hugs, flowers, food. The phone was ringing constantly.

My head was spinning. What did we have to do? We had to address the practical matter of how to bring her home. Should we fly to Arizona? We called our friends, the McPhillips, who own a funeral parlor in Middletown and, thankfully, they took over, making all the arrangements, explaining that nothing would happen until an autopsy was performed. It would be days before anything could be planned. We had no idea when we would be able to plan a funeral or when her body would be released. The thought of an autopsy made me physically ill. I knew it was necessary to establish the cause of death, but it felt like a violation. I found I could not think about what was being done to our precious, beautiful daughter.

Horrified and frightened, I knew this was a big story that would create a media storm. James Ray was an internationally known motivational speaker, immensely popular, on the rise, featured in *The Secret* book and DVD, vetted by national media, and a frequent visitor on *The Oprah Winfrey Show*. My sister Mary's son, Tom McFeeley, who had experience in print and TV communications, arrived on Friday afternoon to help us manage the media and act as family spokesman during those first few weeks. George's nephew, Bob Magnanini, a high-powered lawyer, called assuring us he would oversee any legal issues and speak to the investigating authorities.

When we saw the first reports of the tragedy referring to Kirby as a "middle-aged woman from New York," I thought to myself, "Oh, no. This will NOT be reported this way. 'Middle-aged?' No. We will find pictures to show the world the dynamic, healthy, vibrant person whose life force was snuffed out in that sweat lodge tent." Tom got those pictures to the news outlets before the evening news broke.

On Friday night, our son arrived with his wife, Kory, and two children, Lyle Angela, two, and George, seven months. By then, the story was on every major TV station. Pictures of the sweat lodge tent, audio of the 911 call made by a participant, emergency vehicles arriving at the scene, helicopters medevacing people to area hospitals, and pictures of Kirby filled our TV screen.

No one could really explain why this had happened. However, we knew we had to devise a plan to deal with the media, even as we tried to figure out a funeral. Tom provided some protection for us, especially in those first few weeks. He set up some interviews with the major stations, the morning news shows, and our local station, and had us booked with Larry King three weeks after the tragedy.

As I tossed and turned that night, exhausted from crying, I could not sleep, obsessing, trying to understand what and why this had happened. I never knew that grief could be a real physical pain, a stab in the heart, an inability to breathe, a heaviness that hurt everywhere, a clutched throat that choked on an unuttered scream.

SATURDAY, OCTOBER 10

The sun rose, the morning dawned. How is it that the world continues when one's life has come to an abrupt, screeching halt? Little Lyle Angela, our oldest grandchild, a little over two, snuggled into bed with us; tickles and laughter helped me awaken to the new day. These little ones would help bring us through this nightmare. My sister-in-law Kay was orchestrating food and taking care of everyone in the house. I have always loved sharing our historic Victorian home with others, being the hostess, creating an atmosphere of welcome and ease. Our home is comfortably worn and well loved. Our dining room was originally the formal parlor—the room that juts out and is surrounded by the classic Victorian porch. A bright room with large windows and a side doorway, it is graced with rich wood molding and a lovely carved mantel. Dark mahogany furniture—a china closet and two sideboard pieces that had been handcrafted in the 1920s and passed along to us from George's grandmother—fills the room. The beautiful crystal chandelier adds to the formal feeling of the room. Now, at the table that had witnessed so many celebrations, holiday meals, and Sunday dinners, I began making phone calls and taking notes to uncover the mystery of why this had happened and what we had to do.

I turned to practical matters and tried to think who might have information. She had a truck and luggage at the event. Do we ask the police to protect Kirby's things at the ranch? On Saturday morning, our son, Bobby, made inquiries about Kirby's personal possessions at Angel Valley Ranch. In his conversation with Amayra Hamilton, the owner of the ranch, we were given assurance that Kirby's truck and belongings would be safe while we found someone to recover them. She also suggested to him that he think about this event from a "metaphysical" perspective. Enraged, he started shouting about "these people," who were crazy, unrealistic, "out there," and unconcerned that people were dead! What did that mean, "metaphysical?" Do they think that there is a spiritual purpose—that it was meant to be, it was ordained? I think it slowly began to dawn on me that we were entering a "new age" explanation for a bizarre death. Another layer of unreality settled over me as I struggled to breathe.

I had to focus on some solid realities: Kirby's things, her clothing—how could we get them? What could I dress her in for a wake? Kirby had visited with Mika and Bobby Cutler, good friends who lived in Moab, Utah, before going on to Sedona. When I called them on Saturday, they agreed to drive to Angel Valley and get Kirby's truck and belongings. While they could not drive her truck east, they would ship her personal belongings and clothing immediately. Kirby had left her little dog, Tuffy, with them and they quickly agreed to take care of him. Oh, Tuffy, her little Mexican "chilaba" (how we humorously referred to her mutt, a mix of Chihuahua and Labrador, that she found abandoned on the streets of San José del Cabo). How attached he was to Kirby! Julie Min, a participant and one of Kirby's roommates at the ranch, stayed with her things until Mika and Bobby drove to Sedona on Sunday.

In the meantime, George spoke with one of the police investigators assigned to the case who confirmed that the owners would also protect Kirby's belongings and truck. The other victim, who had been found next to Kirby, was James Shore—a father of three young children. Another woman who was flown out on Thursday night was in critical condition in the hospital. Asking about Ray, the investigator revealed that Ray had left the scene in the middle of the night, refusing to talk to the police and never addressing the participants of the event. There was confusion at the hospitals because people had arrived without any identification.

On Saturday afternoon, Katie and her husband, Mitchell, arrived with their baby, Angus, from Mexico where they lived just around the corner from Kirby's home. Kirby had been present in January at the birth of her godson, Angus, now nine months old.

SUNDAY, OCTOBER 11

As we were leaving for Mass on Sunday morning, News 12, our local news station, arrived at our home with a film crew.

Tom handled the surprise interview. The major news stations began calling. Geraldo called for an interview. It was a surreal chaos, blanketed in a suffocating awareness that Kirby's death in a sweat lodge in Sedona, Arizona, was only too real.

Entering our parish church, I knew people would have heard what had happened. I felt raw, exposed, and naked. There is that moment when the bile in your gut threatens to erupt while you desperately struggle to keep it down. I never realized how hard it could be to allow personal pain to be seen, so that others could help love and heal us.

A friend I had worked with, Chris Onofry, one of many angels in what I call the "days of discovery," stopped by on Sunday with a journal for me to record the information from the numerous phone calls I was making. "Ginny, you'll never remember everything you are hearing." I tried to establish a timeline from Friday morning onward and began making notes for almost every phone call I made. I wrote in this journal for over a year, recording significant phone calls, interviews, important information related to this tragedy. On tear-stained pages I recorded my fears, my prayers, my questions, my own thoughts, as well as the words of others. Without this physical record, I never would have been able to write our story.

Our youngest and newly married daughter, Jean, and her spouse, Mike, travelled from Ontario, Canada, to join the family on Sunday. By Sunday night, everyone was in Westtown. Our old Victorian was filled with our son, Bobby, our two daughters Kate and Jean, their spouses, and children. Our home reverberated with the sounds of three grandchildren under two and a half, the phone ringing, friends arriving—the chaos of care. Kay and Al, George's sister and brother-in-law, headed back to New Jersey, having coordinated meals and household tasks since Friday afternoon. They had driven the three hours to Westtown to be with us and take care of whatever they could as soon as we called them. All the everyday things one does so automatically with little effort or thought, like laundry, food, meals, tidying up, were suddenly unseen, unimportant tasks as this massive weight, this unexpected reality, took over.

On Sunday afternoon, entering the funeral parlor, I was struck by the quiet, heavy solemnity of dark wood paneling and rich fabrics. How did we get here? One makes funeral arrangements for a parent, not your child. How could we bury her, such a vibrant spirit who was not earthbound? Sitting in the parlor chairs, without even discussing it, George and I knew that cremation would be the only appropriate route for our Kirby. We knew we needed a wake, some rarefied time to be upheld and love-surrounded. We knew others also needed a time to grasp this and to say goodbye.

We spoke of pictures for a video tribute and a chose a quote from Philippians 4:8–9 for the remembrance card.

> And now, my friends, all that is true, all that is noble, all that is just and pure, all that is lovable and gracious, whatever is excellent and admirable—fill all your thoughts with these things. The lessons I taught you, the tradition I have passed on, all that you have heard me say or do, put into practice; and the God of peace will be with you.

I knew Kirby would want us to live fully and drink in this life as she did, embracing adventure, seeking growth, expanding our hearts.

The last time we were in Cabo, Kirby and I went to the farmer's market with signs about recycling, instructing others about how to compost, ways to reuse materials, and places to recycle plastic and glass. She was very "green," conscious of our responsibility as stewards of the environment. So I asked Mary, the funeral director, about the casket and we arranged to use a coffin that was used for display and would not be destroyed, needlessly consuming beautiful wood.

The McPhillips, who also knew and loved Kirby, would keep us informed about the autopsy and when she would arrive in New York. It would take a few more days before we saw Kirby's body.

On Sunday afternoon, my four brothers, who had been having a "brothers' weekend" in the Adirondacks, spent the afternoon with us on their way home. I am in the middle of seven siblings. I have two older sisters, one older brother, and three younger brothers. My beautiful strong brothers cried for us and for their loss as well. Horrific, traumatic grief hears no words of comfort, but feels the presence of compassion and abiding love.

On Sunday evening, Connor, the young man who had been hospitalized after the retreat, called. He had been next to Kirby and James in the sweat lodge. He spoke in a strangely detached, unemotional, flat manner.

He explained the activities of the week and the ceremony in the lodge. "Throughout the week, we worked on what we wanted in our life, our seven intentions and then in the sweat lodge there was a round of chanting words and Hebrew songs for each intention. Everyone who got sick was in the same area closer to the steaming stones and had less air."

Reluctantly, he continued, "Kirby was actually encouraging others to stay in the sweat lodge, rocking back and forth continually repeating, 'You can do it. You can do it.' But she wasn't saying it right. We *were* doing it and Ray had explained that the universe only responds to positives."

Listening, I thought it seemed like Kirby was experiencing this as a test of endurance.

Connor was clearly upset that her words of encouragement were actually not in alignment with the universe according to

Ray's teachings. Did she need to be saying, "We are doing this?" The whole "universe" rule seemed quite bizarre to me.

Connor continued, "James Ray was at the entrance of the tent and people could leave between rounds when he opened the flap for a few minutes."

"What did Ray say when people left the tent?" I asked Connor.

"He challenged them with statements like 'You're more than that,' encouraging them to stay inside."

Connor did not think Ray was being coercive or manipulative.

"Kirby was afraid to spend the previous thirty-six hours alone in the desert. She did it and created an amazingly beautiful medicine wheel with feathers, crystals, and stones for the four directions."

My mind raced, a million questions exploding within. I tried to focus on just listening and writing down what Connor was revealing. He described some of the events of the week. Then he said, "I'm sorry if you find this upsetting, but when I was on the ground, there was a metaphysical woman next to Kirby channeling her to the next plain, who reported that Kirby felt wonderful. She forgot her body. They [Kirby and James] were surprised that they were dead."

A metaphysical woman, a channeler, someone who purported to be able to speak to the dead was there?

I was stunned. "Do you really believe that Kirby chose death?"

There was silence.

"When you were being taken to the hospital, did you want to die?"

"No, I was scared."

I realized he was still in shock, traumatized by what he had experienced. Then he said, "Next weekend there is a Harmonic Wealth event scheduled and I'm not sure if I should go or not."

I was shocked that he would even consider going to another

event given by the man who had fled the scene in the middle of the night, never even talking to his "students," the participants of this expensive weeklong retreat, the man who seemed to have no concern that Connor would go to the hospital as a John Doe, the man who never even notified Connor's father of his son's life-threatening condition.

I asked, "What do you think you need to do?"

"I'm not sure," he responded. "I am a little pissed at Ray, but I need to process this experience, release my fear, and embrace my heart being."

The whole "channeling" information confounded me. It seemed to be the "truth" that many participants would willingly believe, absolving everyone—leader and participants—of any responsibility of wrongdoing, whitewashing any lingering guilt.

I sat at the dining room table, looking at my notes, numb. This was not a normal death. This was an unreal, bizarre catastrophe. Oh, Kirby, my very unconventional daughter. She lived "outside the box" and now she was dead having been trapped in a small, suffocating sweat lodge. George was skeptical, convinced that Ray was responsible. I still wanted to believe that this had been a tragic "accident." Thinking that the man Kirby had trusted deliberately put her at risk and then did not care was a reality I could not fathom. I wanted more information to understand what went wrong. In the back of my mind, I kept thinking, "Why did he flee the scene? Not talk to the participants? Why had he not contacted us immediately? How could he allow people to go to the hospital unidentified?"

While I was busy gathering information, George was gathering our broken family. On Sunday night, he initiated what came to be called our nightly "check-ins" after the children were in bed. He summoned all of the family and whoever else was in the house to congregate in the living room in order to share what each had heard and felt during the day. Having run a mobile mental health crisis team for Middletown's psychiatric hospital, George instinctively knew the importance of what is technically called a "critical incident debriefing." Two couches flanked a large wooden coffee table littered with teacups, cookies, chips, and wine glasses. Sinking into the couch or the pillows on the floor, we all talked. I shared my conversation with Connor, and Tommy talked about the morning's interview and other media contacts that were anxious for interviews. Kate and Mitchell, Jean and Mike, Bobby and Kory all shared their impressions, fears, questions. We shared conversations we heard, our feelings of disbelief, grief, anger, rage, confusion, and anxiety.

These evening sessions became a lifeline for all of us. We would eagerly await for others to go home, dinner dishes to be cleared away, children to be tucked in bed to gather in the living room to just talk, cry, and curse.

MONDAY, OCTOBER 12

As another day affirmed the fact of Kirby's death, I wondered if the Shores would like to speak with Connor. I had called Christopher Shore, James' brother, to find out what they knew and share the conversation I had had with Connor the night before. Christopher told me he had been contacted by the police and had to deliver the news to Alyssa, James' wife. Alyssa wanted to speak to others to try to understand what had happened. James and Alyssa had three children who were seven, ten, and twelve years old. Chris explained that James had gone to this event to focus on re-energizing his business and personal life. I connected them with Connor to get a participant's perspective.

Through my calls to those we had met the previous March at the Harmonic Wealth event in Jersey City, I discovered the name and number for the young woman, Julie Min, who had roomed with Kirby and had stayed at Angel Valley to protect her things.

I spoke to Julie on Monday night to thank her for the kindness of remaining at the ranch to protect Kirby's things until Mika and Bobby Cutler arrived. That conversation, like many others, was upsetting and troubling. This lovely young woman, like Connor, spoke without emotional affect.

"I was closer to the door, next to Stephen, who went to the hospital. I understood that the heat would be extreme, and that people might get nauseous. We were told to be responsible for ourselves and our neighbor. James assured us that even though we would be pushed physically, we would still be mentally alert. I think I was in an altered state. I felt the heat but was not suffering. Ray encouraged people to stay in the lodge, saying 'Come on, you can do it. You are more than that.'"

She went on to describe Kirby: "I arrived first, and Kirby just came swooping in with all her stuff. It was my honor to meet her—such a beautiful person, so vivacious, so unabashed and comfortable in her own skin. Everyone loved her open heart, always ready to hear someone's story. … We left everything outside the tent. Kirby had talked about her love life and her struggle to find the right partner. James gave her some special exercises to do and, by the middle of the week, she made her peace with that and then cut her hair. She discovered she could wait for the man she deserved. She put her ponytail on the window ledge and said, 'That is for my mother!' She emanated beauty, love, happiness. She was so amazing."

Julie spoke with little emotion, so I responded, "And now she is dead."

"Yes, it is a devastating loss. There are no answers. Ray didn't talk to us because he was busy with the police."

I told her that the police informed us that he was not cooperating or answering any questions.

After a short silence, she said, "Kirby took her grand-mother's kilt pin with her on the vision quest and had a vision of her Uncle Bob, [Kirby's great-uncle, who was a Christian Brother] telling her to 'Keep it simple.' I think it really grounded her. I can see her heading off with her backpack, wearing her turquoise cowboy hat with the fuzzy trim. She had the most amazing outfits."

"How are you doing?" I asked.

"I'm in disbelief. I am angry, disappointed, frustrated. The whole group is grieving, but we are hanging on to the good memories. We don't want to sit in the dark too long."

"What do you think happened that so many people were injured?"

"I heard that last year, after the sweat lodge ceremony, some people were vomiting and passed out. And three years ago, one person went to the hospital to get medically re-hydrated."

Her affect was flat, and she expressed gratitude at having been with Kirby. She said, "Think happy, positive thoughts. Don't be upset or sad. Kirby was such a positive life force."

I was struck by her unemotional communication. She pre-sented clearly as being confused and numb. As therapists, my husband and I are familiar with traumatic shock reactions. George had worked with the Fire Department of the City of New York (FDNY)—the firefighters and first responders after 9/11—some of whom developed post-traumatic stress disor-der. I have worked with many parents whose life experiences have been so horrifying and unnaturally challenging that real emotions are buried deep within, almost impossible to access.

I asked her, "Now that my daughter is dead, having lost her life while she was trying to expand it, what do you think Kirby would want me to do?"

"I think she would want you to ask the hard questions about how this could have happened."

When I called the police to check on the progress of the investigation, the lead detective, Ross Diskin, told me that Ray had hired his own investigators to figure out what had happened rather than cooperate with the local authorities

Our Monday evening check-in started with George calling everyone into the living room around 9:30. Sitting on the couch, a dram of Bourbon in hand, he asked everyone to share their anger at Kirby. Suddenly, all those questions which we may have felt uncomfortable verbalizing tumbled out: How could she have let this happen? Why did she stay in the stupid tent? Why did she spend so much money to go to this retreat? How could she have believed this fraud? She had so much going on in her life, why did she think she needed even more?

I was worried about the "special exercises" that Ray had given to Kirby. Did she spend time alone with him? What did he know about her private life? If she talked about her relationships, would he twist her words? Would she be judged and blamed for her own death?

George encouraged voicing the fears and rage, giving everyone permission to express whatever they were feeling. Many think cursing the dead is wrong, even blasphemous; yet, George knew those feelings were potent and very real, and if buried they start to corrode and poison us from within. Strong feelings emerge in weird ways when they are not attached to their appropriate origin.

Shouts turned to laughter as we shared funny, weird things that happened to remind us of Kirby, of her presence.

Then, on Tuesday, more dreadful details tumbled in.

Jean

THURSDAY, OCTOBER 8

*O*n *my way home from work, I stopped at a Petro-Canada gas station outside of Ottawa, where I was doing an internship for my master's degree in public policy. These eastern outskirts of Ottawa are very quiet—lots of flat farmland. When you hit that "Welcome to Ottawa" sign right around where I was, there's nothing—trees, straight roads. "This," a newcomer might wonder, "is the national capital of Canada?"*

As I filled up my Chevy Aveo, taking in the afternoon light coming through the trees surrounding this lonely gas station, it must have been about 5:30 pm or 6:00 pm my time, so 3:30 pm or 4:00 pm in Arizona. Kirby and the other Spiritual Warrior participants would have been in the sweat lodge for about an hour at that point. I got back into my car, eager to resume the book-on-tape of Anna Karenina.

But before I started the car, there was a catch, a new electricity in the air, a sudden feeling like something wasn't quite right. I looked around. Went back out and checked to make sure I'd closed the door to the gas tank. Got back in the car. Drove away, still feeling unsettled.

Later that night, I discovered that I'd left my wallet on top of the car at the gas station. I did get it back a couple of days later. But it's amazing how much can change in a span of just forty-eight hours.

FRIDAY, OCTOBER 9

The day after losing my wallet, I drove to work. Other than stopping off to look around the Petro-Canada station on my way into the city, it was a normal day.

But then, sometime just after lunch, my friend and co-worker Waleed came to me. His dark eyebrows were furrowed, but he was relieved to have found me.

"Jean, where have you been?"

Waleed was my friend from my graduate program at Concordia University in Montréal—an all-nighter paper-writing companion and the one who organized soccer teams and nights out for our friends. We regularly played practical jokes on one another in our office at Health Canada. Worried, serious, ominous were not normal states for Waleed.

I'm sure I was smiling. "I was in the bathroom. What's wrong?"

"You have to.... He was trying to call you—Mike. He's downstairs." Mike is my husband.

"Why?" I asked.

He shook his head and looked at the floor. "Just… you have to go down and talk to him."

As the elevator descended the eleven floors, I looked at my reflection in the mirrored wall panels and wondered why Mike was there. We'd been married just three months. Why did he drive two hours from Montréal to Ottawa to talk to me? Was he upset with me over something, so upset that he had to come talk to me in person? Did he have some sort of surprise for me? But that didn't really fit with Waleed's obvious concern.

Did I actually think someone may have died? I don't remember wondering about that, but it's hard to recall exactly what I was thinking. The news he delivered obliterated a lot of details from what feels like a previous life.

When I stepped out of the elevator, Mike's dad was there. This was even more confusing.

He looked at me, wringing his hands. "You'd better go talk to Mike," he said, gesturing outside. His parents' minivan was parked on the street in front of my building. People loitered outside on late lunch breaks, absorbing the sun of the last few warm days before winter.

"*What is going on?*" *I asked when I got close enough to Mike and the van for him to hear me.*

He told me to get into the car, so I slid into the passenger seat while he went around to the driver's side. He faced the front of the car, his blue-green eyes focused on the dash. And then he just started.

"*There was an accident…. Kirby died.*"

Even with so little, it was too much; I jumped out of the van as he was trying to explain and looked around frantically at the people who were smoking, talking, drinking coffee, as though I might find an escape somewhere in between their puffs and sips and conversations.

When I was growing up, I would sometimes—I wish I could find a better word—"fantasize" about one of my siblings dying. It wasn't at all that I wanted this to happen. But I'd imagine the sympathy, the attention, the title of it all. Specialness. Do other people do this? Imagine the response or impact of a particularly awful tragedy? Or does this make me some type of sociopath? I don't know.

But before it actually happened, I guess I could dwell on the rosier aspects of this fantasy because it hadn't happened and the thought of it actually happening was so unthinkable.

"*This will never happen to me*" *is certainly a common thought. Deadly car crashes, sudden life-threatening illness, freak accidents— these things happen to other people.*

Until it does happen. And then what a shift that is. The chasm between reality and unthinkable horror—so unthinkable that I could actually daydream about it—closes as solidly as the minivan door behind me.

"*Jean. Please come back in.*"

Poor Mike. He had driven two hours from Montréal where he worked to tell me the news in person; my parents didn't want to tell me over the phone while I was by myself. His dad came too, so he could drive my car back for me.

I don't remember much of that car ride. The minivan was empty— no back seats—and although I was facing forward, that's all I picture when I think of that afternoon ride: the little metal latches in the floor of the van that the seats click into. Mike and I never talked about how wrenching that ride must have been for him.

After we got home, we went to the grocery store down the street to pick up frozen pizzas for dinner. We were removed from the familial epicenter of grief by a six-hour car ride, so we hunkered down in some sort of satellite crisis mode: easy food, quiet nights in, discussing our "plan."

My dad called while we were in the store. Families were in there, buying snacks and renting movies for the weekend. After a crash or bang echoes through a place, there's that split second where everything is still and silent before chaos erupts. I felt like I was suspended in that moment then—blank, frozen. Maybe I looked scary to the little kids skipping through the aisles. I took the call outside and stood next to the bins of pumpkins as my dad relayed the details that they knew: last event of the retreat, a sweat lodge, after fasting and not hydrating, extreme heat, another person dead, others injured.

SATURDAY, OCTOBER 10

When I woke up the next morning, my first thought as the sunlight streamed through our east-facing bedroom window was "Kirby, how could you be so stupid?"

She had practiced Bikram yoga, which is done in a room heated to 104°F. She lived in Mexico and regularly drove through the desert. She knew heat. She was adventurous, yes, but always cautious and prepared. When we got her truck back from the friends she'd left it with, there were gallons of water in the trunk.

As I lay in bed trying to solve the mystery of her death in my head, I thought back to the time when I was in high school that she had led me in a yoga session in our backyard in New York, on a humid and sunny ninety degree day. It was hot. I tried to blink through the sweat and focus on the lumpy ground under my yoga mat as I pushed my way into Warrior II, tree pose, mountain. I tried to stretch myself through the creeping darkness at the corners of my vision and the heaviness in my head. She was my big sister; I wanted to impress her, and she must have known this. "Drink lots of water. It's okay to sit down if you feel dizzy at all," she'd told me.

So why would she be so reckless, to sit in a steaming hot tent for hours after over two days of no food and water? What was she thinking? It didn't make sense.

Later that day, two days after Kirby died and I left my wallet on top of the car at about roughly the same time, distracted with some ill feeling, a Bank of Montréal branch east of Ottawa called me. Some clever Good Samaritan had turned my wallet into the bank, seeing that I had a BMO bank card.

"I guess we should go get it," I said to Mike. We drove there that afternoon.

After I showed my ID, the teller handed my wallet to me. Everything was still inside. "The person who turned it in left their name and phone number," he told me. "Do you want it?"

I stared at him, wondering why I'd want that. What I wanted to say was, "My sister just died. That's why I look crazy." But instead I simply said, "No, thanks," and left. I realize now I could have thanked the person who turned it in—he or she may have even been hoping for a reward. At the time, though, thoughts like that just didn't come together.

SUNDAY, OCTOBER 11

We drove down to my parents' house in New York on October 11. I'm not sure why we waited those few days. My parents said they were still working out the "arrangements." They didn't know when the coroner in Arizona would release Kirby's body so that we could hold the wake and funeral. Nobody really knew what was happening.

The last time Mike and I were together in Westtown was when we were married in July. As a gift, one of our close family friends who is an artist had painted a picture of the house on the day of the wedding. The little wooden sign with the word "wedding" and an arrow pointing to the purple Victorian with its wrap-around porch was still in the front garden, just as it was in the painting hanging in our foyer.

We brought our things up to the attic where we would sleep for the week. Kirby's high school senior portrait was the first picture up along the stairway to the second floor that I noticed. In it, she holds a single red rose, a portrait that influenced my own school pictures for the next few years; I posed with a bowl haircut and a nosegay of plastic flowers in my nursery school and kindergarten photos.

It was comforting, but also odd to be in the house again where so much was the same: the piece of unattached molding in the kitchen that always clacks when it gets bumped, the rows and rows of books in the upstairs hallway lining the dust-covered sagging bookshelves, the light switches that have never worked. I had spent my entire childhood in this house, and for all of that time, I'd had two big sisters and a big brother. Because Kirby was twelve years older than me, there was actually a lot of time when I lived there that she hadn't, but she was always somewhere in the world. Alive.

Whereas our house in Canada was a cave of isolated grief— we'd just moved into the little brick Victorian in a new town east of Ottawa six days before Kirby died and we knew nobody—my parents' house was a buzzing command center. After the first few days of the news sinking in, the work of figuring out exactly what had happened began. The basic details just didn't make sense. There was clearly more to the story. Kirby wasn't stupid.

As an expat living in Canada, far away from my family, I experienced a perverse sort of happiness at being surrounded by my family back in the home where I grew up. This feeling would repeat itself many times as this event brought us all together on subsequent occasions. There was a warmth there as we all came together.

Those first few days were surreal. Floating around, connecting with family who were already gathered there—my other sister, Kate, from Mexico with her husband and nine-month-old son, and my brother, his wife, and two kids. Cousins and family friends were also arriving. People brought food, flowers, and the support of their presence, to try to help us. At this point, everything was on hold. We were waiting—waiting to find out more, waiting to hear from the police, and waiting for Kirby's body so we could set the funeral arrangements.

In our moments of waiting, filling time was awkward because, although the togetherness was nice, there was heaviness over it all. The reason we were all there together was so horrible. Somehow, we managed to find connection with one another and feel connections to Kirby as well.

On one of these limbo days, Mike and my sister's husband, Mitchell, went down to the lake behind my parents' house to fish. The property slopes down some excellent sledding hills to the man-made lake we'd always ice-skated on in the winter.

Mitchell and Mike brought the only fishing pole they could find in the cluttered barn next to the house—a pink Barbie fishing pole. I stayed back in the house, but I remember when they returned from the lake.

The door off the kitchen, the one that always sticks, flew open with a grunt as Mitchell rushed in. "You guys! You're not going to believe this!" Mitchell was lit up with excitement, his big Midwest boy's body taking over the kitchen as he described the scene.

"We were just down there, fishin', and then suddenly there was a bald eagle and it just kept swoopin' down on us! Can you believe that?

"You guys, it was Kirby. I know it."

Mike, a generally more reserved person, was behind Mitchell. Our eyes met and he was smiling too, confirming the tale.

34

I also had my own moment of feeling that Kirby was there. I was sleeping up in the attic of my parent's house. I love this house, but I've always been a little suspicious that it might be haunted. While I can walk into a dark room in other places without concern, I prefer to have a light on when I head up into the attic at Mom and Dad's. There's just a "feeling" sometimes, the kind of feeling that makes you skip steps to quicken the trip to where everyone else is. On the Sunday after we'd arrived in the late afternoon, I paused a minute at the doorway to the attic stairs on my way down to dinner. Facing the dark stairwell, I thought to myself that I should turn the attic light on so it wouldn't be dark when I came up to go to bed later.

"This is ridiculous," I thought to myself. "I'm twenty-seven years old." I left the light off.

When I went back upstairs later, however, the light—a bare lightbulb in the middle of the ceiling—was on. Nobody else had been up there in the intervening time. I was sure then—I'm still sure now—that that was Kirby.

Jean and Ginny

THURSDAY, OCTOBER 8

*D*uring these first couple of days back in Westtown, I think I was trying to just be. Be with my family. Enjoy the company. And allow the reality of Kirby's loss to sink in. It was so tempting to believe that she was on her way to join us, but in odd moments— brushing my teeth, running down to the basement to grab some extra paper towels, looking out to the lake for an eagle—I'd let the tears of that reality come.

And if only it could have just been that: the struggle to come to terms with her loss. That's enough, really. To have to grapple with a loss that, even removed from circumstances, was so unfair.

But, unfortunately, the circumstances of her death were like a hum in the background of this time when we were trying to simply face our loss in the comfort of togetherness. Occasionally, a note of this quiet but unsettling composition would puncture the coziness with a sharp dissonance. My mother was collecting those errant notes as she called more participants and documented the details in her notebook.

Tuesday morning dawned.

Mika called and told us the box of clothing was shipped and should arrive soon. She also provided some more details about Angel Valley. Amayra, the owner of the ranch, explained that Ray did not cooperate with the police after they arrived on the scene. Mika confirmed that Julie was strangely "unemotional and seemed brainwashed" when they spoke with her on Sunday.

Julie had told me Kirby's camera and journal were not in her room, so the items were probably in her backpack outside the sweat lodge. I called Detective Diskin to inquire if they had found Kirby's knapsack.

Later that day, Connor's father expressed concern that his son was not his usual, vibrant self. He also commented that people in California were taking "pot shots" at Ray. These conversations were mind-blowing to me. Did his father not realize that his son was traumatized, could have died because of Ray's incompetence and lack of leadership?

In a conversation with Bob Magnanini, Det. Diskin delivered more details. The participants were being re-interviewed, and they could not remember what they had said when first questioned on Thursday night after the sweat lodge ceremony. They explained that many people were dragged out of the tent by round four, but by the end people were so depleted they couldn't help each other. James Shore, it was said, had dragged someone out and then went back into the tent. Diskin thought James Shore realized people were in trouble and went back inside to help them. The police were giving priority to interviewing everyone who had been near Kirby and James inside the tent. We learned that one woman, Liz Neuman, was still in intensive care. She had been brought to the local hospital as a Jane Doe. Her family was not notified and had no idea where she was. The hospital had no information about whom to call. It was sometime on Saturday that her cousin asked the local hospital to describe the Jane Doe who was there, only to discover it was Liz.

By Tuesday evening, we still did not know when Kirby's body would be released. We had not heard any official cause of death and we did not know when we would be able to plan a funeral.

The days were awash with tears, little sleep, hugging the babies close, and phone calls interspersed with bits and pieces of information from the Yavapai police. Late Tuesday afternoon, someone who said they were James Ray's assistant called and asked when would be a convenient time for him to call.

Suddenly, the kitchen went into a spin. I gripped the edge of the counter. It was late afternoon. The room was well lit with natural light pouring through all the windows. Our home is set into a slope so that the front door is at street level and the basement door is at ground level at the back of the house. The kitchen is on the first floor. When you sit at the kitchen table, it feels like being in a treehouse with windows on three sides. It is a beautiful, alive room, with a view of trees, fields, gardens, and lake; this room that had always felt comfortably safe suddenly felt foreign. Time seemed to slow down, and I felt terrified, paranoid, convinced that the call would be recorded and that anything I said could be twisted and used against us in the future.

Kirby had led a very unconventional life. Exciting and incredibly vibrant, men were quickly attracted to her. She fell in love easily and then struggled to figure out if that person was truly "right" for her. What did she reveal to Ray? Could her words, experiences, be presented in an ugly way that obliterated the goodness of her heart?

I couldn't save her life, but I was determined to protect her reputation. I kept thinking about what Julie had told me about Ray giving "special exercises" to Kirby.

Bob Magnanini, our nephew, the lawyer, was there and listened as I shared my fears. I asked, "What should I say? I know this man is powerful, well known. I don't know what he knows about Kirby. Could he blame Kirby for her death?"

Bob assured me, "Speaking to him is important. Let's see what he has to say."

"I'm worried the conversation will be recorded. Could he use it against us in some way?"

"Just listen," Bob said.

I'm not totally sure what I was afraid of beyond besmirching

Kirby's character. I think on a gut level I feared he was responsible for this disaster and the eruption of my rage would result in a crazy rant of angry threats.

Ray called at 5:45 pm and asked to speak to me. (Later, I wondered "Why me? Why not Kirby's parents? Did Ray know that I was calling people, trying to discover what had really happened?")

When the call from him came, we were prepared. Well no, we were all completely freaked out. There was an ongoing police investigation. Was Ray cooperating with the investigators? Had he really fled the scene after the sweat lodge? And what exactly had happened—would he be able and willing to explain it all to us?

To speak with him amid all of this uncertainty was scary. We all manned our spots in the kitchen during the call. My mother held the phone and put it on speaker. I was sitting near her, my dad, brother, and cousins; everyone was standing nearby to hear. My cousin Tommy, who'd been helping us handle media inquiries, gripped the edge of the counter with one hand, resting his weight there. My brother stared at a spot about a foot in front of the phone, like he was writing the words of the conversation on the slate blue floor tiles.

I watched my mother take this call. She was very still, although her hands shook slightly—with nerves, I'm sure, though it could have been from the force of her grip on the receiver.

I remember the quiet calm in her voice—a calm that, as her child, I recognized as that last attempt at sanity before the break of anger—when she pleaded with Ray to "just cooperate with the police, please."

The kitchen went quiet. A palpable tension filled every corner.

I felt both numb and cold all over. Shaking, I took hold of the receiver and put the phone on speaker so everyone could hear.

Ray asked, "How are you?"

I replied, "In shock."

He said, "I am too. This is the most difficult thing I have ever experienced in my entire life. I don't know how this could have happened."

"Have you spoken with the police?" We knew by then that he had hired his own investigation team and was not cooperating with the officials in Yavapai. "Please just cooperate with the local police who are investigating."

"I am and, in fact, I have hired my own investigators to get to the bottom of this."

After talking more about how shook up he was, he spoke about Kirby. "Her light," he said, "and love will live on in you. ...You need to know that Kirby was in a really good place."

Good place! "Too bad that place was with you in Sedona."

He expressed chagrin that this terrible accident had occurred. "Kirby gave me a beautiful crystal. I am wondering if you would like me to send it to you."

Kirby and her partner, Nancy, had been making beaded crystal chains to use in the homes they decorated in Cabo. I later found out that she had taken a few, anticipating that she would meet amazing people and wanted to have gifts for those she met.

"Yes," I replied. I never received it. I later discovered it was found in a box that was under a table in the Crystal Hall at Angel Valley.

He also told me he had made a donation to the Surf Rider Foundation. It would take a few weeks before we realized the $100 donation had been made by Meghan Fredrickson, his executive assistant.

"Please call my assistant if you ever need anything."

The call lasted seven minutes.

For as many times as I roll my eyes now at the pathetic assur-

ances and deflections he made on that call, I know I didn't move then, listening to his over-confident voice.

After the call was over—a call that only lasted about five minutes or so—there was a collective letting out of breath and thoughts.

"Wait a minute," I said to whoever was listening as we all relayed our impressions. "Did he even say sorry? I heard 'I'm sorry... that this happened' and that this is the worst thing that has ever happened... to him."

Time had stopped as I held the phone. I remember envisioning his white-toothed, smarmy smile, talking, absolving himself of any responsibility. I don't even remember hearing the words "I am sorry." This was just an unfortunate occurrence that confounded him. Neither he nor any of his staff had informed us on that Thursday night, never took responsibility for shipping her or her things home, never paid for a funeral.

That evening, he was on the stage at an event, declaring that his work was too important to be postponed or delayed by this unfortunate tragedy. He announced that he had spoken to the victims' families.

From the calls with Connor and Julie, it was clear that Ray was in charge of the event, and that he encouraged and pushed people to endure the challenge of his sweat lodge. With this call—so many days after Kirby had died—I began to suspect that James Ray was focused on how this event was impacting him. I wondered if he had any intention of taking responsibility; that certainly hadn't come across in his words.

Beverley Bunn, another participant of Spiritual Warrior who had befriended Kirby, called at about nine o'clock. We crowded around the dining room table where my mother was sitting while talking on the phone and taking notes.

When I went to Vietnam while studying abroad during my under-

grad, I took a tour of the Reunification Palace in Ho Chi Minh City. It was built during the Vietnam War as the residence of the South Vietnamese president. It is best known as the site where the first Communist army tanks broke through the gates at the end of the war in 1975.

The basement of the Reunification Palace contains a bunker and wartime communications center—a crisis room. The stale 1970s air in the rooms holds dust particles in suspension like salt in water. But even stripped of its purpose, its remaining artifacts under Plexiglas, the war room still has a particular energy to it. Places do this, as if they have their own adrenal glands pumping out cortisol to feed the action in moments of stress.

The dining room was the crisis room in our house, and it had this same buzz of emergency. My mother was in command—talking with the investigators in Arizona to glean whatever information they were able to give us, contacting other participants for more details (or trying to—many of them didn't want to talk), tracking down friends of Kirby to find out if she'd said or done anything odd before going on the retreat. The dining table was covered with paper—the shards of truth we were trying to assemble into an explanation.

At 9:00 pm, the phone rang again. It was Beverley Bunn who was with Kirby in Sedona. I took the call in the dining room and started writing down what I was hearing. My journal was becoming my anchor to rationality, allowing me time to process information so that I could respond and not just react.

Beverley was Kirby's roommate. She described some of the events of the retreat. They had both cut their hair, but only after a few days of considering its meaning. Through tears, Beverley kept saying, "I am so sorry."

She described the tent. "It was suffocating. Packed, shoulder to shoulder. We entered together. Kirby was so excited about this final adventure. After the first three rounds, I couldn't breathe. I moved... tried to leave. As I moved past

Ray, he said 'You of all people, you're going to leave? You are more than that.' I was ashamed... stayed inside and found another spot near the opening where there seemed to be a little more air."

Beverley was crying. "People said 'Kirby's not awake. She needs to get out.' I was disoriented. I couldn't see. I heard her trying to breathe. I had no voice to call to her. Ray said, 'We'll deal with that later, at the end of the round.'"

Beverley, who had struggled to survive, was consumed with guilt. She sobbed. Then, she said, "When the last round was over, once I was out of the tent, they poured cold water on me. I looked around. It was total chaos. I helped people who were disoriented, convulsing, vomiting, needing water. A few of us worked together to revive people who were unconscious. I did not see Kirby and I panicked."

She started looking for her. After about twenty minutes, she saw that Kirby had been dragged out of the back of the tent. Someone was trying and failing to administer CPR.

"I tried to get to Kirby. I told them I was a doctor and could help."

Choking on more tears, she said, "The 'dream team' [Ray's unpaid volunteers] held me back. I tried. I tried. They wouldn't let me get to her. I am so sorry. I am so sorry."

As my mother talked to Beverley, her writing became more and more agitated—angular, staccato—as she gripped her pen harder and harder. Her dark eyebrows pressed together and the muscles in her neck looked like they were going to tear through her skin.

And then she screamed, dropped the phone.

Anguish raged through me, collapsing in an immobilizing grief that confirmed all my worst fears. This was no accident. His people were trying to protect him, control the damage, caring less for the lives of the injured. Everyone rushed at me. I tried to tell them what Beverley had said and could hardly breathe. Speaking to Beverley felt like that split second before imminent tragedy, the crunching of the car before the impact, the awareness of a fall that will break a bone, the cry of a child that signals something really serious, and you suddenly know "This is it. There is no going back."

This moment, the shift moment, plays in my memory like a news story you'd watch on TV of a bombing in some distant war-torn country—blood-streaked faces wailing at the cameras in anguish and confusion. Everyone lost the warm energy of togetherness and instead exploded with anger, confusion, and grief, as my mother tried to convey what Beverley had told her. What came through her gulps for air and broken phrases was that Ray had ignored participants who were telling him that Kirby was in distress. Beverley's information suddenly assembled all of those discordant notes into a theme we could follow: James Ray had built a sweat lodge, kept people inside, and didn't let them leave when they were dying.

For me, it was like the minivan all over again, when Mike had first delivered the awful news that Kirby died—a door slamming behind me, those metal holes where the seats click in threatening to swallow me. I ran out of the house onto the front lawn and screamed "FUCK YOU, JAMES RAY!" He had killed her. My sister. She was dead and it was his fault.

I still cannot remember what happened next. I think we had our check-in session after this. After breathing and recovering somewhat, I knew I had to call Beverley to reassure her that I did not blame her and to thank her for being so brave, calling us to tell us what had happened. She was the only person I spoke to that week who seemed human, with real emotion and understanding that what happened was wrong, criminal.

We did speak the next day and I was able to convey our gratitude. She came to Kirby's funeral the next Saturday, flying from Texas with a friend—an incredible kindness I will remember forever.

George started. "Okay, let's talk about what we have learned from these two important phone calls."

The anger expressed on this night was now focused on James Ray, the architect of this disaster: his arrogant hubris, inability to be honest about the police investigation, and his continual reference to this as an "accident" that totally baffled him. Beverley's revelations about Ray's refusal to stop or check on anyone during the ceremony and the chaos afterwards with no appropriate planning or care for those harmed, had us all reeling.

While George was rightfully furious, he was able to keep our session focused, allowing everyone a chance to express their anger.

On this Tuesday, five days after Kirby died, we gained a clearer picture of what had happened from Beverley and a chilling perspective on Ray's character from his call. The whole tragedy moved from being just horrible to being horrible and probably criminal. The fact that Ray wasn't cooperating with authorities and wasn't taking responsibility for what happened caused his image to loom up like a wall—a wall between us and the truth, between Kirby and justice. The thought of a contentious legal battle became inevitable.

Then, the paranoia set in. I remember standing up in the attic with my sister-in-law, Kory, talking about the newest details. We were looking out the front window of the house, toward the parking lot of the church across the street.

"These are powerful people," she said. "It's kind of scary."

There was a strange car parked across the street and I was struck with the sudden feeling that we were being watched. This was total paranoia, but the feeling had parked inside my mind: James Ray's smooth evasions on the phone followed by Beverley's revelations made me feel we were dealing with something more sinister than we'd first realized.

That night, I couldn't sleep. I just kept reliving and reviewing the conversations with Ray and Beverley. I must have fallen asleep at some point because I thought I saw Kirby in the distance and, although I couldn't reach her, she seemed okay and peaceful.

Chapter 2

" I am so grateful for this life I have created.
I am blessed and surrounded by angels.
I give thanks to this earth, to my loved ones who
have passed, to all of my relationships, to all of my
experiences. "

— *Kirby's Vision Quest Journal*

Jean

In high school, I saved up and bought myself a Discman. Because I was buying it with my own money, it wasn't a purchase that required parental approval. But my father let his feelings be known. "I don't like this," he told me. "It promotes solitary activity." While my mother was the coordinator in the family—the one who'd organize our activities and plans—my father fostered the sense of togetherness and family bonding.

My parents are both counsellors, so there was a professional side to how they cared for all of us during this time immediately following Kirby's death. Even in this time of horrible grief, when my dad must have felt disembodied in his own way, he still made sure that none of us was retreating too far inward into solitary anguish. We would grieve together.

Dad slipped from father to counsellor during his check-ins. We'd talk about what had happened during the day and how it made us feel.

When we discussed the details of what had happened to Kirby, I would shake—not just a small tremor in my hands, but a full, deep-body shake that came from my very core. Death is so basic, so elemental. It makes sense that it strikes right at the most primitive part of our brain, the amygdala. That's where the "fight or flight" adrenaline comes from and, oh man, the adrenaline would pump through my body so fiercely that my teeth chattered too. But I was just sitting still—sitting still, trying not to run. So I shook.

In addition to the effort to keep from falling apart that week, we started preparing for the wake and funeral. We gathered photos of Kirby for a slideshow that would play at the wake. I called my wedding photographer—I hadn't even gotten the thank you cards that were part of the package because our wedding had only been three months before—to ask her permission to use photos she'd taken.

"Of course," she said when we spoke. And then later, in an email, she went on: "I've shot numerous weddings and honestly, I can't say that I remember everyone's siblings/bridal party, but Kirby definitely stands out. ...After your call, I looked through your wedding pictures; she shows up in many of the shots, because she was everywhere and with everyone; enjoying life. Although I only spent a day in her presence, I am truly honored to have crossed paths with such a beautiful person, who so happily walked me around the house and introduced me to everyone, making sure that I was comfortable...."

In the days and weeks after Kirby died, I got a lot of messages like this—friends and new family members who had just met Kirby on the day of our wedding, but on whom she'd left such a strong impression. My brother-in-law, quiet and reserved, told me about how Kirby had seen right through his "tough guy" persona and had made him feel welcome at my parents' house. Even on a day that was insanely busy for our family and for Kirby as my maid of honor, she'd managed to interact with everyone there in just the way that had meant something to them.

While organizing the photos for the slideshow, we discussed background music. Louis Armstrong's What a Wonderful World *was a given; it has been sort of an anthem for my family for as long as I can remember as the background of brunch on Sundays and the song we'd all danced with our parents to.*

But we needed a second song. I thought about other music that had been important to our family and to Kirby. Music she'd shared with us, albums she'd bought and stacked next to the stereo in the house. I thought about the beachy vibes of Jack Johnson, the album playing in her Toyota 4Runner while we drove around the Baja on a spring break visit. I thought about the jazz vocalists she'd told me to start listening to and the Grateful Dead she'd played in her room when we were growing up.

Then I had it.

"What about Into the Mystic?*" I said to my brother. Van Morrison was a regular performer on our household stereo.*

"Yes," Bobby said. "That's it."

Van Morrison has said this song is simply about being a part of the universe. In one of those examples of great art, it's a song that can resonate with so many people and their individual experiences. The idea of a "gypsy soul" "coming home," and not fearing the mystical unknown at the end of that journey—these words will always be about Kirby, for me. I can't think of it without getting chills or tears and it was years before I could even listen to it again.

Kirby's death wasn't some metaphysical journey she chose or some kind of karmic reckoning; it was wrong. But even then—even in a death marked by injustice, criminality, violence—there is a peace at the end that waits for all of us.

In the quieter moments of that first week, when we weren't making preparations or discussing our new reality together as a family, I started researching anything that related to Kirby's death. I Googled sweat lodges. The Native American community was already fuming about the cultural appropriation that had bloodied a sacred spiritual

ritual. What I learned in my research sessions, usually late at night when I couldn't sleep, was that James Ray's tent was an irresponsible and erroneous re-creation of a real sweat lodge.

A real sweat lodge isn't covered in plastic tarps. A real sweat lodge holds no more than about six to ten people. A real sweat lodge is led by someone who has apprenticed for years to learn how to safely conduct a lodge. A real sweat lodge is never conducted for money, because it is too dangerous to have people seeking a certain value out of their experience. A real sweat lodge is never regarded as a test of physical endurance.

Even after reading a few articles about sweat lodges, it was clear that James Ray had abused a sacred tradition, used it for monetary gain, and had done it in a manner that was so irresponsible it had killed people. He presented himself as qualified to lead a sweat lodge when he had never received the proper training to do so.

The other threads of information I began to find were about the wider self-help industry. I started to see bits about "large group awareness training" and seminar experiences that are designed to make attendees more likely to buy further into a program—more events, books, CD series, personal coaching. I started to read about neurolinguistic programming (NLP), a teaching technique based on neuroscience which uses intense verbal repetition to create alignment between teacher and student.

Some of these details reminded me of a book I'd read for grad school, Naomi Klein's The Shock Doctrine. *In this book about the "shock therapy" effect of modern neoliberal economic policies on developing nations, Klein talks about the CIA-funded MKULTRA mind control experiments conducted by Dr. Ewen Cameron in the 1950s and 1960s. These experiments formed the basis of the KUBARK interrogation manual. Cameron, in a horrifying experimental "therapy" program, used shock therapy, but also sleep deprivation, light and sound manipulation, and other forms of sensory deprivation to attempt to "erase" the psyche of the patient* and make them more amenable to suggestion in the course of their therapy.

As we learned more about Spiritual Warrior, I saw these threads fusing together and a pattern forming from this tangle of confusing details—a pattern of events wherein James Ray had manipulated his participants to follow him by limiting their sleep, water, and food, and by cultivating their cooperation in this closed group environment.

The information I was finding, along with all of the other details we'd gotten from the police and other participants, settled within me like sediment, building layers of feeling. If you cut me open, the cross-section would reveal these revelations of truth, but also bands of anger, sadness, horror, piled on top of one another and compressed into a striated lump in my gut. Breaking that mass into pieces and redistributing them so they can't sink me has taken a long time.

It's important to understand: the event that Kirby attended wasn't a cult, but James Ray massaged the compliance of his customers with cultish tactics.

And yet, Ray was clearly distancing himself from any responsibility at that point. When we heard about a call that he had held with other Spiritual Warrior participants and the "channeler" who explained that Kirby had chosen to die, I really started to get pissed. Kirby hadn't chosen to die. She had done exactly what she was told to do by James Ray all week and it had killed her. During one of our evening check-ins, I described it like this: Ray was a product that needed to be recalled.

Ginny

WEDNESDAY, OCTOBER 14

At 6:00 am, after tossing and turning most of the night, George and I talked about the night before. How could this have happened? All of my thinking coalesced into one idea: Kirby Brown meeting James Ray was the perfect storm: the perfect confluence of Ray's arrogant ego, his power trip of challenging others to push beyond their limits, and Kirby, who had played "full on" since birth. She rarely backed down once she committed herself to something. Fearlessly approaching kiteboarding, surfing, horseback riding, she worked on refining her skills with a single-minded tenacity. She was determined to finish college in four years even though, after graduating, when I asked what she learned as an English major she said, "I learned I could finish something I hated." A fiercely loyal friend, she extended herself in extraordinary ways to help others. She was physically and mentally strong in her yoga practice. His hubris clashed with her physicality, her acceptance of challenge, her determination to make changes in her life, her drive to always do more, be more.

Beverley Bunn indicated that Ray prompted his participants to go beyond their body in order to experience the promised "breakthrough," to discover one's real inner self and maximize their investment of time and money.

The idea that this had been the perfect storm suddenly made some sense to me—a partial explanation for the question "Why Kirby?"

Bob Magnanini, in speaking with Detective Diskin the night before, learned that the Mercers were the fire tenders. Debra

Mercer discovered that there were three bodies still inside the tent fifteen minutes *after* the ceremony was concluded. Ray admonished them for picking up the back of the tent, saying it was sacrilegious to do so. She dragged Kirby and James from the tent anyway, pleading for help. Jennifer, a volunteer, started giving Kirby CPR. Those fifteen minutes could have meant the difference between life and death. Obviously, Ray never "dealt with it later," as he had assured people he would when they expressed concern during the ceremony.

I spoke to Tommy about our response for the Associated Press and my concerns about media at the church. We called Detective Diskin to find out if help was being provided for the traumatized victims and shared the details of the call we had received from Ray the night before. I called Christopher Shore to check on his family.

Kate had arranged for us to go to the Bella Vista Spa in Westtown that afternoon. She knew we needed some TLC. Everyone in the salon knows us and knew what had happened. The last time I sat in that chair to have a pedicure was the Friday before Jean's wedding in July. I wanted to turn the clock back to that day. I remembered sitting in that chair, looking out on the beautiful valley before me, filled with hope and excitement for Jean's wedding. How could I escape the reality of that day, the day before a wake for my oldest daughter? After receiving a fabulously relaxing massage, the masseuse said, "You should try the sauna." I visibly recoiled; the suggestion seemed so insensitively insane. Noting my reaction, he said, "I thought, given the circumstances, embracing the heat might be healing." I realized then that people would do and say things to help, even if the sentiments are not welcome or helpful at the moment.

Tommy discovered that Sandy Andretti had been a participant at the retreat. She is the mother of Marco Andretti, a skilled racecar driver and grandson of the famous Mario Andretti. I was shocked and intrigued that a celebrity had been at the retreat. He contacted her and learned that Ray had set up a conference call with participants from the retreat that day. Sandy Andretti lived in Pennsylvania within a two-hour drive from us. Tommy arranged to meet at her home to listen to and record the call. I was fearful that such an action was illegal and, yet, we needed to know what was being said, how Ray was explaining this debacle.

Before Tommy had even returned, that same evening, we went to the funeral parlor to see Kirby. The autopsy had been completed on Tuesday night and her body flown home on Wednesday. Time stopped as George and I looked at our beautiful daughter bruised and burned, hair shorn, life gone, almost unrecognizable. I gently traced her distinctive eyebrows to assure myself that yes, this was Kirby. Our children looked on with horror at their sister silenced in death. Were we somehow clinging to the possibility that this was all a mistake?

I had learned from Julie that Kirby had cut her hair, so we were prepared to see her long blond streaked locks gone.

I understand the significance, the symbolism, of hair-cutting in retreat-like settings. It is an ancient spiritual practice, sometimes signaling humility or submission, often a metaphor for leaving the past behind to grow into a new reality. Knowing Kirby, I assumed she would have done this for the latter reason. Still, I was surprised. Kirby was vain about her hair. She had purchased a professional grade hair dryer; she dressed up in ways to show off her hair. But she was serious about wanting change, moving forward, embracing expansion and new growth.

I asked the funeral director to see if they could find a wig before the viewing, knowing that her short hair would be upsetting to everyone. I did not have any clothing for her yet, so I offered a beautiful top that her friend Deborah Goldstein had given me to dress Kirby in.

We returned home in silence, numb. As I walked into the

living room, our friends were there, waiting for our return. Liz Holst had been coordinating food all week, her husband Ed was helping to plan the funeral Mass. Mark and Fran had returned home from Florida two weeks early to be with us, helping with the little ones and all the people in the house. I was so grateful for their presence. I couldn't speak, could not share what we had seen. They cried with us and we were comforted by their sorrowful embraces of love.

After our friends left, George gathered us into the living room.

When we moved to Westtown in 1981, wanting to be more self-sufficient, we decided to purchase an efficient Vermont Castings wood burning stove to heat the entire house. The previous owner of our home had removed walls and hall-ways between the entryway, living room, and kitchen to create a "great room" which allowed the heat to rise to the second floor, naturally traveling up the stairway. Over the years, George would fell trees, chainsaw logs, teach our Bobby to split wood, and the entire family would stack and carry wood into the house all winter. That night, George had started a fire in our wood-burning stove to take the chill off the troubling revelations and experiences that day had brought us. Tommy discussed the conference call.

"One of the dream teamers," he said, "reported a 'chan-neler' sat next to Kirby and James Shore. Believe this shit? The channeler 'revealed' they were having such a good time that they chose not to return to their bodies."

How convenient! How incredibly convenient—an abso-lution. I was stunned that people could actually buy the explanation that these two amazing, very alive people would actually *choose* death! Kirby spent her savings to expand her life, not lose it. James Shore had a wife and three young children, and we are to believe he chose to leave? This confirmed James Ray's malevolence: he allowed himself and these traumatized participants to embrace a fantasy. It was such a simplistic inter-pretation for his depraved indifference and reckless behavior. Facing this kind of behavior made me ill and terrified that this evil was being visited upon my family.

Tommy said, "The guy actually warned against going to a traditional, licensed therapist. He provided a name of a 'like-minded' counselor who might help anyone needing to process this…this bullshit!"

George realized we all needed to talk about how we felt see-ing Kirby's body. Talking about it that night helped that image from being too firmly implanted and magnified over time. The finality of touching her lifeless body was another layer of con-fronting this reality.

THURSDAY, OCTOBER 15

I woke up Thursday morning after my first night of decent sleep. Cleaning up the kitchen with Jean, after breakfast, I felt a growing energy. Threads of an angry defiance began to weave together to create a steely resolve. Standing in the very place where I had heard James Ray's pathetic declaration that this had been an "unfortunate accident," I decided: This was NOT going to kill US! There would be no additional victims taken as a result of James Ray. We were going to do this thing… a wake, a funeral, a beautiful tribute to show the world our daughter and what had been done to her! This strong sense of purpose still walks beside our grief and devastation as we struggle to expose danger and fraud in the industry that so needlessly took her life.

Later that morning, a large cardboard box arrived from Mika with things they had recovered in Sedona. I asked my friend Debbie to open the box with me. Sitting on my bedroom floor, we looked at the box knowing that pieces of Kirby were inside. Tentatively, I began to unwrap some clothing items and jewelry.

Finally, I saw her hair, a ponytail about five inches long—her beautiful blond-streaked tresses. The perfume of patchouli oil permeated her hair and possessions. Drinking in her scent, Debbie held me close as I sobbed for what seemed like hours.

Another item arrived in the mail that day: a sympathy card from James Ray with a $5,000 check "in honor of Kirby Brown" written in the corner. (Not nearly enough for transport or funeral arrangements.) An earlier sympathy card with a standard message of sympathy had arrived on Tuesday and been flagged as "suspicious" because we could not clearly discern the signature. It was also from James Ray. Bob Magnanini told me that if I cashed the check, it could be construed as compensation—a settlement—making suing difficult. I held her hair. I did not cash the check. My stomach churned.

Amidst it all, we had to focus on the funeral arrangements.

Ed Holst was handling the requested readings, songs, and booklet. I called Kirby's godfather, Fr. Larry Hinch, the priest who would say the funeral Mass. Larry has always been an important member of our family. George and I had met at St. Paul's Cursillo Center in Greenpoint, Brooklyn, in 1967 when Fr. Larry was in charge of the retreat center. After Kirby's birth, we had asked Larry to be her godfather, to make him an official part of our family. George loves to tell people that we met in a "priest's bedroom." The truth is, he was teaching in a Catholic girls' high school in Brooklyn and had come to the center to learn about a school retreat. I was working on the leadership team for the next retreat and we were all in Larry's room, sitting on the floor, talking over a pizza when Fr. Larry introduced George to the team. The students George later sent to the retreat decided we would make a "good couple." How insightful high school students can be!

In Westtown, we live across from the Westtown Presbyterian Church, our wonderful neighbors. They offered their hall for us to hold a reception on Saturday afternoon after the funeral Mass in Otisville. Liz was coordinating food for the reception. Donations were coming from Holy Cross and Holy Name, two Catholic churches, and the Presbyterian Church. So many people were involved in showering us with support.

Thursday afternoon would mean seeing Kirby laid out and greeting the first of hundreds who would arrive to mourn and try to comfort us. Walking into the room with the immediate family felt so unreal—how could this be real? We learned that Jodie, Mary McPhillips' daughter (who was Kirby's friend), had been contacted by a friend in Minneapolis; the friend told her that her cousin, James Shore, had died at a retreat in a sweat lodge in Sedona. Then and now, coincidences and connections continue to surround this event, causing us to constantly wonder and question our role, our purpose, and convincing me that I must be Kirby's voice which was silenced by James Ray. I asked Jodie to find out the arrangements for James Shore's funeral so we could send flowers.

When we walked into the viewing room at the funeral parlor, we saw Kirby wrapped in a Mexican-looking shawl. Jodie and Mary McPhillips explained that, due to the severe dehydration, her body did not embalm properly; her body cavity sucked up the fluids which caused bloating. Kirby looked better than the night before, but the lovely top Deborah had given me to dress her in didn't fit. The shawl, Mary explained, absorbed any possible leakage from the autopsy incisions. Makeup covered the bruises and burns. Jodie had found a wig, but I struggled to find Kirby in it—the length and swirl of the hair were not Kirby. Without movement, without smiling, laughing, or giving orders, this body was far removed from the daughter, sister, friend that everyone was coming to mourn.

George and I held each other and sobbed together. The room vanished and only this tragedy, this chasm of loss, engulfed us.

Knowing I needed to pull myself together, summoning every ounce of internal strength, I braced myself for those who would be arriving. They will be mourning too. I reached inside to summon that steely resolve.

A few questioned me about her appearance, her hair in particular. I think the wig was still less shocking than her shorn head. Somehow, I needed to see her for a few more hours before her body was consumed.

At home, exhausted, George called us into the living room to share our experiences of the wake. I warned everyone the night before that people would not know what to say. They might even say something that would be insensitive or offensive, especially when asking for details. We would be consoling others who had no words for us.

We were all awed at how many people were there: old friends not seen in years and people we did not know who knew Kirby. Joan, George's sister, and her husband, Bob, had flown in from Los Angeles and were staying at a local hotel. This was a huge sacrifice for them because Bob was struggling with numerous medical issues and this trip was clearly a physical strain. Seeing them at the funeral parlor, I immediately thought of all the cross-country camping trips we had shared with Joan and Bob and their son, Jimmy, when the children were young. Many people had stories to tell of how important she was to them. I have always felt that a wake should be a way to pay tribute and honor the deceased as well as provide support to those grieving. The music and slideshow were beautiful. At midnight, we went to bed.

FRIDAY, OCTOBER 16

Another day. After showering, I checked to make sure everything was set for Saturday's funeral Mass.

She looked better, less swollen, in her own shirt and jewelry. They drained her body and re-embalmed her to control the bloating caused by her dehydrated cells.

More people to grieve, more stories to hear, more tears to shed.

After our pastor offered prayers at the funeral parlor, I invited people to publicly tell stories. For about twenty minutes, a few people shared their Kirby experiences. I wanted the telling to go on for hours, to hear her impact on others and feel the vibrancy of her spirit. I didn't want to leave that moment.

When we got home, George again called us into the safety of the place where everyone could share what we had seen, heard, and felt during the day. Now, his nightly check-ins felt like a normal, expected part of our days. We talked about who had been at the wake, stories that had been told, the preparations for the funeral Mass, managing media at the Church, and how this tragedy was shaping our lives.

Tommy later shared with me how important those evening sessions were to him, allowing him to be part of the family's "inner circle" and see how we were processing this tragedy.

Jean

*W*e made preparations—*ones we had spoken about and ones we made on our own—without Kirby's body physically there. When she finally did arrive, we went to see her.*

Having grown up Catholic, I've seen many dead bodies at open casket wakes. These bodies have a particular look. Layers of specialty make-up, carefully chosen clothing, jewelry, all composed to render the person as they were in life, perhaps sleeping peacefully, with color in the cheeks, a soft expression.

When Kirby's body finally returned from Arizona after the investigators had finished their autopsy and examination, we went to the funeral parlor where the wake would be. I'm actually not sure if this is normal—for the family to see the deceased prior to the body being prepped for the wake—or if the owners of the funeral home, the McPhillips, did this for us because of the circumstances and because we knew them personally. But we went—my immediate family—to see Kirby as she had arrived in her raw state.

We entered the funeral parlor from a side door closest to the viewing room where she was and where the wake would later be held. It's a room like most funeral parlors—soft colors, lots of drapery, the accordion room dividers to open or close up the space depending on the size of the crowd, that lingering smell of commingled flowers like irises, roses, daisies that I have always associated with death. We walked through the entrance to the room and turned right toward an additional room whose walls were pushed open to increase the space. This room is oriented perpendicular to the main room, with the chairs here facing toward the sides of the other chairs.

Kirby's body was laid out on a rolling table at the juncture of the two spaces. I had thought maybe I'd recoil from the body, afraid and angry. But instead I felt drawn to it. I wanted to hold her. I wanted to feel her. I circled around the gurney, picking up limbs, feeling the weight of her arms and legs. I held her hands and pressed my fingers into them, feeling that leathery texture of her dead flesh.

I held her head in my hand, ran my fingers over her closely shaved scalp. I asked in horror what the large gash on her skull was, sewn up so that it felt like two pieces of hide pulled together, like on a football. "That was from the autopsy," Mrs. McPhillips told me. But there were other injuries that I inspected—a scrape on her forehead (she'd taken a fall during the retreat), scratches on her cheeks (from pushing her face into the dirt for cool air?), cuts and bumps on her legs.

I knew this body wasn't her. You can feel that immediately with dead bodies. But still it drew me in. It wasn't exactly affection I felt for this body. It was more like protection. I examined her body like I'd somehow be able to answer all the lingering questions about her death. I was looking for clues.

The most telling signs of her death, however, were no longer there: the organs removed in the embalming process. Those organs had been cooked.

But there was one visible sign of the trauma that this body had undergone. As the funeral director explained to us, one of the reasons for the delay of her body's return to the East Coast was that it had reacted strangely to the embalming fluid. Having died of heat stroke, the body was severely dehydrated. When the coroners in Arizona first injected the embalming fluid, the body soaked it up like a sponge. Because the cells in the body were so dehydrated, they'd shriveled up like raisins—they were unable to absorb the fluid. Instead, the liquid oozed into the tissue spaces between the cells.

When the body arrived in New York, the McPhillips actually had to drain the body and then repeat the process to be sure that the fluid would work properly to preserve the body for the viewing. As a result, Kirby's body was puffy and bloated, adding to the surreal look a corpse takes on in comparison with the person as she looked in life.

Later, during the trial, when James Ray's lawyers would try to sow doubt in the jurors' minds by offering alternative explanations for the death, like poisoning from insecticides, I would think of that day, seeing Kirby's body, bloated with embalming fluid because of how the withered cells were incapable of accepting any liquid offered, even after they had been so thoroughly cooked to death.

But those moments of silent fury, ruminating over the reality of what had happened while listening to the lawyers attempt to spin a fantasy in which Ray was completely innocent, were months away.

First, there was the wake and funeral.

One of the strangest sensations that stands out from these events was the feeling that my immediate family was somehow in the role of comforting everyone else. I didn't think at the time of how peculiar and backwards that is—aren't these events held in part so that those closest to the person can be comforted by others? Shouldn't we have been receiving the hugs and reassurances? And, of course, that did happen. But the feeling that I had to console everyone else was much stronger than the impulse to seek comfort from them.

Kirby was the sort of person who acts as a pillar in the lives of people close to her. Her loss was devastating to so many who had relied on her to walk them through their own problems as well as share in their joy. Kirby was that special combination of loyal and useful. She was the person who got shit done.

This is what she was to people, so I think that the idea that she could be vulnerable to the sort of death that claimed her was deeply unsettling for everyone. When she died, my immediate family instinctively knew that her death was shocking not just because of her age or how she died, but because of how largely she loomed in the lives of people close to her.

The wake was held a week after Kirby died. There were still so many unknowns at that point. I tried in my hugs and smiles to offer reassurances to others. I was certain even at that point that Kirby's death was not her own fault and I wanted people to understand that.

So I steeled myself. It was like an acting role—I put on a mask of strength, checked my posture, and held myself up so that I could help hold everyone else up. We all did.

As we stood in that ever-awkward receiving line in the funeral parlor, the casket that held Kirby's body was now the focal point in the main room, to the right of where I stood. She had been made up in that way that dead bodies are, so that people could remark on how "good" she looked. We'd settled on an outfit that didn't feel quite right, because so many of her clothes didn't fit properly. Kirby had loved jewelry and had a huge collection, so we put a statement necklace on her. But nothing looked right. I resisted the urge to make adjustments to her hair and clothing during the hours of the wake itself.

From where I stood in the receiving line, the spot in between the two rooms where Kirby's body had rested on the table earlier that week was at my back and it seemed to hold a presence there—hanging like the electric outline of an image left on your eyelids after you close them. I felt like I was guarding that spot of lingering energy while I shook hands, gave hugs and air kisses.

Because, although I wanted to reassure people that Kirby was still who they knew her to be, there were things I couldn't say or didn't really want to say. For example, we'd decided to put a wig on her body, thinking the sight of her shaved head would be too disturbing. That stubble prickled like a secret in the casket. For those who could tell the hair was fake, it was a whispered message: "We're not quite ready to talk about that just yet."

With the inevitable legal proceedings, both criminal and civil, we also had to guard some of the answers we did have. At one point, one of Kirby's friends from high school approached me. He introduced himself.

"I'm Jim—I graduated from Minisink with Kirby."

"Oh yeah, hi, how are you?" I said, after managing to connect the late-thirties, slightly pudgier and wrinklier face in front of me with the portrait of a boyish eighteen-year-old from the

senior yearbook of Kirby's that I had studied as a kid.

In the awkward silence that came after the initial small talk, I could feel the "What happened?" before he even asked.

"It's just—it's so hard to believe. Kirby.... So, it was some sort of enlightenment retreat or something?"

"Yes." I said. "She'd been there for five days. This was the final event—sort of a sweat lodge."

"Crazy," Jim said. "And the guy who was the... leader?"

"Yeah, we're not really sure at this point. The detectives out there are working on it." But I knew. I knew that Kirby shouldn't have died, that it wasn't just an accident, that another person was responsible for what had happened. I knew. But I couldn't say that yet.

Leaving the wake that night, I passed the little table at the entrance where we'd displayed pictures of Kirby. I had put a poster I'd made in kindergarten, which I'd fished out of the sideboard drawer in the dining room at my parents' house. It was one of those "Who I Am" fill-in-the-blank posters children make in school. "When I grow up, I want to be... paste a picture of your family." Kindergarten for me was the same year that Kirby was a freshman in college, five hours away at Geneseo University in Western New York. In the spot that asked me to explain my "greatest wish" I wrote, "I wish Kirby to come home." I really wanted that poster on the table at the wake, because it was exactly how I felt then.

On the way to Kirby's funeral, on Sunday, I remember my mom's speech to us in the limo, encouraging us not to be led by anger. As she spoke, I looked at the houses out the window, century porches blurred by our movement. I nodded. Because I got it—I knew what she was saying. I don't think I met her eyes, though, because I also knew I wouldn't be able to honor that request right away. I'd be keeping anger close for a while... including right in that moment. At Holy Name Church in Otisville, the parking lot is off to the right when you face the church from the street. Leading up to the front door of the church is a long, straight drive right through the cemetery. That long drive is only ever used for infirm parishioners, or the limos arriving for a wedding or a funeral. I had just been driven up that straight drive for my wedding three months before in a white limo instead of the black one we were in now.

This is bullshit, I thought.

Along with that anger, everything was overwhelming—the FDNY honor guard, the media, so many people. The wake had felt intimate and I felt in control there. But at the funeral, it was like the whole situation had slipped away and ballooned into something else, floating away from us.

I don't remember the readings or Fr. Larry's words. But Bobby, my brother, gave the eulogy. And that I remember. I'd offered to help him write it during the week, but it was clear he didn't need any help. He knew what everyone needed. Nobody needed to hear about who Kirby was or what she'd done in her life; everyone already knew all that. Anyone could have written that eulogy.

Because Kirby's death was so sudden, so shocking, so wrong, what we needed was to hear from Kirby. So Bobby let Kirby speak through him. Through Bobby, Kirby told us not to cry for her, but to laugh and love and learn and live for her. Through Bobby, Kirby spoke to our sister Kate, to me, and our parents with messages and gifts for each of us. I remember feeling honored that I was described as graceful—I'm the youngest in the family, always a bit outside of the loop and clueless, or feeling stupid for messing up a phone message. Graceful wasn't how I saw myself. These words touched me so deeply and are a constant source of inspiration still, as though Kirby really had spoken them to me.

I can't even remember what the weather was that day. But when I think of my brother standing up there delivering his eulogy, I remember that the church was filled—with people but also with light. Behind the altar, there is a floor-to-ceiling stained glass window of two reflected rainbows and Jesus sitting on the Earth in the middle. The walls in the church are white and the space is sparse and open. On that day, while Bobby spoke, that room glowed.

Everyone was weeping when the recessional began. Over the summer, when we were all in Westtown for my wedding, Kirby had shared a DVD of the George Harrison tribute concert that his family had organized at the Royal Albert Hall in London. I can picture Kirby grooving in the living room, arms out and eyes closed, while the Eastern-infused strums of George's music twanged with peace and energy. It was one of those times when Kirby's joy was so meaningful for her that she had to share it with us.

So the song choice for the recessional was a bit of a coup. Catholic priests usually insist on "liturgical" music in church— that is, selections from an official hymnal. But our parish priest at the time was from Vietnam and I believe it was the language or cultural barrier that allowed us to suggest George Harrison's My Sweet Lord *for the recessional song. A chorus singing "Hari Krishna" is definitely not a Catholic liturgical hymn. But it was just the right send-off for Kirby.*

After the funeral, we had a reception in the hall at the Presbyterian church across the street from our house in Westtown. More grains of information about Spiritual Warrior and the "sweat lodge deaths" trickled through the sieve of media reports throughout the week, sparking new lines of inquiry from friends.

For example, the question of Kirby's hair had come up and was now unavoidable with the presence of Beverley Bunn. Beverley is an orthodontist in Texas—very successful and driven. She is like Kirby in many ways—adventurous, hard-working, goal-oriented. And rational. Like Kirby, she'd leapt ahead of the "standard" path of James Ray events, having attended only a short weekend event where she signed up for Spiritual Warrior, an event normally only open to people who'd attended a number of Ray events. Given her independent personality and perhaps this lesser exposure to James Ray, Beverley was one of the only Spiritual Warrior attendees brave and clear enough to speak the truth about what had happened to her and Kirby and the rest of them. To me, Beverley did what I feel certain Kirby would have after the event, had she survived. Like Beverley, Kirby would have been outraged.

But the hair—Beverley's close shave was like Rudolph's nose, Rudolph's nose before he saves Christmas, when he was ostracized and ridiculed by the other reindeer. And I understand why the hair was alarming for people. It screamed "cult."

I wanted to shield Beverley from any prying because, after all, her testimony was a beacon of truth for us. And despite her own personal suffering, she had come to share in ours as well.

After the more formal reception across the street, the gathering continued at my parents' house and loosened up. We moved furniture and made space for musicians. Again, it was fun and beautiful and sad all at the same time. Beverley sat on the stairs, out of the way, and I was very conscious of her presence there.

I don't remember how long I stayed up that night, but there's just one moment that was everything for me. We'd moved the couch back against the staircase. At one point, when I looked toward the stairs to check on Beverley, I saw Kirby's friend, Eric. Eric was the boyfriend (now husband) of one of Kirby's dear friends, Tami. Tami sparkles. She's energetic and lively—she'd always be right along dancing with Kirby at the concert or the bar or the party. Eric, on the other hand, is a wallflower. At that point, I hadn't spoken much with Eric and the match felt odd to me, as it had to Kirby until she'd gotten to know him better. She'd assured me he was "cool," but I'd not had more than polite small talk type conversations with him, even when his family helped out with my wedding.

But when I checked back to see Beverley, it was Eric I saw there on the couch. He sat still, his hands in his lap, with very little expression. But tears were streaming down his face. That was the first time I had really seen him. Naturally, Kirby had shown me.

Ginny

SATURDAY, OCTOBER 17

I warned the priest that media would be present at the church and asked him to speak to the local police to keep them away from the family. Tommy spoke to the news outlets, agreeing to interviews after the Mass, while making it clear that no cameras were allowed in the church, but reporters were welcome to pray with us. I learned later that some of the cousins had spoken to reporters afterwards. We were transported to the church compliments of Johnny Rotondelli at Windsor Limousine, the limo company that Kirby had driven for after she graduated.

On the Isle of Arran off the west coast of Scotland, there is a sacred place. Off the coast, next to the main road, over fences and through the sheep pastures, circles of huge stones can be seen standing majestically, rising up powerfully from the ground. This is Scotland's Stonehenge. In 2007, on holiday, among these massive slabs of rock, we could feel the powerful dignity of ancient ancestors. Visiting Scotland has been one of our joys and anyone who knows George knows he is very proud of his Scottish heritage. His cousin, Ella McDonald, a kilt maker in Edinburgh had sewed him two kilts which he loves to wear for formal events. Kirby was also proudly aware of her Scottish roots. In college, she had visited relatives in Scotland and on her vision quest she had taken a kilt pin belonging to Nana, George's mother, with her as a sacred item. In the summer of 2009, Kirby had been with us to see George's cousin, Stuart, playing the bagpipes in a local competition. One of my favorite pictures is Kirby throwing her head back and laughing as she tried to fill the bag to play Stuart's pipes.

On the morning of Kirby's funeral, George chose the Dress Stewart plaid and his black jacket with the silver buttons and braided epaulets. We both remarked on how much Kirby loved for him to wear his kilt. George also wore this special garment to bring his parents, his ancestors, and the entire clan with him to the church. We both needed the strength, the warrior hearts, of all those who had gone before us.

In the car, I was aware of feeling that steely resolve and saying to our children and their spouses: "Please remember, while our lives are forever changed because of her death, you cannot allow your sadness or your anger to dominate your life. Otherwise, James Ray will have taken another victim in this family and I will not allow that. We can still live with love and joy. We cannot let our lives end because hers has."

Death also has a way of unbalancing truth.

I was aware that, in death, Kirby was now going to be sainted, so I said, "I just want you all to know that Kirby was extraordinary, but we all know she was also bossy, opinionated, and could be a pain in the ass sometimes."

As we approached the church, Stuart was playing the bagpipes and an honor guard of New York City firefighters greeted us. Two columns of men in full dress stood at attention while we walked up the path. George gasped and his eyes immediately filled up. These were the men George had worked with after 9/11, counseling some of them, helping their family members and other victims of that terrorist tragedy. George often said that working with these brave firefighters was the best job he had ever had. Serving them had been a privilege and now they were with us to share in our pain and grief, to support and uphold us. To this day, remembering this kindness overwhelms George.

As I entered the center aisle, I wanted the Mass to be a tribute to Kirby. I sang my heart out. I read the words of *The Prophet*, by Kahlil Gibran:

Your children are not your children.
They are the sons and daughters of Life's longing for itself.
They come through you but not from you,
And though they are with you, they belong not to you....
You may house their bodies, but not their souls,
For their souls dwell in the house of tomorrow, which you
cannot visit, not even in your dreams....
You are the bows from which your children as living arrows
are sent forth.

I believed this about our children—Kirby, especially, because she always defied a simple, stable explanation. She had always been "on the move." And now she had been moved beyond my sight, flying to the house of tomorrow.

There was a powerful energy in the church—celebration, gratitude, a recognition of a spirit that needs to be lived and carried on. Our son, Bobby, gave the eulogy.

He began by asking how many people were Kirby's "best friend"; most of the congregation raised their hands. He then went on to deliver a eulogy in Kirby's voice.

It was the first time I had ever witnessed people standing, applauding after a eulogy.

As strains of *My Sweet Lord*, the recessional hymn, wafted out of the church, I noticed a woman with close cropped hair, and I knew it was Beverley. She approached us outside the church as people were greeting us and introduced herself. We cried together. I was overcome with a need to be with and protect her, fearful that others would blame her, assault her in some way. Beverley, like a drowning person gasping for air; Beverley, the last person to see Kirby, talk to her—I felt the overwhelming need to ask questions, get more information, understand Kirby's mindset at the retreat and protect her at the same time.

I was in "Momma Bear protecting her cubs" mode. I couldn't

protect Kirby, but I was determined to protect our children and Beverley—the only person from this tragedy who called us and was now here.

That need to protect would resurface often in the years that followed. George and I would both slip into the "protector" mode, trying to protect others harmed in this tragedy and each other.

Back in our living room, I sat on the edge of the couch listening to Beverley's every word, answering questions about the week and things Kirby had done or said. At the same time, I was conflicted, aware that I should be across the street at the reception, thanking people for their contributions of food, support, love; yet, I had to breathe in the air of her words. I could see how Kirby and Beverley had so easily connected. Both are strong, determined, passionate adventurers, drinking in life while demanding personal accountability.

Someone came over to the house to say that we needed to go to the reception—people were asking for us. Seeing that Beverley was ready to greet others and answer questions, we walked across the road to an amazing display of food and people. The hall was filled with friends from Mexico, neighbors, college buddies, musicians, classmates from Minisink where Kirby attended middle and high school, and friends of our other children who knew Kirby.

Everyone was invited back to our house for a celebration. We are a "party" family. All life events deserve recognition and celebration. Our close friends since high school, Ed and Liz Holst, and their children are all musicians and we have spent many an evening with all the kids and adults singing along with guitars. Harmonizing church music, singing Irish folk ballads, peace songs from the 1960s—all would bind our hearts and nourish our spirits. Kirby always loved our family song fests.

To celebrate Kirby, the guitars, fiddles, and bagpipes played late into the night, the singing mixed with tears. Furniture was moved for dancing and more stories were told. Kirby's essence, her party spirit, filled the room with joyous life. Beverley sat on the stairs, watching this family who would celebrate life and never allow Kirby to be forgotten. From that moment on, we invited her into our "clan."

After everyone left, I sat with my nephew Geronimo, talking until 1:00 am. He told me he had come to the funeral parlor the day before, sneaking in between viewings and spent an hour alone with his favorite cousin. My sister Anne's children referred to Kirby as their "action figure cousin," always admiring her adventurous, brave spirit—one who lived life to the fullest on her own terms.

I later learned that Ray had never contacted the Neuman family while they sat that entire week in the hospital with Liz as all her internal organs were shutting down. On October 17, while he was conducting a large group meeting for his World Wealth Society, Liz was declared dead and we buried Kirby. He would carry on in spite of this. He would continue to preach and collect money from whoever would cough it up.

SUNDAY, OCTOBER 18

I woke up to the sound of Lyle chattering on a toy phone. She was in a porta-crib in the room next to ours. Kate and Angus had climbed into bed with us.

Coffee started our day and we talked about the future: What did we want to do, where was this taking us?

Kirby's business partner and close friend from Cabo, Nancy, and her sister Beth Ann arrived for the afternoon. Deborah and Samantha, other close friends, were present as well, as we shared what we knew. Kirby had been left in the tent for at least fifteen minutes after the ceremony. We spoke about the Tuesday evening calls from Ray and Beverley. Nancy doubled over, screaming her rage and anguish. Nancy and Kirby had been working together in Cabo for almost ten years. Their decorative painting business had grown, and their friendship was very deep. They spent almost every day together, working or playing. Nancy taught Kirby all the faux techniques and together they experimented, expanded, and refined their work, creating a strong reputation and a highly desirable business. Nancy's husband, Peter, was a woodworker and a musician who played at the local jazz clubs Kirby would frequent. He was also a surfer who often hit the waves with Kirby. He owned a ranch in Oregon where Kirby had visited on numerous summers when everyone left the heat of the Baja. Nancy was truly lost and overwhelmed by Kirby's death.

Nancy and Beth gave us information about Kirby's new home on "Gringo Hill" in San Jose. She had just moved in and unpacked in early September. This was the first home that was truly her own; previously, she had always lived in houses that she was caretaking or decorating for others. We had to decide when we would go to Cabo to recover her possessions and settle her affairs. That protective instinct surfaced one evening later that week when I lost it after talking to the landlord of this property. He suggested we get to the house as soon as possible because it was close to the road and had been broken into in the past. Her things were suddenly an extension of her which needed to be respected. Kate assured me the place was secure and now properly locked, but she would make sure Kirby's things were not desecrated. She lived near Kirby in San Jose and would oversee her home until we went to Cabo.

Outside, I showed Nancy and Beth the barn that George had built—a two story batten board structure where he worked on our cars and had a woodworking shop. I showed them the stall on the lower level where Happy Dot, Kirby's horse, had been kept.

Further down the hill was the lower field where she pastured her horse. Kirby's closest friends were completely devastated, and I began to see my developing role as their consoler. There would be hours, days, of phone conversations with many friends grieving their loss, even as I struggled to articulate my own.

On Sunday night, as we gathered to process the whole weekend, we began making plans to disperse her ashes. Bobby had suggested we expedite this process and not "drag out" the ash ceremonies as he had seen other families do.

We decided to place Kirby's ashes in both oceans. She had told me that the ocean was her spiritual place, where she met God. Sag Harbor, Long Island, where my parents had lived was Kirby's first ocean, so we thought about a ceremony for the East Coast family the day after Thanksgiving; but I knew we would also need to hold some sort of ceremony in Cabo for her Mexican community to mourn her. Kate would create a spectacular send-off for her sister in January when we would scatter Kirby's ashes in her surf break.

We discussed our role in this tragedy, our need to ensure that Kirby was not a nameless victim, and our desire that her spirit of action and loving compassion be continued in some way. Should we do something to help the others traumatized by this event? After all, George and I are therapists who understand trauma and could maybe help others find local resources across the country through George's firefighter connections. We recognized the results of a carefully orchestrated environment which had created suggestibility and compliance, robbing the participants of their mental acuity. No one at the Spiritual Warrior retreat would say they had been brainwashed or that this was a cult; however, the leader was using cult-like tactics to control them. There was sensory deprivation (limited sleep, sound assaults, lack of hydration), breathing exercises designed to change brain waves, group pressure and control, neurolinguistic programming, and the continual challenge to play "full on" and push beyond one's comfort zone. Individually, these strategies might seem innocuous, but put together they led to a deadly result.

It was from these early conversations that SEEK—Self-Empowerment through Education and Knowledge—was born.

Chapter 3

" I realize that I have been in this world mostly physically and emotionally. I am so very physical—my work, play, helping others. ...I now am the most Spiritual I have ever been, and it only has begun. I thank you for this experience to get my heart open to expand my spirituality, honoring the existence of all energies! "

— *Kirby's Vision Quest Journal*

Jean

*L*eaving Westtown and returning to Canada was sad. I didn't want to leave my family—for their sake or mine. But my life was north.

When I got back to Ontario, I returned to work at Health Canada. Right before Kirby died, the team I had worked with had been dissolved. While I was gone, my whole group had been scattered—my manager went one place, Waleed went somewhere else. I got sent down to a new group. As an intern and a non-Canadian citizen, my future there was precarious. I needed to focus on proving my worth so my new manager would be willing to take on the trouble of hiring me as a permanent employee. Instead, I was numb.

The new work I'd been assigned was uninspiring. It was basically data entry, which was a big shift from the more analytical policy work, writing briefing notes and literature reviews, I'd been doing *with my original group. That work had used the skills I'd developed during my master's studies. In my new role, I could have been a high school summer student. I was working with one other man on this database and it was very isolating.*

It was about two weeks after Kirby had died. I'd missed a deadline for entering a batch of information and my supervisor brought me into a meeting room for a chat. These meeting rooms are meant for small, private conversations that shouldn't happen in the open cubicle spaces. Frosted windows looked into the hall, but the room was otherwise basically a closet with two scratchy, corporate standard issue chairs and a small, round table. My supervisor looked at the wall above my shoulder as he lectured.

"Yes, I'm sure this time has been hard for you. But, these things happen, and we have to just... move on."

I didn't get a permanent position with Health Canada. Once my contract ended at the end of that December, I was done there.

This was also the end of my graduate program. Despite my program being internship-oriented, I still had to write a short, fifty-page thesis that somehow related to my internship experience while testing some of the academic literature I'd covered during coursework. Other universities' grad programs didn't have an equivalent paper requirement and students in my program (myself included) held a strong resentment for this requirement of our degree. I had classmates who'd dragged out what should have been a two-year master's program for years and years.

But, as luck would have it, the department started to crack down on this procrastination and, by the end of the summer of 2009, when I should have been wrapping up but had put off the paper due to our wedding, they were threatening to kick me out of the program.

So when Mike and I returned from our honeymoon in August, I had to get my shit together. I basically wrote this fifty-page thesis in two weeks. The years of all-night paper writing came to play in those frantic weeks in September. I was renting an apartment in

Ottawa with my fellow grad program friend, Nada. My manager at Health Canada let me take time during the workday to write the paper and then I'd rush home to our yellow-walled living room to keep on working.

In fact, my last conversation with Kirby was while I was typing away in that living room. My mom must have told her how stressed I was about completing this project, so she'd called me to give me a pep talk.

I tread a circle around the little wood veneer coffee table in the living room as we spoke, occasionally stopping to adjust a trinket on the mantle of the defunct fireplace. The layers and layers of white paint were chalky.

"I'm freaking out," I told her. "I have, like, forty more pages to write, all this literature to go through…."

"You can do this!" she said. "You're a great writer."

While we spoke, I heard students passing outside on the street. They were unencumbered at this early point in the semester and were busy organizing their dorms and apartments during the day, partying at night. I scoffed at Kirby's encouragement. This paper had nothing to do with my writing ability, I felt; it was a research paper.

This was sometime in mid-September. She was back in Cabo before she would drive up to Arizona for Spiritual Warrior. At the time, I resented the requirements of that internship report because it was useless. Now I resent it because it dictated the last conversation I ever had with Kirby.

I did finish that paper, though, and the final draft got approval on October 6, two days before Kirby died in Arizona. I'm grateful, at least, for that. I probably wouldn't have finished the program if I hadn't finished the paper before October 8.

I still faced a thesis defense, though.

Before Kirby's death, that time was hectic enough—finishing the paper, travelling back and forth between Montréal and Ottawa, and moving into our house on October 2. It was all exciting, though. It was the start of things—our marriage, a new life in a new town, a new job.

I was hopeful. And then it all just stopped. Before Kirby died, all of that was ahead of me. When I returned to Canada after her funeral, that life was gone. I couldn't see what was ahead of me anymore.

Yet, life was still busy. Unplanned trips back to New York, a trip to Mexico at some point, and even a trip to California to appear on Larry King Live.

The Larry King appearance was on Monday, October 26. I flew out of Montréal. I learned, then, that when you fly from any major city to LAX, there's a good chance you'll see some celebrities. While I boarded my flight, waddling my way through first class, I saw Sandra Oh and Jay Baruchel. Sandra had her headphones in; I didn't ask for an autograph.

CNN had arranged all of the details, so there was a car waiting for me at LAX to take me to the hotel. For the first time in my life, there was someone standing at the arrivals gate holding a sign with my name on it. We were staying at the Renaissance Hollywood Hotel, which is just off of Hollywood Boulevard. As I checked in, I wondered if the concierge knew why I was there.

I arrived before my mom, Bobby, and Tommy, who'd been coordinating with CNN. While I was waiting for them to arrive, I took a walk around the area. When I stepped out onto Hollywood Boulevard, I was on the Walk of Fame. The Kodak Theatre, where the Oscars are held, was right there. Madame Tussauds was across the street, next to a Scientology "bookstore." I walked through the mall there—the Hollywood & Highland. I wanted to buy something, but buying a souvenir felt somehow wrong. In Sephora, I bought makeup and my favorite fancy deodorant instead.

"Would it be cliché to eat at the California Pizza Kitchen?" I wondered.

The next morning, I kept obsessing over whether I should do my makeup or not. I knew they'd be doing TV makeup, but I was rolling into CNN studios. I didn't want blotchy, tired-looking skin.

I joked about this with the makeup artist as she prepared us for the interview. Larry was in there when we first arrived. He wore a lot of makeup—more than I needed. Then he scuttled out.

The makeup artist was a pixyish, friendly-looking woman. She had short hair and a bright smile. She asked me how I normally did my hair.

"I'm pretty minimalistic when it comes to hair and makeup," I explained to her. I didn't want to look not like myself.

She smiled, the small lines around her eyes crinkling just a bit. "Well, for TV we have to do a bit more or the lights will wash you out. But I'll keep it natural."

It felt like a long time, but it was relaxing and comfortable sitting in the chair while she pampered me. She asked a bit about Kirby and reacted as many people did—very, very sorry. A bit shocked. But then, she was able to do something tangible for me in that moment and it felt like she was taking that opportunity seriously as she took her time applying eyeshadow and lip gloss. It was very kind.

She gave me a deeper parting in my hair than I normally had. I was wearing a grey mohair sweater. People later told me I looked like a movie star.

I'm not a particularly vain person. I take care of myself and have pride in my appearance, but I certainly don't base my worth on how I look. And yet, I've noticed a bit of a theme in times when I had to publicly face Kirby's death—I felt really concerned about how I looked. I've wondered why. I suppose it was a small detail that I could control—making sure I looked presentable or even good. I think maybe I knew there was no need to appear heartbroken and shattered—everyone would assume that's how we felt. Instead, I've always taken strength from appearing strong and together, in spite of the heartbreak. Larry King's makeup artist probably styled a lot of heartbroken people over the years. She must have intuited all of this.

The studio itself was smaller than I expected—all of that black, shadowy-yet-shiny background looks huge on TV. In reality, it's a small room with a large desk. I didn't know what to do with my hands, so I rested my forearms on the slippery looking surface.

"Jean, where were you when all this [finding out that Kirby had died] was going on? ...Who called you?" This was Larry's first question to me. I tried to speak slowly and clearly, enunciating. Even as I answered, I started worrying that I was talking too much, because this wasn't the important part of our story. It wasn't what we'd prepared to say.

Larry wanted the sappiness. He didn't want to hear about why we knew that James Ray was a dangerous example of deadly irresponsibility in the self-help industry. He didn't want details about how a proper Native American sweat lodge is held. He didn't want to know about the cult-like mind control tactics Ray had used to make his customers pliable and weak. This is what I wanted to talk about. Instead, I retold the story of how I'd found out. And I sat while my mom and brother answered Larry's other soft questions. It's live, so you don't interrupt.

And then we were done. We were supposed to get the whole hour, but Sherri Shepherd from The View was there. Surprise! When we were ushered out during a commercial break, Larry tried to introduce us to Sherri like it was some sort of consolation prize. He actually said, "Here, meet Sherri Shepherd!" and motioned in her direction with both of his bony hands. To her credit, Sherri was sympathetic in those five seconds that I met her, but I was ultimately unimpressed.

How do you inform your extended circle that a family member has died? I mean, do you call friends and say, "So... I just wanted to let you know, my sister died"?

For my family in the States, the story was big enough news that they didn't have to call around telling people. But in Canada, it wasn't as big a story. Some of my close friends in Canada found out by seeing us on Larry King.

People who did know had watched the show to see and support us. This is how it was with the administration of the political science department of my university in Montréal. At this time, I was coordinating with them to appear for my thesis defense.

Three days after our Larry King appearance, I parked the car around the corner from the Hall Building on Rue de Maisonneuve. Just down the street was the pub my poli sci group used to have our get-togethers at, where they made the best bison burgers. Right outside where I'd parked, I had taken the phone call with the news over two years before that we'd successfully bought our first condo in Montréal.

Now, I knew I was unlikely to ever park there again after that day. I had arrived early, so I sat in the car reviewing my notes, my hands shaking. I was nervous, but a bit detached. Part of me didn't care much at all. I also couldn't imagine the professors in the defense being too difficult on me, given the situation.

When I got up to the poli sci floor, I went to the admin assistant, Julie. She is exactly the admin type. After dealing with her for just a few minutes as a new student, you quickly realize she really runs the place—not the head of the department or any of the professors.

She gave me a quick hug and then put on her business voice.

"Okay, they're all already in there," she told me, pointing to one of the windowed conference rooms. There were desks arranged in a rectangle with a big space in the middle, workshop style. My thesis advisor and two other professors, the second readers, were scattered at the desks with pads of paper in front of them. I sat at the focal point of the rectangle and went through a quick verbal presentation of my paper, then opened it up to questions. I honestly can't remember what the reader panel asked. I'm sure I smiled, but the sort of smile that leaves no lasting memory of joy in the muscles.

It was embarrassing. There were some long pauses in between questions, the professors reluctant to ask me anything, and it wasn't because the paper was particularly good. They definitely weren't going to give me a hard time with this. Even my paper advisor, with whom I'd not had a close relationship, was smiling sympathetically, while also pretending to be invested in the reason we were there. They all looked at me like I was a very sad little puppy; their eyebrows lifted into crinkles in the middle of their foreheads, lips pursed off to the side. I could see them all visibly relax when it was done, shoulders slumping with their exhales, as though they'd been more nervous than me. It further impressed on me how much of a waste the final paper had been. But I passed the defense, thereby completing my degree, and it was over.

A master's in public policy is not an easy program. It involves a lot of reading, a lot of writing. It was an intense two years of my life. The end of that program was anti-climactic and it's sad when I think back on it now. I'd worked hard, but when I walked out of that building where I'd spent so much of my life for the previous two years, I just left.

Ginny

O n the Tuesday after the funeral, before fully waking, I saw Kirby in a circle of light. Then I went downstairs to watch Bobby being interviewed on one of the morning shows. Unreality enveloped me once again as I listened to Bobby talk about his amazing sister.

Practical details of death certificates, a visit to the surrogate court to be named administrators of her estate, and the disposing of her cremains filled these days. We discussed the investigation in Arizona with Bob Magnanini, and the possibility of suing civilly after a criminal court case. The police in Yavapai had determined this was not accidental and was actively investigating this as a homicide, but we had no way of knowing when or what exact charges would be leveled against Ray.

I asked Bob Mag, "Can I use the word 'murder'?" I was being perverse. I knew that I couldn't say that. Ray didn't deliberately intend for people to die; he just set up the conditions that made it inevitable. But it has always felt like murder to me.

Tommy set up an interview with Larry King and we needed to discuss what could and could not be said on national TV on October 26. The information about the fire tender discovering the bodies in the tent fifteen minutes after the ceremony ended was not yet for public consumption. George would be with Bob Magnanini in Arizona, speaking with the investigators and lawyers, while we were in California.

Meanwhile, those who had been at this event were struggling with their own grief, memories, fears, and trauma.

Ainsley, the woman who was saved by James Shore on October 8, connected me to Melinda Martin, a fairly recent employee at James Ray International (JRI). She was the event coordinator for the Spiritual Warrior retreat in Sedona. She said that when she called the office on Monday after returning from an overwhelmingly emotional weekend at the hospital with victims of the sweat lodge, she was greeted with, "Good morning, it's a great day at James Ray International!"

She recoiled and was then horrified at how the event was being portrayed. She said, "A spokesperson was declaring, 'Unfortunately, some participants fell ill after the sweat lodge ceremony.' The staff were minimizing the whole thing, blaming the victims. I am not hewing to the party line—I couldn't believe their reactions."

We agreed to meet as she was planning to leave and come east.

Beverley called, frightened and upset at being questioned about her short hair and the assumption that this was a cult. "Cameras are coming. I don't want to be seen as crazy. People do not understand. Ray swore everyone to secrecy. People are afraid. At the retreat he showed clips from *The Last Samurai* for two days, ...all about integrity and showing up in life. In the God game, people die and he's like, 'You can't protect yourself from death. It's inevitable. Showing up in life is what's important!' So, where is he now?"

She paused, then said, "He was always throwing us off balance. Food was restricted, no meat, little protein." Beverley cried, "We wanted him to care about us, to believe in us. We wanted to do everything right, follow his direction. We believed the challenges would help us with whatever we were dealing with. We believed so much! ...When I talked to him... about cutting my hair... he said, 'I don't give a fuck if you shave your head or not!' Talk about being thrown! I was devastated.

"...At the end of each session, we had to forego sleep and write in our journals. Kirby wrote until 4:00 am or 5:00 am. After the God game, we went into the desert, alone—vision quest. It was dark and cold. Ray offered us 'authentic Peruvian ponchos' for $250. Can you imagine! I think a few people bought them, that's how fucked up we were."

Ainsley, Melinda, and Beverley were planning to meet to process their experiences. They continued to provide me with more details about the weeklong retreat.

I spent the majority of the week on the phone gathering both information and condolences. I now had Kirby's list of the smaller group of participants that were in her "warrior group." I made calls and left messages, none of which were ever returned. It seemed clear that the majority of participants at this event wanted no part of us. I knew they were suffering, surely traumatized, but I made it clear I did not believe they were to blame in any way. The lack of response from those with whom Kirby shared the last week of her life was painful. I just wanted to speak with those who had been with her. Talking to them felt like a lifeline to her.

In the midst of this chaos, Kate and Mitchell left for Mexico on Thursday, and Joan and Bob headed back to California. We discussed more details about Kirby's place in Mexico on our way to the airport.

One afternoon that week, lying in the hammock which Kirby had given us for our anniversary that June and looking up through glorious golden leaves at the crystal clear autumn sky, I screamed until my throat was raw. Every time I see or lay in that hammock, I recall that day, venting to the universe.

George called me to come to the phone. We had a call from Angel Valley Ranch. Amayra Hamilton wished to speak with me. She shared her fears about the intrusion of the media on their life, her desire to not appear on camera, how traumatized their employees were, and information that should not be public knowledge. She told me about people who had been hospitalized and reported their stories about the ceremony, as well as her confusion about why so many had pushed beyond their physical limits. Ray's private investigators had already spoken to them. She expressed her anger and frustration that Ray fled in the middle of the night, never speaking to them, leaving this chaos for them to manage. She spent that weekend in the hospital with those who had been in intensive care. Speaking with participants at the ranch, she heard from those who refused to stay in the tent: a couple who had left after the first round, a man who said, "this was not a religious experience."

Amayra had overseen vision quests and sweat lodge ceremonies in the past, but never had participants been without water for thirty-six hours. This shocked her. They had given Ray too much leeway to conduct this retreat on their property. The Hamiltons, having rented the ranch to Ray for the past seven years, had decided that this would be the last year they would allow Ray to use their property because they had "outgrown each other" and their "frequencies" no longer fit. On his own, Ray had already begun looking for a larger venue so that he could hold a bigger event in 2010. Amayra shared that Angel Valley was a special place of high energy with a "thin veil into the next world." She extended an invitation for us to come to Angel Valley for healing.

This was the last place George and I wanted to visit at that moment. I would learn that there had been problems in the past of people becoming sick and losing consciousness after the sweat lodge ceremony. Amayra had called 911 on one such occasion, only to be severely admonished by Ray at the time. "This did not feel like 'good energy' to us."

There would be more phone conversations with Amayra and the Hamiltons visited our home in 2016.

On Friday morning, October 23, Beverley was interviewed on Channel 4. She looked exhausted, ravaged. My heart broke for her.

Ainsley called that day and provided more details. I sat at

the kitchen table to listen and make notes as she spoke:

"Kirby was right next to me. We are so alike. We made plans for lunch on Friday and a visit to my ranch. I was so excited about meeting Kirby. Her intensity was so appealing, her energy rich. We were like ten-year-olds, you know, like you're gonna be friends for life. ...Kirby talked about the summer in New York, the wedding, how much she adored her Dad."

"What happened to you during the ceremony? Where were you in the lodge?"

"I was thinking about leaving; it was so freaking hot, NOT spiritual at all. I was going so far inside myself to just endure it. Then, I passed out. ...I think at the fifth or sixth round, James Shore pulled me to the door. Marta pulled me out. Ray sat right at the door. I think James went back inside for Kirby."

"What happened during the week?"

"Oh, the vision quest—that was powerful. Felt like a time lapse. I worked through some traumatic memories. It was good. I never questioned Ray's motives. A successful businessman does not allow his clients to be harmed, right? I totally trusted him. One night, I stayed up until 3:00 am, but I didn't do that again. Kirby, Kirby was so focused, I don't think she slept much at all. On Tuesday, the Samurai/God game was creepy. There was a lot of confusion. ...I think Ray was getting more and more pumped up on his ability, his own personal success."

Ainsley shared that she had been to many James Ray events, some with her daughter, Eliza, and was aware of his use of neurolinguistic programming. Ray skillfully employed this technique to create compliance in his followers. Ainsley was intrigued by Ray's intellect and ability to synthesize disparate ideas from ancient philosophies, religions, and science.

I wrote furiously to capture all I was being told as Ainsley continued, "That whole channeler thing? Outrageous! Like Kirby's death was her own responsibility instead of Ray's.

Come on. Ray walked away from it. From us. It wasn't about us. It was about him, what he could endure. The sweat lodge? It was like a personal victory for him!"

She and her daughter had attended Practical Mysticism in June and could see each event was more intense. Eliza was well versed in neurolinguistic programming. She was also aware of the deliberate tactics to move people into an altered state, using exhaustion, dehydration, heat, special breathing, and shock, removing the primary directive of the conscious mind for self-protection.

Ainsley explained, "I never knew people had been harmed in the past. He instilled trust with the whole 'living an impeccable life filled with honesty and integrity' thing. And now, he creates a recipe for hell. He could have stopped this. ...I was shocked! No medical support? No risk management plan? This retreat was an expensive, 'high-end' event. Why would anyone put their business in such jeopardy?

"You know, in hindsight, Ray never took a medical history. There was no phone reception, so how do you get help in an emergency? I never thought about that. Isn't that the role of the leader?"

Each conversation added to a growing body of evidence. This was no accident. Ray was culpable. Each conversation drew a sharper picture of the mind-controlling, cult-like tactics used throughout the week to create suggestibility and compliance.

Saturday, one week after the funeral, we had an exhausting interview with Michael Gross from *New York Magazine*. He arrived at 1:30 pm and left after dinner at 6:00 pm. He wanted to use the $5,000 check Ray sent us that we were advised not to cash. Bob Magnanini, who was handling our legal concerns, had it. I felt a real connection to this young man and sensed his true concern and compassion.

This was my first exposure to the fickle media world. The article was never published and, instead, Michael Joseph Gross was given an exclusive interview with James Ray shortly after his lawyers released a white paper which explained his lack of any wrongdoing. His article was published in *New York Magazine* on January 24, 2010, a few days before James Ray was indicted by a grand jury for manslaughter. Reporters work for editors and editors want the marketable story; interviewing Ray was obviously the bigger story.

That day, Beverley had a conference call with her warrior group and gave each of the participants our phone number. None of them called. I also learned from her that Ray had been directed to stop using Holotropic Breathing, a technique developed by Stanislav Grof. Apparently, Ray was not certified to teach his methods.

Suddenly, I realized I had to pack to go to California the next day for the Larry King interview, which was set to air Monday, October 26. In my journal, I wrote:

Lord, guide me, my heart, my mind, my mouth. May I speak with love and compassion and be able to challenge the thinking of those protecting and defending Ray. May I walk in the light of truth. Give me patience. Give me wisdom to be Kirby's voice.

These same sentiments would be repeated many times as we slogged through this morass.

It had been a hard night, and I was unable to sleep after pouring through Kirby's things from Sedona. She had signed up for a Ray event in November—Quantum Leap—and her date book indicated that she was trying to cancel, but JRI would not allow it. In fact, the money she spent for that event (over $3,000) was never returned. They had a no refund policy, which

I guess applied whether you were dead or alive.

After going to Mass at Holy Name, Billy Dahly, another distraught friend of Kirby's who lived in Denver, called. He agreed to go to Moab to pick up Kirby's truck and whatever things were left at Mika and Bobby's, and drive everything to us in New York. I made plane arrangements for him to return home to Colorado.

At 1:30 pm, a car arrived to take Tom and me to the airport. There have been very few occasions when we have hired a driver to take us to the airport. We have always driven ourselves, parking nearby to avoid airport parking expenses. Beverley called while we were in the car to discuss the warrior call of the day before. I also spoke to my partner at work to make sure our program was running smoothly.

Being on a plane headed to Los Angeles, sixteen days after Kirby's death, was unreal. I studied the workbook from the retreat that had been with Kirby's things and statements from Ray's book, *Harmonic Wealth*, picking out key phrases: "Energy flows where attention goes." "Winners take responsibility for their actions and are totally responsible for the results they achieve." "Be impeccable. You alone are responsible for your actions, intended or unintended." How ironic, written by the man who was unable to face his own actions.

We met Jean and Bobby at the hotel, and we spent an anxious dinner discussing what the next day might bring, agonizing over what we could or could not say when interviewed by Larry King. Calling Bob Magnanini helped to clarify what language to use and what to share.

The next day, we all met in Tommy's room for a pre-interview call from King's assistant. We spent over an hour discussing what would be asked and covered the history of Kirby's involvement with Ray, how we all learned of her death, contacting other participants, who Kirby was, and pursuing civil litigation. We decided who would handle different questions. Jean would discuss the effects of sensory deprivation and how that interfered with Kirby's mental clarity to assess danger. She would bring up the need for industry regulation and use the analogy of a product recall. When a product harms, it is removed from the market. Jean wanted to say, "My sister is not finished. We will set up some kind of foundation to honor her."

Bobby would handle legal questions and how the media had legitimized Ray. Ray's appearance on Oprah and national TV news shows had "vetted" him, giving viewers a false sense of confidence in his skill and integrity.

I would focus on our loss, our sadness, and anger, as well as our concern for the other traumatized participants whom Ray had abandoned at the scene. We wanted to emphasize our desire to uncover the truth about what had taken place and do something to ensure that a tragedy such as this would never happen again.

King's assistant reviewed with us how we had heard the news, Ray's call on Tuesday night, and our actions in the first few days.

After this preparation, I was less nervous, but as we sat at lunch at an outdoor cafe in the dazzling sunshine of southern California, I was overcome with the unreality of this situation. Being in California and being on national television was exciting, and that feeling alone was disorienting. We were there because Kirby was not here!

We returned to the hotel to leisurely shower and dress, leaving the hotel at 4:30 pm for the studio. At the studio, I was ushered into the hair and makeup room. The results of the lovely woman who worked on me were amazing. I felt confident and calm, ready to do this interview.

Before going on the set, I was introduced to King's "second" guest. Shocked, I mentally calculated how much of the hour we would have. I thought, okay, we'll probably have forty minutes of the hour. The first segment seemed a bit slow, with King concentrating on how we found out. In the next few minutes, we were able to share some details of what had happened and, then, at the break, we were told the second guest would be introduced after we had a final word. I realized we had only four minutes left in a twenty-minute time frame. I focused on getting as much said as possible. I wanted to make sure we addressed the other participants, letting them know we realized they were in shock. Then we were dismissed after being given twelve minutes to tell the story that was making international news—the story that had forever altered and devastated our lives! Twelve minutes for four people to be flown across the country, be put up in a hotel, meals paid for, transported in a car with a driver. How was this possible? In my financial world, none of this made sense. I felt like someone had exploded a bomb next to me; my head was spinning, my gut retching. The next guest, with her hand on my arm, expressed her condolences as we stepped off the set. We had practiced with his assistant; we were prepared to be on camera for one hour. I felt both numb and enraged.

I cried in complete frustration as I hugged Jean and Bobby goodbye. Both had to leave immediately to fly home due to work and school commitments. Tom and I went to dinner, and then I returned to my room where I spent the night flipping through TV channels to find someone, anyone, covering our story. Instead, I found the rest of *Larry King Live*, at midnight, forty minutes of the second guest, Sherri Shepherd from *The View*, flirting with King, promoting her book, and discussing her abortions. I wanted to smash the TV screen.

I felt deceived and ripped off. There were so many things we were prepared to say. So much time and energy had been focused on this show, and I felt I had failed this chance to be Kirby's voice. The night was filled with recriminations, all the whys. Why Kirby? Why did you believe him? Why someone with so much to offer the world? Why did this amazing opportunity prove to be so much less than it could have been? In my journal, I wrote, "I want to see Kirby's face on every station!"

The only consoling note was my son's wise words when I spoke with him in the morning. Bobby told me the feedback from the interview had been very favorable. He then reminded me that we had agreed to play in the media's medium; it is their playground—an entertainment vehicle and we have to be grateful for any time, exposure or coverage we got. He was thankful for the chance to be on Larry King, but was disgusted that the man never even greeted me before the show.

I called Beverley because I wanted to apologize for not being able to mention her and our gratitude for her bravery in contacting us and coming to the funeral.

Tired, angry, hungry, and frustrated, I decided to watch a movie on the plane. *My Sister's Keeper* was showing. I had read Jodi Picoult's book and was interested in the movie. In the movie, a family goes to the beach as a final request by their dying daughter. Suddenly, sobs and bitter tears erupted as I thought of Kirby's love for the ocean and not having had a chance to say goodbye. I am usually very controlled in public, but this catharsis was beyond my control. I think all the emotions of that experience in California simply took over. Feeling wrung out and slightly ill, Tom and I were driven home to Westtown.

Once home, we got a message from George and Bob Magnanini that the coroner's report showed clean toxicology and massive organ failure due to dehydration and heat. The police investigators in Sedona were convinced: This was an act of reckless endangerment, negligent homicide.

We put out a statement:

For a motivational speaker who teaches others to lead an impeccable life and take responsibility for their actions... we appeal once again for James Ray to cooperate with the police investigation and take full responsibility for the results of his actions.

Once home, phone calls continued to consume my days. Mika and Bobby told me Kirby's dog, Tuffy, was inconsolable, lying under her truck for the last three weeks, eating very little, knowing she was gone. Others from the Baja community called. The Neumans were speaking to the federal prosecutor. Billy Dahly called to discuss the details about picking up Kirby's truck. Participants who had been harmed and the Neuman and Shore families were contacting lawyers.

On October 28, I had a long conversation with Sandy Andretti. She said, "Marco, my son, and the family—they don't want my name associated with Sedona. They're embarrassed. If it comes out... well, they think I'll come off as a crackpot! They're freaked out I shaved my head. ...They don't understand. They think it'll sound like a cult and there'll be all this negative press."

I asked her, "Why did you go in the first place?"

"I've been through near death experiences, traumas. After my divorce from Marco's father [Michael Andretti], I struggled with depression and I have CFS [chronic fatigue syndrome]. I thought the retreat would give me strength, help me heal."

I pushed for more information. "Would you be comfortable sharing what happened during that week?"

"The 'God game?' That was stupid. It was offensive—Ray getting off on playing God. If you broke one of his confusing rules, he'd pronounce 'You're dead,' just like that. I had no idea what was going on."

Still, I pushed. "What did Kirby do during the game?"

"She died early. The other thing was to die with honor. You couldn't move from the spot where you were struck dead. If you did, someone else on your team had to die. Someone told me Kirby had to go to the bathroom, but she didn't move for an hour and a half. Also, you couldn't look at anyone. There was a code of silence. The team was dressed in black robes. Ray's were white—creepy. I should have just left. Why didn't I leave?"

Sandy described Ray's instructions to everyone before going into the tent and the atmosphere inside the sweat lodge. It was hard to listen. "In the lodge—imagine this—he said, repeatedly, 'It's common to pass out.' I remember thinking, 'That's not right.' He told us to go within, 'Don't worry about those around you.'"

Sandy explained, "Ginny, I don't do bugs or dirt. But I wanted to be healed. You know, he sold Spiritual Warrior to women, especially those who had faced traumas and sexual abuse. Many of the participants had significant abuse backgrounds and Ray urged us to trust him. 'Play full on,' he said. 'You made an investment. This is the place for you to transform, to be reborn.'

"When I crawled out of the tent, I was totally disoriented. Everything snapped. I collapsed on a tarp. My body was greenish, fluorescent! I was fighting for my life. I saw people with bluish skin, having seizures, vomiting, foaming at the mouth, shaking, yelling. Ray—he stood there in a victory pose. I think his arms were outstretched. He was flexing his muscles, for God's sake. He sat on a chair, smiling, drinking water, surveying the scene. He did nothing! I was crying. Bodies were lined up—people being hosed down. He did nothing. It was total chaos—a nightmare. Him sitting there as though there was no problem!

"When we were in the tent, we told him 'We have a problem.' Ray goes, 'It's fine. There's no problem, part of the rebirth.'

"On day one, Ray said, 'this will be the most transforming experience you will ever have in your life. How many are willing to do whatever it takes to be transformed? You paid me and trust me to lead you. Are you willing to play full on or just dabble? Be honorable—show it—I've got clippers. If you're all in, shave your heads.'"

"Sandy, what happened to you after the lodge?" I asked.

"In the Crystal Hall where we ate, a dream teamer told us 'Kirby and James made choices.' I thought, 'What?' But I was confused, dazed. I couldn't react. I wound up in an ambulance to the hospital. They put me on IV fluids and oxygen. I called my son and daughter from the hospital the next day. I wanted, I needed, out of there, immediately."

After listening to these shocking details for an hour and a half, I was drained. She confirmed that multiple warnings of trouble were voiced, and Ray dismissed them. Sandy told me her friend Cassandra was speaking for her and was concerned that Ray was deliberately exploiting a very vulnerable population. She reported feeling ashamed and was in shock after she learned of the deaths. I had spoken to Sandy a few times during those early weeks and would speak many more many times in the year to follow. Sandy shared how lost she felt and that speaking with me was "like a lifeline" because no one understood what she had gone through. Sandy, a very spiritual woman, knew she was seeking God and true discernment. I realized that Kirby was also seeking something, someone bigger than herself. Like others who had been in Sedona, her physical symptoms persisted, and cognitive confusions and delays hampered embracing wholeness. A trauma like this for the participants and for me will never "go away and be finished." While this loss is with me always, it has less of a continual, gripping hold on my mind and heart as time goes on.

Each conversation with participants gave me more insight into this nightmare and plunged that knife of pain deeper.

Compelled to know more, I sought out these conversations. I wanted to know everything that had taken place. I needed to know what Kirby's last hours had been like. I needed to clearly understand what had gone wrong.

I listened carefully, without judgment, understanding how traumatized these participants were. I spoke little and wrote down pieces of each conversation.

I spoke to Michael Lynn. Michael Lynn was a man I had met after the March Harmonic Wealth seminar. He shares his healing abilities with others freely. He suggested a visit to help me, and shared how he was helping both Julie and Connor process their experience of Sedona. We spoke about the grief process and the importance of owning our feelings and understanding them to allow for healing. I politely declined his generous offer of help. I was frankly uncomfortable with non-traditional methods and felt strongly that my faith and support system served me well. While open to and curious about other approaches, my daughter had just died trusting in a person and method well beyond her faith foundation and experience with therapeutic professionals.

Ainsley spoke of others who had left the tent and her resolve to focus on herself.

Reports from the few participants I spoke to revealed the confusion and emotional turmoil of that final night, the chaos outside the tent, the agonizing bewilderment inside the Crystal Hall as those who had not gone to the hospital sat awaiting James Ray's appearance. The story about Kirby and James' choice to die seemed to be concocted that night by a dream teamer.

On Thursday, October 29, I attempted to return to work. I stopped in the office to check messages and put away supplies. However, there was more pressing business: mail to read and sort. More calls, lawyers, future litigation. The planning of memorial events in Long Island and Cabo.

I had to order thank you cards to send out to those who had come to the funeral, brought flowers, food to the house, or had sent Mass cards. I chose a great picture of Kirby—one of my favorite pictures of her—with her black cowboy hat, brimming with life. It was an acknowledgment from her.

Friday was a hair trim and then an interview with our local newspaper, after which we had to pick up the death certificate at the funeral parlor. The certificate said the time of death was 6:21 pm, when Kirby was declared dead at the hospital. We knew death to have taken place at Angel Valley in the late afternoon hours. The cause of death read "pending." I didn't understand. She died of heat stroke; her body was totally dehydrated and cooked to death. Why didn't the death certificate simply state the facts?

Over the next few weeks, there were more calls and messages from Kirby's close friends, sharing their pain and distress. We received messages about the ongoing criminal investigation; participants and victims were retaining lawyers, investigating potential civil suits. We had emails and phone calls from the Hamiltons who wanted to avoid any litigation and calls from lawyers. I worried about Kirby's siblings, their confusion and pain, and how this was affecting their lives.

Halloween weekend was a little oasis of normalcy. We arrived at Bobby and Kory's home for Halloween trick-or-treating in their neighborhood in Darien, Connecticut. A few couples came with their young children, all decked out in adorable costumes. Leaving their gray and white Cape Cod style house, two-and-half-year-old Lyle went skipping up to neighbors' doors in her floppy bunny ears, delighted with the candy that was accumulating in her bag. Nine-month-old George, dressed as a ladybug in the stroller, accompanied the parade of toddlers. I had never gone trick-or-treating with a cooler of beer in the bottom of a baby carriage, but that seemed to work well for this group of parents. As I watched Lyle's unbridled happiness, I thought, YES, we can do these simple, fun, ordinary things, despite the constant backdrop of sorrow and longing. We will not shut out joy.

Later that evening, after the children were safely tucked into bed, we sat in the living room. I held a glass of wine and talked with some of Bobby and Kory's friends who wanted to know what had happened in Sedona.

Bobby's friend, Chris, asked, "What was this retreat all about?"

How to explain the unexplainable? "It was a week-long 'self-help' retreat for entrepreneurs and others seeking growth in their lives. People wanting 'more' from relationships, business, personal spirituality; they seek Ray's teaching and leadership. He has a following. He wrote a bestseller, *Harmonic Wealth*. He's been on Oprah. We are still gathering details. Obviously, he didn't know what he was doing with the sweat lodge."

Chris asked, "Why was Kirby there?"

Most people have never heard of a sweat lodge and we all became familiar with how this ceremony originated and was used by Native Americans. It was intended to be a healing ritual, in a lodge tented with breathable materials, not a super-heated environment to test endurance and push people beyond their physical limits as Ray's was.

Kirby was intrigued by the spiritual ceremonies of indigenous peoples. She knew there would be a vision quest, a time alone for contemplation in the desert, and she was excited to experience that.

Answering questions, my rage bubbled to the surface. I started to shout, through tears, "She was there to grow, not die! She wanted to learn, experience, expand. ...She was a risk-taker. She sought adventures, loved experiences. She believed in this man and he took everything from her."

George put his hand on my knee. I could have kept on crying and shouting.

She gave Ray her trust, her hard-earned money, her life! Yes, this man who was promoted, vetted on national TV and Oprah, turned out to be a dangerous coward who ran away in the middle of the night, never addressing his participants or identifying those who went to the hospital. Who would have thought that on this level there would be NO risk management plan, no health checks, no medical support available—untrained personnel who didn't even perform CPR properly?

Yes, my Kirby, my adventurous, rebellious, and lovely Kirby believed a charismatic fraud, a clever manipulator who taught about being responsible and impeccable and was unable to be either.

The incomprehensibility, the unfairness left me consumed with a helpless, impotent anger. How could I ever explain the unimaginable?

On Sunday, Beverley told me Julie Min was really struggling and now had a hospital bill that she couldn't pay. James Ray had been in touch with her, suggesting she speak to a "like-minded counselor." She seemed to still be under "his spell." Meanwhile, Melinda Martin had left James Ray International and was determined to leave San Diego. She had been outside of the tent when everything was unraveling and then had spent the weekend in the hospital with those who were in the ICU. Melinda felt she was being "targeted" by some of Ray's "loyal" staff and was fearful. She reported that Steven Ray, another participant, had brain damage and had lost his job. Others were not speaking out, due to confusion and fear.

When I was about seven or eight years old, I had a recurring nightmare. In my dream, I saw a huge bubbling caldron, filled with an evil, brownish liquid which swirled around while the walls seethed, moving in and out, accompanied by a scary, cackling voice fading in the distance. Those terrifying images often caused me to try to stay awake. My bedroom was in the attic and my older sisters had the room next to mine, so sometimes I would wait at the foot of the stairs for one of them to go upstairs, so at least I wouldn't be alone. (I was also afraid of the dark.)

As I listened to the fear, anger, bewilderment, rage, and confusion swirling through these messages and calls from those directly affected by this tragedy, I was reminded of this dream. This did seem like a nightmare and some days the walls were closing in. Yet those calling clearly wanted to talk to me and I needed to hear and connect with them.

I wrote in my journal:

What am I supposed to be doing? Going back to everyday life? Work? Clients? I know I need some routine, grounding, but life will never be normal again. For some reason we have been placed in the midst of this tragedy. Some good must come out of this. Kirby's memory and life MUST be honored. There has to be some PURPOSE. Lord, guide me, help me know what I should be doing.

Finally, in early November, I had a long, detailed call from Ainsley about the entire week and her feelings for Kirby. She said, "I think I was unconscious for most of the ceremony. I went somewhere else by the fourth round. I remember hearing James Shore say, 'I can't wake her up. Kirby's down.' She was literally forgotten."

This statement would resurface and bring hot, searing tears many days after that.

Forgotten?

When she was in college, dog-sitting for her professor, she was biking along the banks of the Genesee River with the dog running beside her. Suddenly, the dog lost his footing and slid down the embankment into the river. Without hesitation, she jumped off the bike and plunged into the fast-moving, cold water, grabbing her charge, throwing off her jacket. As the turbulent river carried them further along, she told me she couldn't find a safe spot with enough shore to get out of the water. Carried along for at least a mile, she was finally able to get to shore with the wet, trembling pup. Stumbling up the bank, she ran to the road, soaking wet, freezing, waving at passing cars for help. As she related this saga to me, she was laughing. "Mom, people just waved back. No one even noticed our condition and how ridiculous we looked. Man, was I scared. That water was running so fast!"

Fortunately, this call was made from the warmth and safety of her room. I kept thinking this could have been a call from the Geneseo police reporting a very different outcome. She risked her life to save a freakin' dog! But she was forgotten in that sweat lodge; Ray left her, even after being told she needed help.

Ainsley said, "I think Ray was competing with himself. How many heated rocks could *he* stand? He bragged how hot 'his' lodge was, like we weren't even there."

She said, "Melinda Martin needs help and I want to help her maybe get to a safe place, like her parents."

Ainsley was overwhelmed. "Freaking *20/20* and *Dateline* called. I'm not ready for this. My God, I have double vision, massive headaches, body tremors on my left side. The doctors say I need another EEG and more neuropsych tests to identify the extent of the damage I sustained. I can't go on TV! I'm exhausted. I can't write. This is very scary."

She paused and then said, "I have cried and cried over Kirby's death. I feel so guilty. We were going to be friends... for life. She's been stolen from me."

I ventured out to work. I sat at my desk, a small corner space with overhead compartments. I looked over email messages, deciphering what needed attention and what could be ignored. For the past month, I had had excellent coverage for the Strengthening Families Program I ran for the Dispute Resolution Center, a fourteen-session program for teens on probation with their entire families. We serve dinner, have skill-building groups, and end the two hours with a family activity. It is a physically demanding program that produces amazing results, keeping many of these kids out of state placements. My back to the late afternoon sun, I looked at the file with time sheets and started to fill them out. As I looked at the dates—October 9, 12, 13, 14, 15, 16, 19, 20, 21, 22, 23, 26, 27, 28, 29, 30, November 2—seventeen days of missed work, I collapsed in a heap of tears. All these days missed because my life was radically changed, never to be the same again. How was I going to do this—teach these parents, working to change the angry energy in their homes? How was I going to go on and be productive? How was I going to manage all the information, listen to others' grief, and pay attention to my family? This was an epic meltdown which has stayed with me as a sign of that intense struggle to live or succumb, to pull the covers over my head and not get out of bed.

That night, when I spoke to Kate, Bobby, and Jean, just checking in on everyone, I was reminded of the reason I keep getting out of bed: my children who are still here who love me and need me to love them.

Then, we heard about Colleen Conaway—a suicide at James Ray's July 2009 "Absolute Wealth" event in San Diego, the same event Ainsley and the Shores had attended.

I think Tommy discovered this and Bob Magnanini had also learned that a suicide had taken place by a woman who was attending "Absolute Wealth," a James Ray seminar where people were simulating being homeless in a mall. The police never investigated any connection to Ray, even though she was attending his event. Something was clearly amiss. There was confusion about when the team learned of her suicide. There was a report that someone from Ray's event went to the morgue to identify the body because Colleen did not have any ID on her person. They had everyone's cell phones and knew she was not on the bus returning to the hotel where a celebration party would be held the next day. Although they held her phone, there were messages on her phone asking about her welfare after they left the mall area. When police searched her room, there were no seminar materials, no notes or event workbook, nothing to indicate her state of mind or give a clue about her intentions.

A person at the event reported having witnessed a suicide at the mall and was suddenly filled with an overwhelming sense of gratitude for his life. (He later had the word gratitude tattooed on his arm as a reminder.) No one told him that the victim was Colleen, someone who had been with the group all week.

This information felt diabolical to me.

Everything seemed so complicated. The details of getting Kirby's truck from Moab to New York needed to be worked out: We had to take ownership of the car, insure it, give formal authorization for Billy to drive it east. Even calling my family to arrange the service in Sag Harbor for the day after Thanksgiving overwhelmed me.

Could things get more bizarre? Another evening in November, I listened to Beverley on the phone describing her latest call with her warrior group. Members of the group had been contacted by investigators. Totally frustrated, she said: "They discredited me! They questioned my accounts of the sweat lodge ceremony, the chaos afterward. They suggested all sorts of shit. They asked why was I exaggerating and lying, creating hysteria? Was I a spy? Could I be trusted? These had to be Ray's investigators."

She went on to say, "Members of the group were defending the proper action on Ray's part to cancel future events, but I explained to them the events had been cancelled by the venues, not Ray. Then, the group started focusing on the importance of spreading Ray's teachings and I challenged them. 'Look,' I told them. 'HE did not live his teachings. He abandoned us!'"

She then suggested starting a "Survivors' Fund" to help each other heal and recover from this tragedy.

Many more conversations with Beverley over the next weeks and months would reveal an incredibly strong, brave woman, confronting past hurts and courageously moving into her own truth.

Sometimes, when dealing with my growing children, I often thought, "If I just explain something better, they will get it, agree with me, and say, 'Ok, Mom, I'll do my chores, stop fighting, do my homework, etc. …I understand your excellent reasoning." I realize this is a mother's frustrating fantasy. When speaking to those involved in this tragedy, I often felt that same frustration. What seemed so obvious, so rational to me, was obviously viewed very differently by some of these participants who still needed to believe in the man they were following. It was a willful suspension of disbelief because what happened did not make sense. A charismatic teacher who had helped people would not deliberately harm. Sometimes, our actions have consequences we do not intend but for which we must remain accountable.

Now, Melinda Martin was coming to New York and wanted to meet us. Billy Dahly was arriving with Kirby's truck from Arizona. The TV show *20/20* was looking to do an exposé. The relentless aftermath of this tragedy kept invading our lives. Each day, as phone calls or situations arose, I was determined to rise to the challenges with composure and compassion, resolving to be responsive and not reactive.

By mid-November Billy Dahly arrived with Kirby's red Toyota Tacoma. On a quiet Sunday morning, we drove to Riverside Drive to pick up Melinda Martin. In the hour and a half drive to Manhattan, Billy said that Kirby had kind of "saved" him when he had gone to Cabo to rethink his life and his direction. "She always listened. Helped me see what I really wanted out of life."

I have always felt proud when told stories of Kirby's impact on others. We do not know how we affect other people, unfortunately, those stories are often only revealed when the person is gone, and the emptiness of our loss unfolds.

Billy said, "I don't know if you know this, but she told me she wanted to write a book—about saving lives. You know, where she saved people's lives."

I had been in Cabo once when Kirby was called late one night by the local hospital to inform her of a friend's serious pelvis injury after being hit by a car. Maciek lived on the East Cape and conducted the monthly full-moon parties. Her phone number was the only one Maciek had on him when he was brought into the hospital. They were planning to transport him two hours away to another hospital and Kirby was convinced such a ride would create further damage. She spent the rest of that night making phone calls to friends, hoping to organize an emergency medical evacuation. Since he was a Canadian citizen, she called the consulate to see if they could assist in transporting him for better medical treatment. They were sympathetic, but unable to help. As friends gathered or called Kirby back, she was able to collect enough money for an evacuation to Canada. Now she had to enlist the cooperation of his daughter who lived in Canada. Coordinating an evacuation was incredible in itself, but even more remarkable to me was Kirby's ability to convince his daughter after a long period of estrangement to help her father, despite past hurts and misunderstandings.

As she described this exchange to me, she simply stated, "He is her father. Regardless of what has transpired in the past, he needs her help now."

Kirby had always worried that her father and I were not properly prepared for our future, having chosen social work as a profession. Little money, no status, what were we thinking? As I watched her spring into action, I felt so proud of her, realizing that Kirby had clearly embraced the values of compassion and service. I told her two days after that call from the hospital that she was an amazing social worker!

As we approached the city, I was anxious about meeting Melinda, not knowing what new information I might hear about that week in Arizona. Melinda confirmed all the reports I had already heard about the chaos at the end of the sweat lodge ceremony. She had been outside the tent and was upset that as each person emerged from the tent, they looked really bad: eyes rolling, disoriented, irrational, screaming, crying. She was trying to help the participants, wetting them down on tarps. She took over administering CPR on Kirby for about fifteen minutes and was surprised that she wasn't airlifted but put in an ambulance.

"I thought she might make it. What was shocking, really, was that James Ray did NOTHING. Didn't touch anyone. Didn't try to help. He sat and drank water. The police said he didn't speak to them—refused to have his room searched. They got a search warrant—middle of the night."

She shook her head. "Megan? His assistant, she told me to get everyone who could walk up to the Crystal Hall. I snapped and said, 'I'm not a camp counselor, look around you!' Jesus! No identification, no emergency contact information, for anyone! I actually followed an ambulance to the hospital to see if I could identify people. I stayed all night with Ainsley and Liz who were in intensive care."

She explained that a few others, dream teamers—Ray's unpaid volunteer force—came to the hospital as well. These volunteers helped run his events and their reward was to attend without any cost, although Ray did insist on separate checks, even when getting pizza at a planning meeting.

"I was infuriated by that cheery hello at JRI on the following Monday. I challenged them. They said, 'Stop gossiping and scaring the staff.' Talk about denial. I was told not to call again. I was the event coordinator. I couldn't sleep or eat. I was a total mess."

"Were you at the Absolute Wealth event, in July?"

"Yup. ...Ray had this homeless game going at the mall. When we got back, I saw the staff huddled together. They stopped talking as soon as I approached. Unsettling, right? What's going on? 'Everything's okay. No worries.'" She waved her hand. "I asked them about Colleen. 'Oh, she decided to go home.' They must have known. They lied."

She shared her immediate feeling of connection after meeting Kirby and told us she regretted not coming to the funeral. Because she had been so frightened, I was concerned about her safety, but I could see now that she no longer had a job with JRI and she was getting ready to move east.

As Beverley shared more information about the weekly warrior calls, it became more apparent that participants were traumatized and frightened, unable to reconcile Ray's actions with what they had learned from him. Ainsley felt Ray deliberately took high achievers and broke them down. It was clear that internal confusions and warring emotions were making it difficult for these victims to talk to or trust anyone. Lawyers were now being called as participants realized they could not manage their medical bills and were receiving no help from James Ray International.

Chapter 4

" Everyone is full of love and there are so many heartwarming hugs. The march slows and I realize it is perfect. It is always perfect. Slow down. Listen, taste, smell, enjoy life to its fullest all of the time. That's what we have. We have been bestowed upon perfectness. Enjoy this sweet life! "

— Kirby's Vision Quest Journal

Jean

*O*n *the weekend of Thanksgiving, we held a memorial service for Kirby on Long Island, NY. We'd decided to scatter some of her ashes in the Atlantic and some down in Baja, so she'd be on both coasts.*

We went to the bay right around the corner from where our grandparents had lived in Sag Harbor—Long Beach. We went there frequently as kids. The water is calm and easy there, with the sort of gentle waves you'd hear on a white noise track. The broad beach stretches for about a mile, with tons of shells, beach glass, and rocks to find. I loved the colorfully iridescent shells from a scallop-like mollusk called an anomia. These shells are sometimes called jingle shells, because they're used to make the wind chimes that tinkle all over Sag Harbor in homes and restaurants. We'd collect hundreds of these things as kids: pastel purple, white, yellow, amber colored.

But the day we went to scatter Kirby's ashes was not a "beach day." The sky was a deep and angry purple, like the inside of another shell that litters Long Island beaches—the wampum shell.

We had picked out some things to read. My mom kept everything in a manila folder she carried with her along with books, slivers of ripped paper marking the pages of the poems and readings. Across the bay, where water touched sky, the clouds threatened, whipping the wind at our faces like a warning. As we stood on the beach, a flock of gulls that had rested on the sand a bit away from us suddenly took off into the air, almost like they were sucked up into it, fighting together against the chaos. We tried to read the poems and recount some stories, but few words made it through the gale.

We had a rowboat and the idea was that, after the readings, a few of us would row out into the bay and drop this package of ashes wrapped in tissue paper that the McPhillips had prepared for us. The tissue would then dissolve in the water, the ashes carried on the currents, while the bits of bone would sink into the sand and become part of the seabed.

But the usually placid bay had actual white-capped waves that day. Getting the boat out into this water was a disaster. I was in the boat with Bobby and our cousin Zack, while another one of our cousins tried to push us out beyond where the waves were breaking. The wind and the water conspired to soak us all. I pulled with my oar to try to help move us further out, but it was useless. I like canoeing and rowing, though; I kept trying. It felt like I was pushing through sand rather than water. On a final attempt at control, Zack's oar snapped into pieces, jarring us off our balance. I laughed, although the wind was so loud none of them heard me. We looked at one another and shrugged with an understanding that we needed to just drop the parcel there. We were absurdly maybe fifteen feet out into the water. I kept the middle section of the broken oar—its weather-beaten, grey-brown wood with the shock white of raw pine at the shard-like ends.

After the beach, we gathered at my Uncle Joe's house for food. We read some of what we'd intended to say on the beach. But then, something else happened.

At my uncle's house, a golden wood staircase curves up to the second floor. The landing at the curve is like a lectern. My cousin, Bob Magnanini stood up at one point, after we'd all dried off and had something to eat. Bob is a storyteller. A big guy, a colonel in the army, he gets everyone's attention and keeps it.

He drew for us this image of a soldier preparing to ride a horse into battle. "We're going to fight this," he said. "I'm going to fight this."

I stood up, too, and read one of the poems we'd given up trying to read at the beach. Inspired by Bob's declaration of war, I also spoke about how we weren't going to let this just go away.

My family—cousins, aunts, uncles, family friends—looked up at me. "I realize now that things don't always happen for a reason. We have to create reason out of the things that happen."

I hadn't prepared to say any of this, but the storm on the beach felt like Kirby speaking to us. And she was furious. Of course, we'd still be sad. But we were also going to fight.

GINNY

On Thursday, November 26, we celebrated Thanksgiving dinner at Bobby and Kory's home in Darien. Jean and Mike arrived from Montréal and Tommy would join us with my sister, Mary. The next day would be the first of the two memorial celebrations we would hold to distribute Kirby's ashes.

On the beach at Sag Harbor, against the stormy sky and angry sea, a lone piper played and I wondered if Kirby was speaking through the weather. At my brother's home in North Sea, we gathered in remembrance and resolved to have something good come from this unimaginable horror.

In my journal that week, I wrote, "This sadness is so heavy. I have to set it aside to concentrate, to work and focus on other [things?], but it takes so much energy." So many entries say, "I am so exhausted, tired from crying, weary from trying to just function."

In early December, Ainsley, Beverley, and Melinda were meeting in Sedona. The coroner's reports had yet to be released and no one knew if any indictments would follow. These three brave women were trying to decide how to share their experience with others even as they healed themselves. Each would call me with their fears and worries about media coverage—*Good Morning America*, *Dateline*, ABC, *48 Hours*—who to trust and what would happen when what they knew was public? Would they be questioned, discredited? The fears of the unknown and distrust shadowed these women who had been thrust into a nightmare of someone else's making. Their terror was not far from mine, not knowing where this tragedy would lead us.

We spent an early Christmas celebration in Vankleek Hill at

Jean and Mike's newly acquired home. Reading Mitch Albom's book, *Have a Little Faith,* on the drive north and then watching the movie *Julie & Julia* with Jean and Mike were necessary counterpoints to all the sadness, confusion, and fear. Jean wanted to check out a local antique store so, on Saturday, we walked into a huge barn, filled to the brim with wonderful treasures. As I walked through the first room, I saw a pedestal oak table—beautifully carved, gleaming wood, soft to the touch. I had been looking for this table for years, imagining such a table gracing my kitchen. Made around 1880, it had been in the dining hall of a local convent which had just been sold. Years of prayers and polish had been showered on this surface. Extra leaves and additional chairs would allow at least fourteen people to be seated at it. I hesitated, as I always do when making a monetary decision (my children call me "cheap," I like to think I am cautiously thrifty). Suddenly, I could hear Kirby saying, "Oh, for Pete's sake, Mom, buy it. It is exactly what you have always wanted in the kitchen. It is perfect!" Now, as I sit in my kitchen looking out at the field where Kirby pastured her horse, the lake where Bobby played hockey on the ice, the apple tree where Jean read, the garden where both Jean and Kate married their husbands in the summer of 2009, I thank Kirby for helping me choose beauty and utility.

I was to be interviewed by *20/20* on December 21 and I began to organize my thoughts. I was determined to be clear, cogent, rational, so that others would listen and not write me off as the distraught mother. This was a tragedy that never should have happened and could have been prevented.

January was fast approaching. Cabo awaited. I had to end a program and clear my desk. I'd be away for three weeks.

In the vestibule of the church at Midnight Mass at Christmas, I was torn apart with my grief. "Oh, Kirby, what were you looking for? Why couldn't you find your Lord here?" I tried to make

Catholicism real and deep for our children growing up. But I knew, having witnessed scandals in the all too human institution of the church, Kirby had rejected traditional religion. She had to find her God in her own way and time. She told me she felt God in the ocean, in nature, and I know she showed His face to others in how she loved, respected, and served others.

New Year 's Day dawned quiet, slow, tearful, as I searched through Kirby's things to make sure I packed what I needed for Cabo.

On January 1, Amayra Hamilton called.

Amayra said, "My son was born around the same time as Kirby. He died. Meningitis. In '99. He was twenty-eight." We shared pregnancies and the heartbreak of losing a child. We also shared our understanding of Khalil Gibran's words about children.

"Ginny, I'm afraid we're gonna lose the ranch."

In my journal, I wrote:

I wished her a happy year. I don't want her to lose her ranch. She has shown compassion and has reached out to us, even though I know she shares some liability for what happened on her property.

We had a 9:00 am flight to Cabo. The usual excitement of going to Mexico was obscured by dread, loss, sadness, and the anticipation of being there without Kirby. In searching through the things that had come from Arizona, I found a slim book with Kirby's reflections on her vision quest.

JEAN

In January 2010, we held a memorial for Kirby where she lived in San Jose del Cabo, the town just north of Cabo San Lucas, Mexico.

It wasn't financially possible for Mike to come with me, so I took the train to New York from Montréal and then I would fly with my parents to Cabo. I'd taken this train ride many times in the three years I had lived in Canada at that point. While it's ridiculously long—the passenger train travels the rail lines that are owned by shipping companies, so the train regularly has to allow the cargo trains to pass by—it's a breathtaking trip alongside Lake Champlain and through the Adirondack Mountains of New York State.

At the border, passengers remain seated while the US Border Patrol agents comb through the train, checking the documents of each passenger. I was reading The Secret Life of Bees, *a story heavily focused on a relationship between sisters. It was engrossing. I reluctantly tucked the book between my seat and the one next to me when the border agent came to check my passport. It was a routine check—the agent didn't even ask me what I was doing in Canada or why I was travelling back to the US. After she returned my passport, I switched it with my book so I could continue reading.*

The realization that I'd left my passport on the train came over me later when I was at our family friend Deborah's apartment in Chelsea, Manhattan.

"Fuck. Fuck fuck fuck fuck fuck!" I said.

"What is it?!" Deborah looked at me, alarmed, while she stirred soy milk into my coffee.

"My passport—I left it on the train!"

Deborah went back with me the next morning and we begged the Amtrak guys at Penn Station to let us on the train that had taken the trip from Montréal. We zig-zagged through the cars, checked on and under all the seats, but the passport was lost to me forever. It was a shame—that photo was actually a pretty good one.

I was supposed to fly out with Deborah and my family in just a couple of days. Getting a rush passport was actually not that difficult, given that I was in New York City. But it did cost about $600. I tacked that one onto the Grief Bill (which never does get repaid).

Because of the passport debacle, I had to delay my flight by a day and fly to Cabo alone. One of the in-flight movies was the Jennifer Aniston and Aaron Eckhart movie, Love Happens. He's an aspiring motivational speaker, who holds challenges like fire walks at his events. The movie is forgettable, but for me, en route to the memorial for my sister who died at a motivational speaker's event, it was absurd that it should be this movie playing on this flight. Like reading The Secret Life of Bees, it was as though all of the storytelling I was taking in was shining a spotlight on this real-life drama I was living through.

I'd visited Kirby in Cabo just one other time, but I remembered the drive from the airport through San Jose del Cabo, the roundabout near the big grocery store, and then the entrance to La Jolla, a community of homes where Kirby had lived the previous time I'd visited her.

That was a college spring break visit with my mom, a friend of mine from school, and Kate (who didn't live in Mexico yet). Kirby lived with her fiancé at the time, Ross, who has a house in La Jolla—somewhat more modest than the celebrity-level homes Kirby painted, but still beautiful, with a great room that opened out to a view of the water. Kirby had done so much painting in this house—hallways that held unexpected sparkles when light reached in, serene blues in the guest room where we stayed that reminded us every morning when we woke up that we were in paradise.

It wasn't hard to understand why Kirby lived there when we visited her. Everything from the food to the music to the friendliness and familiarity of the people, and then the quirkiness of the town and culture, and living there as somewhat of an outsider—

it's a perfect blend of ordinary and magical that allows you to live and enjoy with ease, but also a sense of wonder that won't run out over time.

One of the days of that spring break visit, we drove around the tip of the Baja to a beach on the Pacific side that had especially good surfing. Kirby had given us a first lesson at a calmer beach in San Jose and we were ready to test our skills. My amateur abilities nearly failed me on that day, though, when the surf was especially rough.

Kirby and I paddled out beyond the wave break, where the water was calmer, to wait.

"Yeah, we'll just wait here as long as it takes, until the right wave comes," she explained.

There were a few other surfers out there and that camaraderie is interesting. The anticipation of the ride connects the surfers, even as there's very little eye contact—everyone is watching the waves.

Kirby took a wave in and then I was alone. After a few more minutes, my wave came. I shakily pushed myself up into a standing position on the board and stood up for a bit. But, once I got in closer to the beach where the waves were breaking, I toppled over and rolled under the wave, twisting and churning in the surf so that one leg popped up out of the water first because I was completely disoriented. The waves were breaking about twenty feet out from the shore, but I couldn't get myself in before the next wave slammed on top of me.

A few more waves rolled me, my board still tugging at my ankle strap, and I began to think perhaps I'd die there. At least it was a beautiful place. Finally, the waves let up enough for me to swim in and crawl up onto the beach. An older man who looked like Santa, probably in his sixties, sidled over to me.

"Ya did good there. I was watchin' ya."

I just nodded, breathless and still too full of saltwater to answer.

"Next time, just make sure ya stick yer arm up when you come out of the water, so yer board doesn't getcha in the head."

I nodded again. Then Kirby came over.

"Hey sweetie, that got you good, huh?"

More nodding. Grinding my palms down into the sand was helping me feel less dizzy.

"Yup, she's all right," Santa said.

Kirby helped me up and carried my board as we walked over to our towels.

"Yeah, these old surfers—they always have your back. You did okay, though. I was watching."

Now I was silent out of embarrassment.

"It's okay," Kirby said. "What we learn from getting rocked is usually more important than what we get from a perfect surf."

I modified my excitement as we drove past Kirby's friend, Sheila's, restaurant on the edge of Gringo Hill and the thin span of road along the beach before you hit Palmilla, the gated community where my sister Kate lived. All of the feeling of my previous trip was returning, but this wasn't a vacation. This was getting rocked in the surf.

Before the memorial, there were a few days of finalizing the event plans and visiting with Kirby's friends as more of the East Coast friends and family gathered. And we had to go to Kirby's place.

We'd been preparing ourselves particularly for this day. Kirby had just moved into a new rental three weeks before she went to Sedona for the Spiritual Warrior retreat. She had paid her rent ahead by months and the landlord, a friend of hers, had agreed to leave the apartment until we could go there to collect her things.

But before dismantling it, we just took it in. A few people had warned us to be prepared for what we'd see.

Kirby had moved around a lot since she'd lived in Cabo. In keeping with her typical resourcefulness, she would often live in a space where she could do painting work in lieu of rent. Or she'd house-sit for any of the many people whose Cabo home was a vacation home.

At one point she even lived in a palapa, a palm-leaf-roofed lean-to, attached to a friend's house on the beach.

This rental house was the first living situation that had felt like a place of her own. She was clearly proud of that, because she had made it a home in such a short span of time before her Sedona trip.

Many of the homes typical of Cabo don't necessarily have a conspicuous grand entrance. More often, your approach into the house is more circuitous, through a garden or courtyard, and then you sort of just find yourself inside. Kirby's house had lots of lush vegetation outside, surrounding a small little door. The entrance was tight, with a bathroom to the left, then the master bedroom on the right, another larger bathroom after a few steps through a hall, and then a step down revealed the wide-open main living space. It felt like crawling through a tunnel before stepping into a great room. Out the windows at the back of the house, facing east, was the beach where she frequently surfed and the Sea of Cortez beyond that, where schools of whales breach in the spring.

There was a lot of terra-cotta tile and stucco—very Mexico. But, mostly, there were layers of Kirby everywhere. Her art collection turned the off-white walls into a gallery; her Elizabeth (Lizzie to Kirby) Rosefield flower oil paintings were prominent: a stargazer lily, a silky white datura. Objects from all of the world—all of her travels—sat on window ledges, punctuating stacks of books, elevated countertops. I noticed many things she'd gotten in Thailand when she visited me—Buddha statues, teak elephant carvings, silk pillowcases, a lacquered flower painting I'd bought her in Ho Chi Minh City. Everything was so carefully arranged: clothing in the closets (so much clothing!), toiletries and beauty products in the bathroom (so much pampering!)

Downstairs was a small kitchen, another lounging area, and an entrance to outside. On a doormat next to the sliding door were her hiking boots—cracked, dried mud falling off in clumps as though she'd left them there the day before.

While we were there, a few of her friends showed up. We sat in the main living area and talked a bit. Nancy told us about how she'd talked with Kirby before the Sedona trip.

"She didn't even want to go," Nancy explained. "She'd tried to get her money back."

I mentioned that I felt it was strange how she was so attracted to James Ray. "I don't think she was driven by a quest for wealth," I said.

"Oooh—yes she was," one of her friends, Sheila, the restaurant owner, interjected. Some of Kirby's other friends nodded. "Kirby wanted to be rich—for the right reasons. But she definitely wanted money."

I suppose working in so many huge houses gives you that perspective. I also realize, now that I'm a bit older, at a point you want some sort of security. And, though she wasn't materialistic, Kirby definitely did love beautiful things. That was clear from how carefully she had curated her possessions over the years, how she'd saved things even during multiple moves, how she'd arranged and displayed everything so artfully in this home she'd only spent a few weeks in. God, that was heartbreaking.

During that trip to Cabo and at other times talking with friends of hers, there were little discoveries like this—little pieces of who she was, pieces that weren't familiar to me. I still feel angry that I don't get to ask her about those things now.

Because, even with the insight from her Cabo friends, it was still a mystery. Kirby always struck everyone as such a strong person. Many people had, still have, a hard time understanding what it was she was looking for at James Ray's events. I wondered too. I thought about it a lot that week, and in the months and years after. I'd stand in the shower, grab at my hair while warm tears blended with the water, and just ask "Why?" Why did she need to go? What was she looking for?

A passage from her vision quest notebook has helped me understand it a little better—I think. In a space along the curve of her medicine wheel, she detailed an "offering" of her vision of the future:

My beautiful creation, my reality. A beautiful home with lots of animals and loved ones (my family). Horses and dogs, chickens, goats, pigs, cattle… a ranch.

There is an art studio… one for pottery and the other for beading house jewelry and chandeliers. It is so magical… the creativity flows like the river.

My relationship with my family and friends is of highest standard. There is unconditional love and support. We all have so much fun together!

My relationship with my lover is amazing, passionate, loving, kind, supportive, compassionate. We grow together through good times and difficult times.

…My businesses are running smoothly, efficiently, and making lots of money. Nancy and I still do homes but only one big one a year. The rest has taken over.

I am fit and healthy. We surf all the time and have our own yoga studio. It is truly a most outstanding life.

I believe Kirby felt she was at the foot of the next level in her life—even this home she'd created right before she left for Spiritual Warrior was so close—but there were things holding her back. While she appeared strong and in command from an outsider's perspective, she had doubts and fears like all of us. She had chosen a different life path, one for which she didn't have a clear example or roadmap—she was charting it herself. She was so strong for so many people and she needed to release some of that responsibility so she could move forward. Creating those boundaries was hard and scary. She had searched for a life partner, maybe searched too hard, trying to make herself fit into someone else's life. I think she had decided instead to focus on creating the life she envisioned for herself, trusting that the right partner would follow.

With all of these desires and tasks in front of her, I think she felt she needed guidance—a push to help her get to that next level. The messaging of James Ray really resonated with her. The idea of the "Law of Attraction"—that you need to clearly visualize what you truly wanted so you could manifest it in your reality—hit home for her, because she'd often gotten caught up in the needs of the people who relied on her. Ray's ability to convince people that he had the answers, that he was the one who could push them ahead toward that vision (if only they were committed enough) was seductive. The intense motivation that was always a part of her personality made it easy for her to "play full on," as Ray put it.

When I look back on her vision for her future, it makes me so sad. And angry. Her vision is so beautiful, so pure. To come into contact with a person who lacked the integrity he claimed—that was her ultimate downfall. It's so tragic. I just have to believe that she's on that ranch now, so that I don't hold that sadness too tight forever.

My sister Kate, who has experience in the food and wine industries, organized the main party. During the week before the memorial, I went on errands with her as she finalized last-minute details. By the time we'd arrived, most of it—the venue, music, the color of the tablecloths, the type of cups we'd have (they were compostable)—was already arranged. Kate had done a lot of work for this send-off.

On one of our outings, we stopped at a small shopping center near her house. Some artisans were selling jewelry, clothing, and other small objects outside.

Kate picked through the merchandise on the tables.

"I want to get something for Beverley," she said. She was arriving that afternoon.

This surprised me. I'd been a bit nervous about how Kate would react to Beverley and her being there. Kate is the fiery one in our family—the one who won't let anyone get away with any bullshit. She has a protective exterior.

But I realized, while she selected a ring and small pouch decorated with shells, that on the softer parts inside, she was feeling some of the same protectiveness I felt for Beverley. She wanted her to feel welcome.

Kate's week had been filled with details—of the party, of people flying in and guests staying at her house—but that she still had space for this small detail touched me.

The week felt like the lead up to a wedding. People were gathering at Kate's house—some staying with her, others (like me) at neighbor's places, some in hotels. We would hang out in the daytime and gather in the evenings for dinner. Every meal felt like a party.

And then there were actual parties. One night, we were at Havana, the bar owned by Kirby's friend, Sheila. Kirby had taken us there on my first trip to Baja to listen to music. The restaurant tucks into the rocky hillside, with tiled steps leading up from the tight parking lot into the restaurant.

We danced that night, the week of the memorial. A band played—musicians whom Kirby had supported over the years. I recognized one of the musicians—he'd been about fourteen when I'd met him on my first trip. Kirby had introduced us then, proud of him. He was shy at fourteen, and still shy then when I saw him again, but he remembered me too. We awkwardly held onto this memory of Kirby together.

One of Kirby's signature moves (so often referenced by friends and family that it's almost cliché now) was that when listening to a band, she'd always get people up on the dancefloor. She'd basically coerce people with her enthusiasm. And then, when the music was done, she'd flitter around with the tip jar (even if the band wasn't especially good). Bands loved when Kirby was at their gig, because they'd inevitably make more in tips when she was there.

For that particular night, we commissioned a special tip jar from the local glass blowing factory (another stop on Kirby's Custom Baja Tour). I tried to carry it around a bit, but I felt like an imposter.

Kirby's tip jar shtick was so effective because it came from such a genuine place—it was her reveling in the music and her experience of it. You can't fake that.

When a surfer dies, fellow surfers honor their friend with a special ceremony called a paddle out. They literally paddle out beyond the wave break to the calm water where they form a circle and sing, share stories, splash, whoop, and sometimes scatter the ashes of the deceased. It's a sacred ceremony among surfers and a big honor for one who's died.

This was the culminating event of our memorial in Baja. People gathered on the beach at Zippers, one of the surf spots right in San Jose del Cabo at the foot of Gringo Hill, where Kirby and most of her community lived. On the beach, Lizzie Rosefield (the painter) led a Native American inspired prayer service and the surfers gathered to swim out to the ceremony in the water.

I went in a boat, one with a motor this time, along with my parents, to meet the surfers off the beach. Bobby, on one of Kirby's boards, and Kate were among them. The surfers' tans and bathing suits and the designs on their boards painted a brilliant circle in the aqua water.

In the boat, we floated a bit away from the surfers and watched, and then finally dropped the parcel of Kirby's ashes into the water. Unlike the day of the Long Island ceremony, this day was bright and sunny. The splashes of water from Kirby's friends and neighbors sprayed into the air and sparkled in the sunlight. Their cheers and cries built inside the circle and splashed out, too, with a primal sort of energy. I had never witnessed or even heard of a paddle out before, but I am so grateful for this tribute to her. Even amid the confusion, anger, and bald sadness of Kirby's death, it was important to celebrate her too—to feel joy in having loved her. This is where I felt that joy.

During the party following the paddle out, there was an odd reminder of the new-aged wackiness Kirby's death had introduced in our lives. At some point during the party, some of Kirby's friends told me I need to speak to Sunny.

"Jean, she's just…. You need to go talk to her. She has something to say, something really important, and you should really listen," one of Kirby's Gringo Hill neighbors told me.

So my mom and I went out onto the beach. Sunny was sitting in a spot. She wore all white and had a shaved head—like some sort of mystic.

She smiled, big and toothy, with clear blue eyes and a sunworn but radiant face. She certainly did have a presence.

She started by introducing herself.

"My name is Sunny." She then mentioned a well-known cosmetics company and simply told us, "I founded that company." I wasn't sure how she wanted me to respond to that, but it was an odd introduction that I've often wondered about. What did she want us to take from that claim? She then explained that after leaving "that world," she'd found peace and discovered her true gift.

Then, she'd told us that she had a message—from Kirby.

"I was meditating and this being of light came to me."

She gave a lengthy description about her vision and then explained that Kirby had an urgent message for us.

"Kirby wants you to know that she's okay. She's in a peaceful place and is joyful. Everything is as it should be now. But she also wanted me to tell you a secret. 'You have to tell them,' she said."

Sunny paused, building the gravity of this "secret" from Kirby.

"The secret is that the answers are within you."

While we sat there, the sun was starting to fade, but I focused on a volleyball net set up nearby. We were on a broad, deep stretch of beach, and it felt like the sand just went on and on forever. I found it difficult to focus on what Sunny was saying because the surreal-

ity of the situation was so distracting. My mom was similarly still, kneeling in the sand with her eyes fixed on Sunny. I believe I get my patience and tact from her.

"Wow. Thank you, for that," I managed to say, when the monologue was over.

My mom and I looked at one another, and then walked back to the party in silence. What else was there to say? Perhaps Kirby was at peace. But we weren't.

When describing the big secret to my dad, my mom was a bit incredulous.

"That's it? The answers are within? I've always told you guys that!" she said.

Having heard about James Ray's "channeler" trying to dissolve the horror with mystical explanations of what had happened at Spiritual Warrior, I couldn't help but wonder if there was an ulterior motive from someone like Sunny relaying a message like that. I wondered, would the whole self-help world—people who earn their living and build their power from selling their experience in the metaphysical, the spiritual, the alternative—would they be threatened by what happened to Kirby? Would they be threatened by her death and what it implied about their livelihoods? And, if we were going to speak out about how fucked up it all was, would they be threatened by us?

Removed from that beach by years, now, the message feels… nice. Not hostile. But as with many of the well-meaning but "alternative" people we met in those months after Kirby died, her timing sucked.

Before we went to the airport to take our flights home, we gathered at the house where my parents had stayed during the week. The house overlooked the beach. A wooden stairway led down the cliffside to a shallow stretch of sand and rocks. I looked out to the water, the same water where we'd left Kirby's ashes the day before. Bougainvillea petals floated everywhere, little dots of magenta flecked the waves. I picked one out and kept it. The crisp-dried petal is now faded, broken flakes, tucked into a little teakwood box I keep near my bed.

GINNY

I could not help but stroke the pages of Kirby's notebook. Written on special Nepalese paper from the Daphne "lokta" tree, the pages are soft yet durable, delicate and strong, very much like Kirby herself. It begins with the words:

Magic, the ability to create willful change in the fabric of your universe both spiritually and physically. Namaste.

There is a description of her medicine wheel—the organization of her hopes, dreams, and thoughts on that last night of her life.

She described her "pouches," the offerings she was preparing to bring into the sweat lodge. One detailed her emotional hurts and regrets, another contained her vision for her future, her future home, partner, relationships, work, purpose, joys. Her desire for transformation in her thoughts and actions filled her other offerings. I wept through her ideas about changes she would make, and what she wanted to acknowledge and embrace. I wept for the internal beauty my daughter was just discovering and my loss for what I had always known.

She wrote of the stillness, the silence, the rain-soaked earth, the setting sun, and approaching darkness. I felt like I was there with her, drinking in the beauty of the slowly changing sunlight into the "rose light" of dusk. I have always been fascinated by light, noticing the changes especially at the rising and setting of the sun. And Kirby had always been a daughter of the earth and sky, appreciating the physical beauty and magnificence of creation.

I was most intrigued by her descriptions of her surroundings in the silence of the desert. She wrote:

The silence creates a stillness. It slows all energies to a rhythmic, conscious movement that offers awareness... the wind flows through the trees... the leaves glisten and sparkle in the sunlight. ...The sweet and darling chirp of the bird... all of these rhythmic dances are healing to the soul.

She described the setting sun, her appreciation for its warmth and creative power:

As the sun sets, the light slowly changes coming into "God light" or the Rose light time, my favorite... reminding me of Spiritu Santu [a mission in the Baja that some friends were rebuilding into a place of retreat, a place Kirby loved to visit]... now the sounds of the night have appeared... now the crickets are singing their night time song. It reminds me of Mom and Dad's house, a beautiful home. ...I am so grateful I have been able to spend so much time there when I live so far away.

Her last written words are,

Slow down. Listen, taste, smell, enjoy life to its fullest all the time. That is what we have. Enjoy this perfect life!

Recently, we were in Bar Harbor, Maine, and on the summit of Cadillac Mountain. I could see ten-year-old Kirby facing the rising sun. In the early 1980s, while camping at Acadia with our young family, she was the only one who was willing to rise at 5:30 am with me to greet the dawn, the first sign of the morning light on the eastern coast. Seeing that sunrise from the top of the mountain meant leaving a toasty warm sleeping bag, suffering the predawn chill, and driving twenty minutes in the dark to join the "sunrise club." As the sun illuminated her face, I remember falling in love with her as I had when holding her infant self in my arms at her birth. I have experienced that overwhelming swell of love and gratitude when witnessing a moment of intangible beauty, sensing a purity that reveals depth in my offspring. The sun appeared over the water, the sky was washed in brilliance, and all witnesses erupted in applause. I remembered that moment of silent exchange when we both felt the awe of natural beauty. Kirby would always live with a passionate appreciation of nature and all things beautiful.

Oh, how I miss her! How I miss seeing her excitement! How I miss sharing thoughts and dreams! Reading this journal reminds me of holding a precious stone that has never been set into jewelry. I weep and know I will never stop missing her, but want so much to live with the purity of intentions she expressed in this slim volume.

On January 4, 2010, some family and friends joined us on the flight to Cabo. This would be a final goodbye with the Cabo family who were such an important part of Kirby and Kate's lives in Mexico.

I nervously approached the airport security, carrying a canvas bag containing Kirby's cremains—just dust, just ashes that felt so incredibly heavy, the remains of a whole person, a whole life. I carried a letter of explanation from the funeral parlor in case I was questioned. Thankfully, no one inquired about the odd package which I had to "carry on" rather than check with our suitcases. That bag stalked me like a shadow companion and the usual excitement of going to Mexico was obscured by loss and sadness, knowing that we would not see Kirby in the flesh; she was beneath my feet.

Gringo Hill in San Jose is only about a half hour from the Los Cabos Airport. The best approach to the hill is actually through the arroyo which goes under the main highway, a dusty and dry roadbed except in hurricane season when angry rains fill the huge gully.

Homes of all descriptions populate the hill where so many American expats live. There are RVs, a few mobile homes, and large cinder block structures with verandas looking out to the ocean. Winding around the hill, one may never know that behind fences and gates covered in luscious bougainvillea, there are virtual Shangri-las, homes with gardens, in-ground pools, sprawling ranch-like structures with large open living areas covered by palapa roofs. There are hidden gardens around every corner, interspersed with abandoned vehicles and packs of stray dogs.

The community is similarly diverse: entrepreneurs who operate online businesses, local artists and craftspeople, retirees from the States, and families with young children. I often joked that some neighbors were lovely "burned-out hippies from the sixties" who woke up one day to discover they were living on valuable real estate. Many people on the hill barter for goods and services. Mercedes, a good friend of Kirby's, operates a large heated palapa studio where she teaches Bikram yoga, a favorite gathering place. Phyllis has a beautiful palapa home at the top of the hill, where you can view the ocean while getting the most amazing manicure or pedicure. Nancy, Kirby's business partner, and her husband, Pete, have a home that overhangs the hill, touching the sky while looking down on the ocean.

Kirby had lived in a two-story home as a caretaker, managing the property until the owners who lived in San Diego retired. She had decorated and painted every surface of this home in lieu of rent, bringing gray cement to life in design and brilliant color. When the owners would arrive for a few weeks' vacation, Kirby would move to the ground floor where she had created her own little apartment with a bedroom, bath, a kitchen, and an outdoor living room.

By September 2009, she had finally realized a dream to have her own home and had rented a two-story octagonal building that she made her home in a few short weeks before going to Sedona. I wanted and simultaneously dreaded seeing her home, knowing how excited she had been to have everything set up, even the garden, before she left on the Spiritual Warrior retreat. It was a very unusual space, right off the road; I approached the entry, walked through the front hallway, and was assaulted by light—windows on every wall looked out to her surf break. Standing there, I was dazzled at the beauty she had created in those few short weeks before leaving for Sedona.

A winding staircase where she had placed colorful wall hangings led down to a kitchen and eating area that opened out to a patio and a garden with beds ready for planting. The butcher block table and kitchen implements were also ready to create the next party. My heart broke when I saw what she had hoped to return to.

We had to decide what we wanted of her things. Internally, I cried out, "Everything!" but knew that was completely unrealistic. She owned a 4Runner that she used on the beach on the East Cape and we packed it with the items that would be brought back to New York. Geronimo, Kirby's cousin and Alyssa, his soon-to-be wife, had agreed to drive it home for us. Kirby and Kate often were "hosts" of parties on The Hill. Thanksgiving gatherings, hurricane parties, Christmas and New Year's Eve celebrations were often at the Browns'. I continue to use Kirby's tablecloths, placemats, napkins, and lovely ceramic serving bowls. I am so proud that my girls carried on the Brown party tradition, the open door, the givers and gatherers of festivities.

As we looked through her things, behind a wall in the open living room there were quite a few large plastic containers, all labeled. For a young, single person, Kirby had an incredible amount of stuff (clothing, toiletries, shoes, memorabilia, and gadgets); yet, she was very deliberate and organized. We found three bins labeled "journals." My heart stopped. I suddenly felt like I would be able to "touch" her, know her every thought, desire, question. I could feel a tangible draw toward those volumes, pulling me, beckoning me to read her most private musings.

When my children were growing up, I often reflected how awesome it would be to open up their brains; maybe I could see their thoughts, plans, dreams, memories. Mysteries would be solved. Maybe I would finally understand my amazing but often elusive children; maybe I could remove a few bad memories of me from their brains (you know, those days you regret when you lose it).

As I began to act on that "itchy" curiosity to start reading, George stopped me from opening the first volume.

He said, "Did Kirby ask you to read her journals?"

"Well, no."

"Do you think she wrote them for others to see?"

"No, but they are here. This is an opportunity—to know her!"

George, her protective father, wisely said, "A journal is kept to write down private thoughts recorded at a particular time, often to vent anger, frustrations, and other feelings. She might have changed her mind after committing them to paper. A journal is static. It might not really reflect the whole person."

He was right. Kate agreed, noting that there would probably be a lot of shit written in there about her. Kirby and Kate were very different from one another and, although very close, had been through some rough times in their "sisterhood" journey. We decided these journals were not to be read but should be burned instead. They did not belong to us anymore than Kirby ever belonged to me. It is interesting that her vision quest reflections seemed different to me. They were her "final words" and seemed more like a gift to me. But the diaries of everyday life are the recordings of that ongoing struggle to understand one's self.

We would sort through and make decisions about her home and possessions after the memorial service. First, we needed to gather this family of relatives and friends to celebrate Kirby and honor her life.

Kate and Mitchell had moved from the Hill to Palmilla and we gathered there every day. Our son, Bobby, surprised us on Friday, arriving unannounced. It felt wonderful to be together. Some friends and relatives had come, and Beverley also joined us to see Kirby's Mexican life. That evening, Kirby's friend Sheila, who operated Havana in San Jose, opened the doors to host a great evening of food and musicians who created a raucous event to celebrate the girl who had helped Sheila open and decorate that jazz club.

Kirby stories were told, and I heard about an amazing rescue that Kirby participated in while swimming in the mountain pools north of San Jose. After a friend dove in, he began to struggle and appeared to be in trouble. Seeing his distress, Kirby said she was sure that he had injured his spine. Calling to the others in the group, she knew they needed to hold him in the water while someone got medical help. Apparently, it took a few hours before help arrived. The emergency workers said that keeping him suspended in the water prevented further damage and may have actually saved his life. Billy Dahly told me that this was one of the stories Kirby had relayed to him about being involved in saving someone's life. While visiting Kirby in Cabo, I realized that wherever we went—to a taco stand, a tienda, the gas station, a restaurant, or just walking down a street—we would meet someone who knew Kirby, often a musician. Everyone seemed to know my daughter. I mentioned this to one of her friends; he simply laughed and asked if I had ever been to a musical venue with her. He told me that every musician in Cabo knew Kirby Brown because when she showed up at a gig with her tip jar, they made at least three times more money for the night.

The next morning, one of Kirby's friends anxiously approached me to tell me that when Kirby had spent some time at Spiritu Santu in March, she had said if she ever died, she wanted her ashes scattered at the renovated mission. This beautiful place was captured in the last pictures on her camera. However, the boat was ready to take us out to her surf break, the paddle out was already planned, so I decided maybe we could honor her request in another way. I suggested that everyone could write a letter to Kirby—a goodbye, a thank you, whatever was in their hearts. Some friends later took all the letters, burned those sentiments of love and loss, and scattered those ashes on the mission grounds which became the recipient of the love she had inspired in others.

The next day was the paddle out. Out in the water just beyond the breaking waves, surfers congregated while Stuart played his pipes on the shore. Once the boat slowed, George shouted above the sound of the engine and waves: "Kirby we commend you to the sea... to the eternal sea and to eternal life!" On the beach, a large group had gathered to venerate Kirby with a ceremony that Lizzie (the local priestess and artist) designed; she honored the directions and the earth, and saged all the participants.

Once on the shore, we headed to CJ's, a friend who had offered his home on the beach for a celebration that would rival any wedding. Kate had made all the arrangements for this incredible celebration of her sister. She had worked for weeks with local vendors and friends, getting donations and gifts to put this amazing tribute together. Gorgeous flower arrangements, tables decorated with linens and flowers, a tent set up for us to address a crowd of at least 250 people. The gathering of people included some folks who live on the beach, the head of an international bank, CEOs, gardeners, artists, musicians, local professionals, children, and maids, all who knew and loved Kirby. Maciek, who organizes the monthly full moon celebrations up on the East Cape where he lives on the beach, acted as the DJ. A group of flamethrowers put on a performance once it got dark. Hula hoops, dancing, great food and wine filled the night.

I had set up a large basket on a table with paper and pens, and invited people to write their notes to Kirby that would later be burned and scattered at the mission. By the end of the night, it was filled to the brim. There was a large envelope with drawings and letters from the kids who lived on the hill who were members of Kirby's little riding club.

Wherever Kirby went, she found horses that needed to be exercised. She loved to ride and always found a way to barter a ride. She farm-sat to ride; she sniffed out neglected but beloved animals that needed attention to ride; she mucked stalls to ride. In the Baja, on Gringo Hill, she found some neglected horses and, after approaching the owner, was riding them a few times a week to keep them in shape. She told me that the kids on the hill would follow her to the beach and beg for a ride on the horses. She decided to approach their parents to ask if they would like to have their children learn to ride. She was able to gain the permission of the owner of the horses, and found a little piece of open, flat land that could be fenced and used to set up a riding ring. The owner agreed—an unused patch of land was donated, and the parents organized it to create Kirby's riding club for the kids on the hill.

One day, while visiting, George and I went to watch a lesson. I climbed up a small tree and perched from a branch, watching her work with a half dozen young children. One of the boys, six-year-old Miles, was seated on the horse and, suddenly, as the horse was trotting, the saddle began to slide off, sending Miles toward the underbelly of the horse. Before Miles could even yell out or the adults scream, Kirby's strong, capable hands had snatched him out of the saddle and she exclaimed, "Miles, that was amazing. You are like a superhero. You didn't panic or scare the horse. Wow, you are so strong and brave!" Before the child could even speak, his look of abject fear became one of pride as he yelled to his mother, "Mom, did you see that. I'm a superhero. We have to tell Dad!" I jumped from the tree, amazed at her quick thinking and immediate action.

These same children would write her love letters, drawing pictures for her that filled that large envelope. One wrote, "I will love you forever and never forget you." I cry when I think of the joy she created and the pain her death brought upon us all.

The rest of that week, as family and friends left for home, we dismantled Kirby's home. As we tearfully walked together through her dwelling, we made some decisions about how to distribute her belongings. Possessions reveal a lot about the values and character of the owner. Between books, journals, artwork, beauty products, shoes, beautiful clothing, surfboards, safety equipment, and paint-splattered work jeans, we could feel her life. Her home truly reflected her life—filled to the brim with fun, adventure, beauty, celebration, work, and introspection.

The kitchen was filled with dishes, bowls, glasses, and gadgets—items that Kirby had always remarked were needed in Kate's woefully understocked kitchen. We packed and brought some of her kitchen up to Kate's house in Palmilla. Having hosted many events on the hill for their Cabo family, both Kirby and Kate knew how to prepare delicious food and create fabulous parties.

Mirrors, artwork, rugs, a few selected pieces of furniture, and clothing were brought to Kate's house for us to sort through to incorporate into the Palmilla house or to pack to be returned to New York.

One hotly contested piece of furniture was the butcher block table on wheels that Peter, Nancy's husband, had made for Kirby. The table had served as a kitchen island and was beautifully constructed of cherry and oak wood, with a knife drawer and lower shelf for serving bowls. Many vegetables were chopped, and many salads were prepared on that surface. I pulled the "mother" card and claimed the table. We packed that into Kirby's 4Runner, which Geronimo and Alyssa would drive back to New York for us.

I still invoke her spirit as I prepare meals on the same surface in our home.

Kirby loved vintage jewelry and clothing and had often shopped with Nancy at what they called the "Gucci Will" in San Diego, a thrift shop which was filled with discarded goods from wealthy donors. Her closet was filled with wraps, furs, amazing dresses, and clothing Kirby had had tailored for her in Thailand. Fortunately for me, Kirby and I are the same size, so I inherited a new wardrobe and have worn much of her clothing over the years.

We were not the same shoe size, however, but she could have opened a shoe store with her boots, shoes, and sandals.

I found two teddy bears that were made by a local craftsperson from pieces of old coats and sweaters. A crystal was sewn onto an embroidered fabric heart in the center of the bears. Kirby had gifted me a similar teddy bear for my birthday the year before. These are not soft bears that you cuddle with or give to a child. I found them a little odd, almost scary-looking, but Kirby had explained to me that the artist was just starting out and Kirby wanted to encourage and support her. Geronimo took one to keep on his dashboard for the trip to New York. He named it "Trucky"—a Kirby talisman.

Surf boards, a bike, kayak, mountain climbing, and safety equipment needed to find new homes for another's adventure.

I know it is just "stuff," but it was HER stuff and seeing it, touching it, felt like her. These days of cleaning out her things were both torture and a gift. I cried for what she would never return to, the life she would not continue to live in her beloved Baja; yet her things were also a consoling presence which I wanted to respect and protect.

Her Cabo community also wanted some of Kirby's things, important mementos attached to rich memories or useful items that they felt Kirby would have wanted them to have. The rest we left for Kirby's friends to choose; everyone wanted something of Kirby, something to help their broken hearts. I could not go to the house the day her friends descended upon it to pick over the leftovers, to divide up her things, treasuring pieces of her life.

Leaving was another finality. I wanted to stay in the place she loved, with Kate, Mitchell, and Angus. I wrote in my journal:

Lord, stay with us and guide us through this pain… loss, sorrow, anger, thanksgiving, joy, laughter, small miracles, beauty, an amazing journey. Be with us to balance our purpose, time, intention, emotions. What an incredible two weeks. Its finality wrenches and yet I am filled with pride for Kate, Bobby, and Jean. While our family is diminished, I think we have been made stronger and are more fully focused on our love and need for each other.

Upon our return from Cabo, I was reminded that our loss involved a larger reality; I began receiving calls about wrongful death parties suing James Ray. Lawyers were being hired to represent the Neumans and Shores, and others who had been injured and were trying to recoup some of their losses from hospital bills and lost wages. There were also messages and calls from *48 Hours, The New York Times,* and an AP reporter from

Flagstaff. It was almost four months since the deaths and still no charges had been leveled. Four months seemed like forever, waiting for Ray to be held accountable. The memorial services certainly consumed my attention and prevented me from obsessing about an indictment; however, with every phone call from those victimized by this event, I became more and more sure of Ray's depraved indifference and his criminal culpability. We were so fortunate to have Bob Magnanini handling the legalities. He was interfacing with the other lawyers and investigating Ray's assets to determine what course of action should be taken in any lawsuits.

In the midst of this numbing grief, the news finally came. James Arthur Ray was indicted for manslaughter in early February 2010. I felt some relief, but also renewed horror; this was a confirmation that these deaths were not an accident but caused by willful negligence. That day, the phone rang off the hook—calls from reporters, friends, the other victims. I did an interview for a Phoenix station. Bob Magnanini called to tell us the grand jury had indicted Ray for manslaughter sixteen to one and the next step would be a bail hearing, then a hearing for pre-trial motions and, finally, a trial date would be set. I remember shaking all over, wondering how all this would unravel. *Dateline* called, as did *The New York Times*, NBC, 12 News Phoenix. There were pictures on the news of Ray in orange, cuffed and shackled doing the "perp walk." I felt relief that finally we would hear the truth of what happened that week in Sedona. Little did I know then that truth, even factual information, can be quite elusive when highly paid lawyers are defending your case.

For the next few weeks, bits and pieces of information started to come our way. Angel Valley Ranch was in bankruptcy, which was one of the reasons the Hamiltons had allowed Ray to do the retreat in October, even though they were growing increasingly uncomfortable with him. I knew there was talk about suing them and, while I agreed there was some culpability on their part, I also felt they had supported the participants after Ray left and Amayra had reached out to me with real compassion. I did not want them to lose their ranch.

Bob Magnanini found a private attorney in Arizona to represent us. When he told us that the lawyer retained was Mike Murphy, I inwardly chuckled at the synchronicity. My mother's brother was Michael Murphy who served as the NYC Police Commissioner in the 1960s. I felt that we were in good hands.

There were now nine claims representing the family victims of Sedona and eventually eight others who had been harmed would join the suit. A forensic accountant was hired by the court to determine Ray's net worth in order to set bail, because Ray's lawyers were protesting the amount ($5 million).

We learned that an investigator was checking out Ray's insurances and knew Ray had contacted other Spiritual Warrior participants to offer deals and have them sign releases, to prevent any further suits for the tragedy in Sedona. I was confused about that; I didn't think that would be allowed.

The bond hearing was set for Tuesday, February 23, from 3:00 pm to 5:00 pm EST and finished Wednesday, February 24, from 1:30 pm to 3:30 pm EST. This hearing was necessary because the original amount set for bail was being protested by Ray's attorneys. We were invited to listen to the proceedings via phone. Ray had established a separate corporation to handle the sale of his books, tapes, and seminars (White Wolf International); another corporation, set up in March of 2009, purchased his Beverley Hills home, valued at $5 million (Quantum Shift); and another corporation handled monthly income/expenses (Global Harmony). The bondsman was evaluating collateral property because Ray was presenting no assets. His properties were leased or in foreclosure, showing a destitute individual with no liquid capital.

Sitting at our kitchen table on that gray winter day, George and I strained to hear and understand the forensic accountant for the state and the comptroller for James Ray International attesting to Ray's cooperation in giving full disclosure. I looked past the bare branches of the horse chestnut tree which are a brief reach beyond the kitchen windows—a gray landscape, a lonely field sloping down to a dark, silent lake, an overcast sky. The cold seemed to seep inside me, and I felt removed, numb. So many times, I asked myself, "How did I get here? How could this be my life?"

I returned my focus to the phone. Suddenly, a voice from across the country addressed us, asking if we had any questions. I was struggling to process the information about properties, possessions, and the amount of money being discussed. Feeling anxious, scared, my stomach in knots, I listened to the man— who had boasted on stage of having an internationally successful business, making tons of money—say he was indigent.

My hands and voice were shaking as I asked, "Mr. Ray, I heard you last year on stage bragging about your net worth, having earned $10 million the year before. Were you lying then or now? Are we to believe that you are truly without any monetary value, destitute?"

There was no answer.

Based on the information given, the state reduced the bond from $5 million to $500,000, of which he had to post 10% to get out of jail after he had been indicted. I should have seen that as an indication of how the trial would unfold. His passport was confiscated to restrict travel. At this point, Ray had served three weeks in jail.

Now, we had to address a lawsuit. Bob Magnanini was investigating Ray's insurance policies which could be used to settle a claim as opposed to a civil suit if Ray had no available assets. He coordinated the lawyers to work together for the seventeen people who were now attached to the lawsuit. It was time for us to introduce ourselves to Mike Murphy who would be representing us.

In a conversation that week with Alyssa Shore, she told me that her brother-in-law Chris was the one contacted by a sheriff thirty hours after her husband's death, who then delivered the devastating news. Ray called her on Sunday night, three days after he had refused to respond to James' request for help before he died next to Kirby. She exploded at Ray. Both she and her husband had gone to a few of Ray's events and had invested a considerable amount of their money in Ray. How could he have allowed this to happen on his watch? They trusted him and not only had he not protected his participants, but he had not even notified her of this tragedy. The depth of her grief and anger was beyond description.

On a bleak, cold day that month, I thought of a woman who I had met in March and remembered that she said she had joined James Ray's World Wealth organization. This organization was set up by Ray as a high-level networking opportunity for motivated entrepreneurs. It also allowed for closer access to Ray on special trips to sacred places. I gave Kerri a call and she explained that she had gone to Peru the year before as a member of the organization, but had only joined for six months due to the expensive entrance into this exclusive group (I think the cost was $60,000 to $75,000 per year). She was very insistent that Ray was one of the persons closest to "source" on the planet. She could not believe this tragedy had occurred because of his authenticity as a shaman with healing powers.

She explained that it had been revealed to her that, "Our past lives follow us into the present and James Shore, Kirby Brown, and Liz Neuman had been key players in an earlier life during the Middle Ages, and were responsible for the execution of Ray's wife and his wrongful death."

She explained to me that these deaths in Sedona were simply "the fulfillment of a sacred contract to satisfy universal karma."

I was astounded that she would explain this to me even as she conveyed her condolences on Kirby's death and suggested I go to a place for healing my grief. Are you kidding me? Basically, you are telling me she got what she deserved?

I put down the phone and sobbed in a despairing disbelief that there were people who could actually believe such a fantasy to support their need to believe in this charlatan.

This was a world I did not know and wanted no part of. Feeling that creepy fear overwhelm me, I prayed to the God I know for protection, insight, and right purpose.

Part II:
Grief

Chapter 5

❝ Our loved ones that have passed are with us. ❞

*—Kirby's words in the voice recording
before going into the tent*

Ginny

**❝ Whatever happens today, learn from it.
You may need it tomorrow.❞**

*—Wise words spoken by my mother-in-law,
Josephine Brown*

DEATH/GRIEVING:
WHAT AM I LEARNING?

In the late summer of 1983, I watched my dear friend, Sue Damiani, die of breast cancer. She was a college friend and, after graduating, our parallel lives of marriage and motherhood deepened our friendship as we shared confidences about the joys and struggles of being a spouse and mother. At the end of her illness, her daughter, Kate, was five years old. In her final days, as I sat on her bed holding her feverish hand, she whispered, "Please pray that this pain will not change who I am. I need to be able to let Kate know how much I love her. I still need to be me." I still hear her voice.

149

On a plane trip in the summer following Kirby's death, looking through the clouds below, I realized that the solidity of my life had become hazy, often unreachable and sometimes unrecognizable. My life would never be what it was. I was ungrounded, floating, displaced. I kept wondering if death has a gestation period similar to the birthing of a child. It takes nine months for the baby to become real. Maybe it takes at least nine months for a death to become as real as life. I know I was not in complete shock or denial. But like pregnancy, in the early months, you know you are expecting, you feel the baby moving, you see your body changing, you imagine and anticipate this new life. And then, after nine months of development, the baby emerges; what you knew was happening is suddenly completely real. There is a new life with needs and demands that will change you forever—a new life that will change the priorities of your time and will impact and shape you in unimagined ways. You have a new identity. Can anyone prepare for motherhood—or sudden, traumatic death?

On October 8, 2010, the first anniversary, I was suddenly aware that I had been holding my breath for a full year. I realized I had been thinking, "I can do this for a year. I can pretend she's in Mexico and will be coming home soon. For a year, I can do this."

But after a year, a new level of knowing shows up—this IS my life. She will not show up as she did in the past. She will not be here physically, surprising me, or orchestrating some amazing adventure. I thought: Maybe now, after almost a year, I truly feel the REALITY of her death. And now, I am changed. With these new demands, what do I have to learn? And will I still be me?

George has often said, "This is a club no one would ever look to join, but which has irrevocably connected us all."

This kind of grief sets one apart from others. It is a unique type of grief. My brother Frank told me about a short story he'd ready by Colum McCann in *The Best American Short Stories 2015*. Frank wrote:

> The story's title is 'Sh'Khol' which is a Hebrew word that translates to 'bereavement,' but actually means the loss of a child. The author describes the word as onomatopoetic: starts with 'shh'—no one should speak of it—and ends with 'kohl,' a harsh and disruptive sound. It is odd that there is no word for the loss of a child in English—no corollary to the word 'orphan' or 'widow.' The fact that this experience is not named in our language, I think, reflects our culture's inability to come to terms with it.

In the first year, I knew I had to survive, but there were a few days when I was unsure if I would. I felt ravaged, hollowed out with a longing that was a physical pain. Often during those first few years, living in an altered reality, shrouded in a misty fog which obscured clear sight, I wanted to look rational even though I felt crazy inside. I wanted to be in control of my actions, not do or say things I would later regret. I needed to be ME even though I was in an emotional blender operating at high speed. When being interviewed, I didn't want to be seen as the crazed, grieving mother who would simply be written off as understandably upset. I wanted to be heard, seen as an intelligent, sane person who now understood this never should have happened.

A month after Kirby's death, I returned to work and found that it allowed me to focus on something else. It did not diminish my sorrow but allowed me to be distracted from it. I discovered that I could still do good work that helped others and that helped me. Working with clients, planning programs, or teaching a class helped me to feel real. This trauma had caused me to feel untethered; good work helped me to touch the ground again. Horrific sudden loss scrubbed me raw. I needed to have real feelings that were not about me, in order to help me find myself in the tumult of grief.

In November of 2009, I was reading, *Stones From the River* by Ursula Hegi and I came across this quote:

> Once someone has been in your life, you can keep that person there despite the agony of loss, as long as you had faith that you could bring the sum of all your hours together in one shining moment.

That thought helped me struggle out of the abyss. I have always found reading to be helpful in pulling me out of myself to restore balance within.

Reading can also bring solace. Like "comfort food," I sometimes seek out comfort reading. A few months after Kirby's death, I read *Anne of Green Gables,* a sweet story with lovely characters, oozing with simple goodness. Beach reads and stories with well-drawn but good, courageous characters boost my belief in humanity, helping to banish dark thoughts. I have sought out Netflix streaming series to satisfy that same need to escape haunting memories and angry feelings. Carefully chosen movies and books can be like a healing emotional massage.

There was a time after Kirby's death that George and I were addicted to watching *Cold Case*, the TV show about detectives investigating old, unsolved deaths. The final scene would always show the person who tragically died looking from the past into the present, a shadowy image finally at peace. It was the mission of the investigators to honor the deceased through their work, ensuring that those who had died would never be forgotten. That is what resonated with me.

That first year was a curious mixture of interminable days of bleak sadness and fast moving events that propelled time forward. A year of firsts: holidays; visiting Kate in Cabo without Kirby being there; February 8, her birthday; other family celebrations of birthdays; Mother's Day; summer vacation—all experienced in that chasm of loss. A year since she is gone—how could that be? It was the first time in my life that I longed to turn the clock back, back to before October 8, 2009. Could the demands of death be the struggle to allow the life of today win over grieving the past? Even in that first year, I was very conscious of that struggle to let in the joy of the moment, to share laughter with another, to see beauty, despite the tinge of guilt on the edges of every experience. It is okay to be happy even if she is not here. It is okay to feel both happy and sad at the same time.

On a trip to Cabo, a year after Kirby's death, we arrived at the Los Cabos airport and I was suddenly paralyzed. I couldn't get up, leave my seat, disembark. I was hyperventilating, frightened, sobbing, and just could not move. What was happening? George sat next to me and took my hand; after a few minutes, through tears, I choked out, "She won't be here to pick us up. There won't be a margarita to greet us. She's not here. I just can't face that."

So many times, we had traveled to Cabo to visit and Kirby's contagious spirit of adventure and excitement would greet us, always with a thermos of something tropically delicious to start off our vacation.

I tried to breathe to calm down. Focusing on the windows of the plane, I looked out at the brilliant sunshine and I slowly emerged. With shaky legs, walking down the steps, I felt the warmth of the Mexican tarmac beneath my feet. The suddenness of that gripping fear, acknowledgement of reality, sense of overwhelming loss, both terrified and confused me. Trying to regain some equilibrium, I quickly headed for the ladies room to wash my face and get composed. I didn't want Kate to see how upset I was; after all, she had been living in Kirby's Baja for a year without her sister and she was picking us up. I was excited to see her and Angus, now two years old. Once we got though the terminal she was there with a brilliant smile, an all-embracing hug and a margarita!

I could be happy, enjoy life and my family even during this sadness. However, I still felt uncertain, unable to grasp my new identity as a mother who has lost a daughter. When I was working, giving a presentation, how was I to introduce myself? In the first two, three years, I felt it was essential to acknowledge that, yes, I am the woman you may have seen on the news, I am the person who has been affected by this big international story. I am the mother of the victim whose case is being tried on Court TV. At that time, most people in the surrounding tri-state area just north of New York City had seen the news coverage. I would try to work this information into the purpose or theme of my talk, without falling apart, and share something I was learning in the resulting grief journey.

A FRIEND, NEEDING FRIENDS

I have always tried to be there for others: supporting, helping, listening. In dealing with this tragedy, I now needed others to hold me up. I looked at our dear friends, Bob and Barbara Driscoll, both therapists, as we sat in their living room a few months after Kirby's death. Bob's twenty-one-year-old daughter had been murdered almost twenty years earlier. They knew this landscape and we needed to know that we would eventually be okay, we would survive.

Barbara said, "Everything from now on will be 'bitter-sweet.'"

I now understand how sometimes the "sweet" of life is so

elusive because the "bitter" is so real. Being with them helped us to face those internal questions: can I laugh and smile when she is gone, when the unimaginable has uprooted our world? Does feeling happy diminish this sadness?

So many good people surrounded us as we struggled to gain some stability. Four months after Kirby's death, Allison, one of Kirby's grade school friends, sent me a quilt that she had made. She explained that all the fabrics were from "their era," clothing worn in the late seventies, early eighties, the primary and middle school years that they had shared together. Sewn into this patchwork of red and blue patterned materials were scripture passages to provide comfort and encouragement.

He heals the brokenhearted and binds up their wounds.
—Psalm 147

Rest in the Lord and wait patiently for Him. Do not fret because of him who prospers in this way, the man who brings wicked schemes to pass. Cease from anger and forsake wrath. It only causes harm. For evildoers will be cut off, but those who wait on the Lord, they shall inherit the earth.
—Psalm 37

Do not fear for I am with you… I will strengthen you… I will uphold you.
—Isaiah 41

The Lord is my Shepherd….
—John 6:47, Psalm 23

In the day when I cried out, You answered and made me bold in my spirit.
—Psalm 138

This beautiful quilt still sits on the iron-framed bed in the "blue bedroom" that Kirby painted for me with Maria. Kirby had found a drafting table in an antique shop in Princeton, New Jersey, where Maria, my good friend from my college days, lives. This was the genesis of the idea to do a room makeover for me. Kirby had been encouraging me to paint, something I have always loved, but as a busy working mom had never found the time to pursue. Knowing how busy I am, she decided it was time for someone to do something for me and, because that bedroom was no longer occupied, this could be my own room, where I could paint, read, dress, relax. She and Maria spent an entire weekend transforming this bedroom—painting, color-coordinating carefully chosen pictures and objects on the shelves and bookcases—a total makeover, just like on TV! The walls are painted in two tones of a very soothing, restful blue. A full-length mirror stands in an oval wooden frame in the corner next to the closet where I have all my clothing. The windows, sans curtains or drapes, allow light to flood the room and provide an unobstructed view of the lake as well as the moonlit night sky. The drafting table with drawing tablets and paints is set in the sunny corner, awaiting creative action. This room has always been special to me, my personal space and a constant reminder of Kirby's thoughtfulness and generous, take-action spirit. In the first year after her death, I would often curl up on that bed and cry, covering myself with that quilt because Allison had written, "Do not put this away or display it. Use it to 'wrap yourself in His Word.'"

That blue bedroom became the place for some of the paintings Kirby had collected while living in Mexico. There are three framed watercolors of Mexican doors, by local artist Jose Cue, and a striking oil on canvas of a 1959 Chevy on a Cuban street. Three smaller paintings by Kirby's friend, Jill Logan, who had a studio right next to the Hotel California in Todos Santos, hang next to the bed. I had purchased two of those lovely prints of palm trees, beach, and sky painted with scrumptious, vibrant Los Cabos colors on various visits to Mexico. Jill gifted me the third print after Kirby's death. I was in the studio and was drawn to a print of multicolored low-lying beach brush set against a brilliant cobalt blue sky with a cloud that stretched out resembling someone dancing.

Jill saw me looking at the print and said, "Looks like Kirby to me. Let me wrap that one up for you."

That painting never fails to make me smile. One year while visiting, Kirby brought us to the Gringo Hill home of Lizzie Rosefield, a beautiful older woman friend, an artist, with whom Kirby had bartered, exchanging her work for a few of Lizzie's flower portraits. Kirby wanted Lizzie to paint one for our anniversary. I chose a gorgeous salmony pink hibiscus, set against green foliage and blue sky, that was growing right there in her prolific garden. She snapped a picture of the flower and, within a few months, that lovely canvas was hanging in this same bedroom. On another visit, Kirby and Kate gave me a two-day painting experience with well-known modern expressionist, Ezra Katz, as a birthday present. My humble attempts at painting the estuary in San Jose and the mountains to the west are also in our artist gallery above my drafting table.

The closet in the bedroom houses my wardrobe, which now includes a number of pieces from Kirby: two suits that were specially tailored for her in Thailand, some fancy tops with fur collars, a few Thai wrap pants, a light gray jacket, and some comfy sweaters and tops. I am forever grateful that we were the same size. I have been wearing her leather coat for a few years. Somehow, wearing her clothing and her jewelry has always felt comforting to me. However, as the years have gone by, items have worn out and I remember that my memories, love, and loss will never wear out.

In those early days, I also received a few "prayer shawls" from friends whose church communities had knitted or crocheted lovely soft, warm lap blankets while praying for me, the sufferer who needed this gift of supportive encouragement. I will never forget such kindnesses and the incredible thoughtfulness of the creators. The words, "What can I do? I don't know what to say. Call me if you need anything," pale against loving actions. I felt supported by others throughout that first year. The compassion of others did not fix or take away grief but, suddenly, I was not walking alone; others were thinking of me, praying for me, remembering Kirby.

One lovely, warm day, a day bright with orange, red, and gold foliage, I sat in my girlfriend Liz's gazebo and played a game of Scrabble. We didn't talk about Kirby, about sadness, anger, or the case, the progress of the investigation. My beautiful friend just allowed me to be there, doing something very ordinary and everyday. Doing something so "normal" helped me feel normal—not crazy or so strange and different from everyone else. She was simply present, there for me.

For the first two years, I cried and screamed every day on the half hour drive to work. I often joked that I bought more makeup in those two years, because I was constantly crying it off. I would wake up, determined to have a good day, get behind the wheel of the car and fall apart. Driving was my "white space," my small piece of daily time when no one was watching, when I did not have to do something for another, when I was alone with my anger and loss.

Some days, I yelled at Kirby, "Why did you believe you needed to be more? Why did you spend all your savings? Why didn't you wait to find that special piece of property in the Baja? Why didn't you leave? Why wasn't what you had, enough?"

Other days, my rage was directed at Ray. "Why didn't you help her? You knew she was in distress? Are you delusional, a sociopath, or just plain stupid? How could you have allowed this to happen? How could you run away from your followers, let them go unidentified to the hospital? You preached being impeccable, responsible for your actions, intended or unintended, can you not live what you teach? You left her and James in the dirt? How could you have done that? You did not lift a finger to help Liz Neuman, who had volunteered for you for seven years, helping you make money, achieve success, and then you let her go to the hospital unidentified, never contacting her family. You preached that you were omnipotent, but all you proved to be was impotent! You knew what you were doing was dangerous—others had been harmed in the past—but each time someone was there to revive the unconscious."

Sometimes, my anger was at life. Why Kirby? Why not some other participant?

James Shore had saved another woman, dragged her out of the tent unconscious; why did he lose his life? Why did no one assist him to get Kirby when he asked for help, only to be told, "The door is closed, not now, at the end of the round"—promised help that never materialized? By the end of that round, both James and Kirby were dead. Why? Why? Why?

Exhausted, I would finally pull into my parking space, re-apply my makeup, breathe, and talk myself into focusing on someone else. Even when thinking, "I cannot live without her. I cannot live with this public reality," I would remember her energy, her desire to live large, to learn, grow, and share with others. How can I do less than that? I asked Kirby to help me be all I can be, even in this very public, painful place.

On one of those breakdowns, driving into town, I found myself suddenly struggling to breathe. Tears streaming down my face, memories of Kirby flooding my brain, I was hyperventilating. I kept thinking, "I cannot swallow this. How will I go on? How can I be available to the rest of my family? How can I keep working, helping others when I feel so empty?"

Gasping for air, I directed the car to my friend's therapy office. When I got to Barbara, her all-enveloping hug assured me that I would survive. I just needed her warm, reassuring presence to get me back to the present. Fortunately, I have been surrounded by many wise, loving, supportive friends.

My head often hurt as I muddled through my thoughts. I want life to be normal; but I want my sorrow to be acknowledged. I want others to remember, to be affected in some deep way. Yet, in grieving I often do not know what I want, other than to go back in time, have my precious one alive.

A curious thing happens as others share how much they miss your child. You want to know that others are mourning her, but you don't want their pain to be bigger than yours. You don't want to be "out-grieved" by others. For me, in the beginning, I knew I would be comforting others; I think with time, I have grown less patient with others expressing "over-the-top" devastation. After all, this is my loss which has altered my life. I guess I'd rather hear the sad, funny, quirky, inspirational stories of how she impacted someone else's life. Learning about pieces of her life I did not know brings her closer to me, giving me another little window into my daughter's world. It is comforting to know she is missed, but maybe it is more important to know how she is remembered by others.

As a person who has often been comfortable being "the giver," I have had to learn what friends I need around me, what my physical and emotional limits are, and how to graciously accept the love and help of others. I am not alone.

MYSELF AS A MOTHER

A sociology major in college, I had taken some child study courses preparing for the family I knew we would start once I graduated. I had married at twenty and I had decided to start a family before pursuing any other career. Kirby was actually on her way, ready to burst into the world, as I received my undergraduate degree.

In many ways, I felt that Kirby and I grew up together. While I was her first teacher, she was also mine. She was teaching me to be a mother. I was learning to combine that incredible love that swept over me as I held her in my arms immediately after birth, with some thought and skill to manage an infant, a toddler, a child. She was irrepressible from birth, strong-willed, determined, and challenging to a young, clueless first-time mom. And I was determined to do a good job, loving her and teaching her, introducing her to the amazing world we have been given.

George and I married young. He worked as a teacher in a Catholic school and I was still in college; we never had the money to go out anywhere. We entertained friends in our apartment—being together and building a life together was enough. Once Kirby arrived, her care was all-consuming, and she was our entertainment. Watching her grow was amazing, every milestone a discovery for us as well. I am grateful that we never had a chance to become too self-absorbed, because I never felt that we missed anything. I never regretted the personal sacrifices that children demand on our lives. I have learned that the love children pull out of us both refines and matures us.

I have repeated the story of "the night" many times.

It was around 2:00 am; eight-month-old Kirby was crying. As I dragged myself out of bed, I did the "multiple guess" (as George called it). Is the baby hungry? Wet? Needs a change? Frightened? What? Why is she crying again tonight at 2:00 am? This had been going on for months.

I decided I would nurse her back to sleep (first time parent mistake #1 or just a survival tactic?) I picked her up, groped in the dark for the rocking chair and, suddenly, we were both on the floor, Kirby screaming and me sobbing. I looked at her and said, "Kid, you are doing nothing, absolutely nothing, to make me love you!" And in a sudden flash of revelation, I knew that, regardless of what she did, I would give my life for her. I then thought, "The God I believe in feels the same way about me! My parent God has already given His life for me to live." Overwhelmed, I realized that this parenting journey is also my spiritual journey. Perhaps parenting would deepen my understanding of the life force that had birthed me. So began many spiritual lessons taught through my Kirby and my lifelong career as a mother.

Throughout her childhood and while parenting Kirby's three siblings, I reflected on my understanding of God, Abba, Divine Father, Mother, Creator. My children have come from me but are not me. Even with our combined DNA, they are separate and unique. George and I wanted to influence and teach our children to be the very best they were created to be. I believe my creator, the life force that brings all into being, imprints a divine spark on each of us and is, in fact, our divine parent, who gives life, and loves and desires the best for each of us. Parenting awakens us to a reality much bigger than ourselves. The love we struggle to give our children is always a pale reflection of my divine parent, continually birthing me.

This conviction that parenting is a sacred, spiritual journey, a true vocation, has been the main message I have shared throughout my professional career as a parenting educator and therapist. I have loved working with parents—mothers especially—to help them experience joy in their parenting.

MY "SECRET RELATIONSHIP"

The parent/child relationship is totally unique. All parents, mothers especially, have a secret relationship with each child.

All the hopes and dreams for a child as they await their arrival, the pain, the worry, the lost sleep, the small and large sacrifices, all influence and shape a relationship with the child who is blissfully unaware, who simply soaks up the love that is given. I would never be able to repay my mother for her gift of love, but I would be able to pass that selfless, freely given love onto my children. It is in this mystery of love that we begin to catch a glimpse of our parent God's relationship with each of us—a secret parental love story. I am connected to my offspring in a way that I will never be connected to another person.

As a mother, I have been acutely aware that as I grieved the death of my daughter, I never wanted my living children to think that their sister was more important to me in her death than they are in life. I didn't want them to feel responsible to ease my pain, to wipe my tears, and yet, I wanted them to know that if one of them had died, I would cry for them every day too. The undeserving lost deserve our tears. I believe it is living with that "secret parental love story" that makes this death of my child unlike other deaths, even the deaths of my parents, my in-laws, or close friends.

My relationship with all my children has taken a weird shift. As my children have grown into adulthood, I now appreciate that when I was busy raising my own family, my mother was still thinking about me even as I was consumed with laundry, homework, soccer games, worry about each of them and work. Now, my husband and I are, appropriately, on the "edges" of our adult children's lives; we are the fringe. They have spouses, children, jobs, homes, friends—a life that does not include us. We live on the periphery of their lives.

However, now that Kirby's life has stopped, I kind of "own" her life. She is no longer physically here to "do her own thing," to relegate me to being the observer. Now, I hold her life in order to feel her. I look at photos of her while the others are making new pictures. I reminisce while the others are creating new memories of their own. I cry for what will never be, as the others are being, moving, alive. When life leaves and the spirit departs, one is left with the shell and the past. Meanwhile, the living—teeming with life—keep moving on.

I think I have also come to understand that in the uniqueness of each of my children, no one can replace another. I have that "secret relationship" with each of them, but each relationship is different. As a parenting educator, I often encounter mothers pregnant with a second child who often worry that because they experienced that incredible depth of emotion for their first, there would not be enough love for the next child. Time is a finite reality that must be divided and shared, but I believe love is an infinite reality that simply multiplies. For me, I think I have understood and loved each of my children differently, sometimes according to what I perceived was needed. I hope I have given each of them what they needed growing up; however, I am acutely aware that each person has their own idea of what was needed and what was not provided by their parents. I have often said, "I believe it is the task of adulthood to correct our parents' mistakes." I am sure I made many even while trying to do my best.

When I was a young mother, I was focused on raising our children; I was not thinking a lot about my own mother or what she might need. I was not aware that she might often be thinking about me. I believe my adult relationship with Kirby was impacted by the fact that Kirby did not have her own family. She did not have the same responsibilities and preoccupation that my adult children now have in their lives as they raise their children. So now, some of the things she either did for me or encouraged me to do, like the relaxing massage, the indulgent mani-pedi, the hike in the woods, the delicious cosmo or margarita, I now need to do for myself. Kirby accompanied me a few times when I was giving a presentation. She had also taught some communication workshops to parent and teens with me when she was in high school. As a result, she was very aware of the work that I did and was my unwavering cheerleader, encouraging me to publish my reflections and insights about parenting. That summer of 2009, she called me her "princess warrior"—an affirmation of admiration and respect. Now, I am working to be "her voice" since her tragic death—to tell her story and mine.

As each of my children entered the world, it took time for me to learn each one's unique smile, cry, need. Every child is different, and every parent is different. The confluence of two distinct personalities shapes the resulting relationship and then morphs over time. I wonder if grief is similar? Each death is unique; the circumstances surrounding that death belong to that person alone. Like the parent, the one grieving is also unique: a person with past experiences, qualities, strengths, weaknesses, vulnerabilities, and resiliency.

I think grief grows and changes over time and the reality of this loss emerges, revealing itself over time. Being a parent is part of my identity. Grief and loss are also shaping me, maybe pulling out of me what I never could have imagined.

With time, the demands of her death have emerged as questions: Can I accept the unacceptable? Can I feel the joy and pain of others or has the weight of this emptiness erased room in my heart for others? Can I be her voice? What is death pulling out of me? How will this death change me? Each of my children challenged me to grow up and now Kirby, in this death, challenges me to become more understanding, compassionate, loving, forgiving, and braver, more open, inventive, aware, and appreciative of the beauty of each person, each moment. Grief can bring a growth spurt, a maturing.

Myself as a WIFE

I think men and women grieve differently. My husband has said, "Women need to talk and seem to want to talk much sooner than men." I'm not sure if that is stereotypical, but for us, yes, I wanted to talk: to talk about Kirby, to talk about how I felt. I think on many days when I needed to cry, George needed to curse and swear. I cry; he causes the "curse-o-meter" to go off the chart. Does that arise from a man's need to protect their children and families?

George has always said men are naturally designed to "secure the perimeter." Therefore, he hears the "outside" noises at night, while I would hear the "inside" sounds of a child's cry, the dishwasher running, the beep of the dryer signaling the end of its cycle. He hears the truck rambling past the house at 2:00 am or the sound of a tree limb hitting the ground in a high wind. Does that need to protect create a rage of impotence in the face of a tragedy that cannot be undone, fixed, changed? I think since Kirby's death, George has become more protective of me, offering to drive me places, encouraging decisions about work and time to ease stress. Some days, that feels annoyingly invasive; however, understanding that desire to protect me when he couldn't protect Kirby is a loving motive for which I am most grateful.

I guess I have always seen my role in our partnership as creating a comfortable, safe, and orderly interior environment. That first year, I would fall apart on Saturdays, my day to clean the house, do laundry, cook, and tend to outside gardening chores. Saturdays became another "white space"—uncluttered, mindless time when I could cry alone and rage. For me, aggressive cleaning and scrubbing have always been a great way to expend angry energy. The look and feel of our family was clearly altered, never to be the same again. I know, on some level, I wanted to wash away this reality, scrub clean my heart and mind, mend my broken heart, and weed out those feelings of dread and fear. While this was cathartic, maintaining an orderly environment was also something I could lovingly do for George, keeping our everyday life comfortable and predictable. Cooking, baking, cleaning, and beautifying our home grounded me in the present, giving me a sense of control and competence in the midst of what had been totally bizarre. Sometimes, doing simple, ordinary things helped me get through a day that demanded extraordinary strength.

We tried to give each other the space each needed for our own personal grief. We could hold each other and cry, but sometimes when one saw the other upset, allowing privacy was also an option. There is no right way to grieve; however, we do know that this kind of trauma can derail a family and destroy a couple. As mental health clinicians, we also know that isolation is not a healthy option and, while everyone needs some privacy, people grieving need connection to dispel the sense of separate "otherness." Others may not have experienced this same loss, they may not understand, but we still need to be surrounded by loving, supportive friends.

I also think that children are attached to their mothers differently than their connection to their fathers. After all, a child grows within a woman's body; we are physically, psychically connected. Psychologists will reference the importance of fathers in the early years of a child's life as helping the child to "separate" from the maternal attachment so that it does not become unhealthily enmeshed. Fathers also act as the bridge for their children to travel from home to the outside world during adolescence. Therefore, the parental experience is essentially different for each parent. One of the many reflections I share when teaching my parenting classes came from Kirby, my first parenting teacher, and illustrates this difference:

It had been a long and tiring day—teacher conferences, mountains of Monday morning laundry, carpooling for soccer practice, dinner, homework, interspersed with my other part-time job; a normal day for a thirty-nine-year-old mother of four, ranging in age from four to sixteen. It's ten o'clock; I stop at my daughter's door, books strewn about, freshly folded laundry in a corner, radio jarring the night air. We sit, turn down the music, and I get filled with the details of her sixteen-year-old day, as well as some information on the current romance and some questions about schedules and when she can use the car, etc.

It is now 11:00 pm as I crawl into bed; my husband sleepily asks, "Where have you been? We came up to bed an hour ago." My response is automatic, "I was giving Kirby her ten o'clock feeding." We both laugh, because Kirby is now sixteen.

But the hour I spent with her was in fact a "feeding." I sat on the edge of her bed and on this night, she wanted to talk. When she was a baby, I would often nurse her at about ten o'clock. Rocking her, I remember a floating feeling, thinking all she needs is my breasts. I don't have to do anything else but be here. As she happily sucked, her stomach filling with milk, being warmed in my arms, she would contentedly drift off to sleep—satisfied, full, warm. At sixteen, I now feed her with my ears, listening to her accounts of the day: friends, teachers, sports, events, conflicts, plans, requests. As she chatters away, I sit and just listen. I dare not speak or have an opinion. My input hasn't been sought. She just wants my presence and my ears. Now, she is ready to sleep—emptied, having expressed feelings and anxieties; now she is satisfied.

The baby feedings were scheduled and somewhat predict-able. The signals and times for the teenager's feedings are more subtle. A baby's cry is intended to be jarring, but a teenager's belligerence or withdrawal is much more easily ignored. Why walk into that lion's den? But, maybe, they still need to feel safe, connected, comforted, less conflicted, less afraid, loved.

Feeding takes time. A rushed "yeah" while cooking dinner is very different from sitting on the side of the bed, without an agenda to preach, and just being there to listen. I used to throw the Cheerios on the highchair tray to keep her amused while I prepared supper, but when she was really hungry and I had to nurse her, everything else would stop and we would rock until she was satiated. It's hard to know when a teenager is satisfied. It seems as though they are always complaining, moaning, and groaning. But somehow, listen-ing to all that, without excuses for self or defending others, seems to dissipate the restlessness a bit.

I can't apply Orajel to her broken heart as I once did to her swollen gums. I can't make everything okay by a fresh change of clothing, a hug, or a kiss. But I can listen. We are growing up together, not easily or without challenge. She will never again cuddle into me and fill me with that wonderful sense of purpose. She is growing to be her own person now; she has to stand alone and maybe challenge me to grow a bit.

In the work I have done as a parenting educator for the Archdiocese of New York, George and I often gave presentations in various Churches throughout the ten counties surrounding New York City. George is incredibly insightful and very funny, so often when talking to a group of couples about relationships, male and female differences, or parenting issues, I would do the preparation, write the outline, create the reflection sheets and the handouts, and George would—as he likes to say—"just show up and follow my lead." So I would introduce the topic, share the information and research, and George would slip in a truly funny story that would have everyone on the floor laughing in recognition of some simple, commonly experienced truth. Or he would add an amazingly profound thought that would be long remembered. It was teamwork that had great chemistry and flow.

As the media began to invade our lives, George stepped back and let me take the lead. He would be available but would often defer to me to carry the interview. While I would be struggling to stay in control and sound rational, he would often come off as more emotional than me. And many times, it was the tearful father that was shown in the three-second snippet of reporting. He still finds it very difficult to "go there," be in the moment of discovery, or talk about the emotional impact on our lives. He was diagnosed with Parkinson's in 2005 and strong emotions often bring on the tremors and uncomfortable symptoms of PD. As a result, I have done a lot of media on my own. However, he has walked beside me on this journey, sharing his wisdom while encouraging my public face.

Just as George has been more protective of me, taking on that public role has been a way for me to protect him.

I often wondered if his reticence was due to the strength of his anger, possibly fearful of being seen as too aggressive in public. He has often conjectured what he would like to do to the one responsible for Kirby's death and George is the one who had the violent and vivid dreams, especially in that first year. There is a dent in our refrigerator door. When the light catches that particular spot, I am reminded that George is responsible. I believe he made that while watching Court TV during the year of the trial. I think it is hard to dent stainless steel.

When Kirby was leaving her home in early October to travel to Sedona, she called to consult with her dad about her best travel route. Both George and Kirby were always map people, so before the days of pervasive electronically guided travel, George was Kirby's GPS, the two of them conferring daily on the phone as she traveled the Baja peninsula up to San Diego, northeast to Moab, Utah, and finally to Sedona, Arizona. The maps were still strewn about the coffee table, Rand McNally prominently displayed, when the trooper arrived at our door on October 9.

Parents always want to help their children through life, giving advice, sharing wisdom, offering options, accommodating and supporting their desires. I think fathers, especially, seek to guide and direct their offspring. George has always wanted what is the absolute best for our children. When we lived in Brooklyn, and our three oldest children were young, he was in graduate school. Going to classes, working part-time, doing an internship, he was rarely home. But when he was there and the children would swarm around him, clamoring for his attention, no matter what they asked for, he would always say, "Yes." However, the promised trip to the park, treat, toy, or puppy never materialized because we either didn't have the resources or he didn't have the time. Disappointment and anger was eventually reframed as "your father has a heart that is much bigger than his head!" In his devotion to them, he has always endeavored to be their GPS.

MYSELF AS A THERAPIST/EDUCATOR

As a therapist, in recent years, I have been sought out by other grieving parents looking for counseling. Sometimes the issues are related to the loss. Sometimes the issues are unrelated, but my clients need to know that I understand that huge part of who they now are that has been forged by the depth of this pain. Sometimes other grief-stricken parents just need to see someone who has survived. What I know and what I have learned through experiencing Kirby's death gives me credibility when working with others in pain. I hope that what I have learned can be helpful for others.

Some who have grieved the loss of their children become impatient with the complaints of others, knowing that they have not experienced the "worst" that can happen. Some do not want to face others, their questions, their pity, their sympathy or advice. It can be hard to see the good intentions of others, actions borne of love and concern, when one feels totally devastated and lost. Sometimes, it is difficult to listen to the stories of others as they share their children's or grandchildren's successes, accomplishments, and milestones, knowing that your child, no longer alive, will never have these experiences—you will never share in those joys. It is almost impossible to describe to others how life has been altered, your identity changed.

Some struggle with the reactions of others. Good, well-intentioned people confronted with another's untimely or tragic loss don't always know what to say. They may feel guilty that their children are alive and yours is dead. They may be curious but feel uncomfortable asking questions, so they say nothing or avoid you. Those who love you do not want to see you hurt, sad, depressed. They want you to "move on," be "okay." Sometimes, friends and family try to rush you through your grief as if it were a temporary derailment in your life. Depending on the history of your relationships, those around you may need you to be okay. Maybe they have depended upon you in the past and they cannot tolerate you being less than strong, capable, able to cope, or emotionally unavailable to them. As a therapist, I know that other people may truly care but cannot tolerate the intensity of tragedy, so they may stumble and look away, almost afraid that tragedy is contagious. It is important to identify what you need and learn to ask for it. Sometimes, I encourage a client to limit contact with those people who may inadvertently offend, but to try to reframe and understand their awkwardness, their sense of powerlessness.

It has been said that anger turned inward becomes depression. Those who are grieving are often angry, not being able to change the reality of their loss and consequently struggle with depression. In those early days there was cement in my veins. I woke up tired even if I had slept all night. Many days, I struggled to find a purpose for the day ahead of me, to focus because nothing seemed to really matter. As a result, I have come to think of grief as a pit of a seething, moving mass of depression, despair, confusion, and rage. I have learned from others that when you experience an intimate, untimely, and traumatic loss, you are stalked by a shadow with long arms that pulls you in, with legs that threaten to trip you up, and suddenly the air is squeezed out of your lungs as you struggle to breathe. The sheer intensity of these emotions becomes the architect of this pit, making it both imagined and real. Naming this reality, feeling its pull, helped me to acknowledge its presence, and then tentatively dip my toe in without getting totally consumed.

Each person who grieves this unimaginable kind of loss needs to look into the pit and decide how much threat it will impose and, therefore, how much power it will wield. I know that it is both essential and healthy for feelings to be acknowledged and not buried. Yet, some of these emotions seem too hot to handle. When you are walking on the edge of the pit, you are engaged in battle. Is it possible to just live, to breathe, to see beauty, feel compassion, experience joy? Can that be done, even while you allow yourself to hurt? Can I allow the negative emotions to be seen and felt without being swallowed up in the "pit?"

I often describe those difficult, uncomfortable emotions as a pack of little, needy, annoying children constantly clamoring for attention. Each one is shouting for recognition, trying to edge out the others as less important.

"Pay attention to me! Losing her is huge, you are now missing out on all you shared together!" my sadness screams.

Longing argues, "She'll feel closer if you give your full attention to me."

Anger jumps up and down, bellowing "This was unfair. I will help you express that injustice! You deserve to be angry!"

Each emotion wants to be heard. Sometimes, one voice is screaming over the others. They collude with other thoughts and feelings to strengthen their cause. Sadness sometimes wins when physically tired, presented with another loss, or sharing another's grief. Sadness can be easily triggered by a song or memory. Longing takes over when feeling restless, uncomfortable with the quick passage of time, aware of one's own aging, and feeling nostalgic for the past. Anger emerges when disappointed, confronted with other injustices, frustrated with feeling ignored, diminished, or silenced.

These emotions are real and need to be acknowledged, but they cannot be permitted to dictate one's entire emotional state or behaviors. I share with clients that you can say "hello," pat them on the head, soothe them a bit, and then decide to get on with your day. You can make an "appointment" to listen later. By the time "later" comes, sometimes the feelings are less intense and perhaps the fresh air of good work or fun with a friend has moderated the mood. Those pesky feelings will probably always surface, but I believe they should only be visited, never invited to "move in." We can have a cup of tea together, ruminate a bit, feel some mutual recognition, but they cannot be invited to spend the night, dictating one's entire mood. They do not serve or strengthen.

Often the idea of "closure" when grieving a loved one is discussed. I have personally learned one never really "gets over" this kind of loss. However, time does affect the grief journey. I have said I would never "accept" Kirby's death. It was sudden, untimely, tragic, unnecessary, preventable, ridiculous. But I have started to get "used to" her not being physically here. It took a few years to stop anticipating her phone call, letter, or surprise visit.

Barbara told me, "You get a pass for the first year. People will forgive all kinds of things that first year."

The implication is that after one year, people expect you to get back to being "normal." But life will never be the same or feel normal again. I think the firefighters after 9/11 coined the term "the new normal" as a way to describe moving on. People are changed by this traumatic grief and will never be the same again.

The pit awaits when happiness presents itself. There is a challenge to feeling happy, not allowing the loss and longing for her presence to extinguish the moment to feel the presence of joy. When each new grandchild has been born into our family, I wanted Kirby to see that new baby, to see her sibling parent a new life.

George has often said, "She sees us. She knows all the little ones."

I think that may be true, but I still want to see HER seeing them, to see her delight. I have often imagined what she would do with her nieces and nephews, the games she would play, the adventures she would have created. Sometimes that fantasy comforts and other times it tears. When I experience that wrenching longing and overpowering sadness, I have often prayed for those feelings to be replaced with gratitude for her life, for all she taught me, for all she brought into our family and, ultimately, gratitude that I have been so blessed that another life could provoke such strong emotions in me. I think love lives, heals, and hurts, but always, ultimately, must be chosen.

In teaching people to be aware of their vulnerabilities, I have had to examine how clueless I can sometimes be to my own vulnerabilities. One day, almost eight years after Kirby's death, I realized that for the past three months I had been cloaked in an unshakable melancholy. Why? How can the intensity of this pain feel so fresh? While weeding in our garden during this time, I was pulling out a particularly insidious, pernicious, fast-growing weed which cloaks and chokes everything with a sticky, clinging web. This uninvited guest was covering a hillside of my beautiful tiger daylilies. As I pulled out the weeds, which came out easily but clung to me, my hair, garden gloves, clothing, I was thinking about this grief that appears uninvited, grows quickly, and threatens to overshadow all other emotions. Why now?

Upon careful reflection, I realized that we had been faced with a number of wakes, funerals, burials, deaths in those past few months: friends, parents, and siblings of close friends—some predictable and some untimely deaths. One young woman who had graduated with our son was a vibrant, brilliant, record-setting athlete who had battled brain cancer for seven years. The parallels between her adventurous, indomitable spirit and Kirby's were not missed by others who commented on the unfairness of the death of two who lived life so fully.

We have also experienced a few close friends selling their homes and moving to retirement communities, changing the look and feel of our everyday life—another kind of loss and another lesson in this grief journey which is now part of my life.

Death, uninvited, unwelcome change—these experiences

reignite the emotions of sadness and loss, intensifying that constant companion which will never really disappear. Sometimes, I can conjure some idea of the why, but the more important questions remain: "What now? What to do with these feelings? How to deal with the crippling pull of depression?"

I share what I know, because I have been here before, many times. It is an act of the will to choose to feel, for a short time, the sadness and the grief, to allow this uninvited guest to visit but not move in. The feelings are real; they do not have to be denied, judged, or banished, but they cannot be allowed to cover my hillside, choking out the emotions of excitement and joy in living.

I believe one has to do something they love, be with someone who loves them, and feel gratitude for all the beauty and goodness in their life. Allowing oneself to be fully present to a different experience does not diminish loss; rather it invites another dimension and other emotions to grow. Mindfully drinking in the beauty of the sunset, feeling the contagion of a child's laughter, focusing on another's need, and doing the routine, mundane activities of daily life will allow the miraculous to flower.

Sometimes, as time moves on, it can feel as though the one lost is being left behind. While I never want to relive those first two years, somehow during that time she felt more imminent. The fullness of life had not yet invaded my sorrow. I now understand why holding onto that sorrow can sometimes bring the lost one closer.

Scott Peck, in his book *The Road Less Traveled*, describes falling in love as a total collapse of ego boundaries as one merges with their beloved. That complete enmeshment is powerful and all-encompassing but, over time, the ego must re-establish itself to deal with the realities of everyday life while still loving the other. I think something similar happens with catastrophic loss. Over time, the totality of this grief begins to take a place amongst the other realities and responsibilities of one's life. The intensity is softened, feeling less immediate. But, like love, the deep emotions still remain. Moving on does not mean we are leaving our loved one behind. As the daily demands of life emerge, I have to broaden my attention, expand my physical and emotional energy, to fill my days with a worthy life—loving others, while striving to be my best self. I am always asking myself, "What would Kirby want me to do? How would she want me to be living? How would she want me to remember her? How can I best honor her?"

As the person who was always brimming with life, I know she would want me to LIVE, to love, to enjoy, to celebrate, to play, to laugh, have adventures, to make a difference, to share what I know, to be present to each and every gifted moment. To honor her, I choose life. Living with purpose, passion, and joy can exist next to sadness and longing.

Me: Bitter or Better?

I sometimes look out my kitchen window and envision Kirby running down the hill, Happy Dot in tow, pasturing her horse in the lower field, ice-skating on the lake, or sledding the hill at breakneck speed. I see the summer of 2009 when Kirby came home to help prepare for Jean's wedding.

Jean wanted a country-like wedding on our property. She said it should be simple and elegant, charming, with fairy lights in the trees and natural-looking flower arrangements. My brother, Joe, who owns a successful landscaping business in Long Island, brought his crew to Westtown and performed a "property makeover" in preparation for the wedding. Our backyard had been transformed, properly graded, and beautifully planted. Jean, ever practical, ordered her wedding gown and all the flowers on-line. We made beautiful arrangements with tea lights hanging from willow branches secured in vases filled with sand. A tent for tables for dinner would be set up in the lower field and another tent for a dance floor and band would be on the terrace above. Everything was ordered. Then, it began to rain.

It rained for twenty-five days in June. The wedding was to take place on July 4. When the big tent was set up, mud dripped from every surface, so the young men setting it up took out hoses to wash off the mud, making the situation even worse. The tent guy was nowhere to be found; the electric kept short-ing out and everything was wet. The caterer was apoplectic, screaming that the surface was unsuitable for her tables. Jean and I surveyed the muddy field the morning before the wed-ding. It was an epic mess and we both cried.

The bride and wedding party were scheduled for a spa day: manicures, pedicures, with a special luncheon before the rehearsal dinner. I was calling the tent man to find out what he was planning to do. Could he put a floor over the mud? Carpet the area? The caterer was demanding answers, wanting to know when she could set up the tables. Caught in the middle, I was at a total loss. Finally, in the early afternoon, after her manicure, Kirby appeared just as the owner of the tent company arrived at the scene. Discussing the disaster with him, Kirby asked if hay and cedar shavings would work to absorb the mud, and then an indoor/outdoor carpet could be spread over the entire area. He agreed that was the best solution, but it was 2:00 pm on Friday afternoon. My action-oriented daughter went into solution mode. She and her cousin, Tom, jumped into the truck and visited every farm in the Westtown area looking for horse bedding and hay. She had worked on most of the local farms at one time or another and many of the horse farm owners knew Kirby. By 4:00 pm, the entire area under the tent was covered in hay and a green carpet was being laid over the lumpy but dry surface. The rehearsal was set for 5:00 pm. Walking under the tent felt like traversing a waterbed and the centerpieces Jean and I had made could not be placed on such an unlevel surface, but tables could be set up and guests would not have to mud wrestle for their food. The next morning, a friend sorted out the electrical problems and Kirby took all the vases with the willow branches and tea lights and buried them into the bank along the side of the dining tent.

And the next day was full-moon magical: fabulous music, great food, tents for dinner and dancing, twinkling lights in the trees and along the bank, flowers, and fireworks overlooking our small lake.

The whole debacle leading up to July 4, the actual wedding, is now one of our favorite Kirby memories.

Two weeks after that unforgettable event, our home was hit by a real summer tornado which uprooted a forty-five-foot blue spruce, a few other trees, removed screens and roof shingles, and swept through the house depositing debris. The house looked like it had been ransacked by demented forest burglars depositing small tree branches, leaves, dirt, and piles of dead bugs from the first floor through to the attic.

Beyond the house, our view of our lake suddenly looked naked and raw without the comforting framing of the blue spruce. The roots were exposed, and its magnificence lay across the lawn. Suddenly, our view was unobstructed and open.

Sometime after Kirby's death, while walking outside one day, I remember thinking that just like the view which had been forever changed by the tornado, but was still lovely, our family was still beautiful, intact, though forever changed. There was a huge hole, a chasm actually, that would never be filled. We were all feeling naked and raw, torn open, but still individually strong, talented, loving, and beautiful. And over time, we are all finding our clothing, ways to cope and live well.

When Liz, knowing we would be cremating Kirby, suggested a place of remembrance in the arboretum at our county park, we met with the arborist to plan a suitable spot. Learning about Kirby, he proposed a solid slab of granite on a wooden base in the Alpine grove—very organic. The plaque on her bench sits next to water tumbling over boulders. It reads: "Kirby Anne Brown 2.8.71—10.8.09. Surf's Up." Across the stream is a tree with another marker at the base: "Kirby: teaching us beauty, adventure, love." The soothing sound of the running water and the solid feel of that rock provide the perfect place to peacefully reminisce; it's also a great spot to toast her with a cosmo, one of her favorite drinks, on her birthday, February 8.

I often reflect on one particularly memorable Thanksgiving, Kirby arrived home suddenly, unannounced. Every Thanksgiving, I can still see her when she walked into the kitchen with a mischievous grin, as I was rolling out pie dough; she loudly proclaimed, "Surprise!" Every Thanksgiving, while baking pies, I look over my shoulder for her to surprise me. One year, I opened a kitchen drawer and found a long-forgotten card with a picture of a house with gingerbread trim on the cover. In it she wrote:

> This card reminded me of our house. Thank you for the childhood you gave me. I love how we grew up. When I meet others and learn about how they grew up, I am so grateful for what we were given. Thank you, always.

I don't remember putting it there, so I guess she still is capable of surprising me!

Those who are grieving struggle to allow happiness to seep into their experience. The holidays when everyone is supposed to be brimming with joy can be especially challenging. I have always loved the holidays: the season of gratitude, giving, and gathering.

I love Christmas, the lights, decorations, preparations, the music. *I'll Be Home for Christmas* always makes me cry. My children have always laughed at my easy emotional responses to movies, songs, even commercials.

Christmas Eve has always been special for the Brown family. We have been sharing a favorite meal (sausage and peppers with fusilli—I don't know how that menu got set in stone!) for over 35 years with Ed and Liz Holst, our dear friends since high school, their children, Jenny, Sarah and Eddie, and now their grandchildren. We exchange simple gifts, and then sing carols with our good neighbors at the Presbyterian Church. Some years we have then gone to Midnight Mass at the Catholic Church a few miles away (we like to keep all bases covered!)

Traditions and celebrations change over time, but some remain steadfast. As we join together on Christmas Eve, I know we are often remembering those times when Kirby graced the table. We still feel her presence in our celebration.

One of my all-time favorite Christmas songs is *Mary Did You Know?* sung by Kathy Mattea. The words ask Mary questions about her cognizance of the future. Did she know what would happen as Jesus grew up to be a man who would perform miracles, heal the blind and lame, walk on water, calm storms, and ultimately save humanity?

As I listen to the song, I am reminded that we do not know what is ahead; we only know what has happened. Would knowing the future make living today easier or more difficult?

Did we know that one we love would be taken suddenly, too soon, traumatically? Did we know what that loss would feel like and how it would forever change our lives? Could we have imagined the energy and support we would need to still live with joy? Whether we celebrate Christmas, Hanukkah, another religious feast, or the coming of the New Year, whatever the occasion, this is a season where we are supposed to be happy, feel loving, and give to others. There are decorations, people are shopping, holiday music is blaring. Did we know that the grief we experienced would change how we entered this season?

Now, the question that needs to be asked is: Now that we know this heartache, how will we allow this grief to shape us? Will we allow that pain to make us bitter, isolating us from others, or better, connecting to those who love us (even if they do not fully understand our pain)? Can I learn from my grief to be more loving, understanding, forgiving, reaching out to others struggling with the sorrow of loss? I know I chose to decorate our home, make gingerbread houses with grandchildren, laugh, and celebrate with family and friends, even though I will cry when I hear the song, *I'll Be Home for Christmas*. And I will be forever grateful that I did not know what was ahead, but that I have had the love and support to live with what has been.

When tempted to ask all the whys, I remember George's wise words, telling us all that "why" is unanswerable, the wrong question. Now we must ask, "What now? What do we do now? How do we respond?"

Eileen Murphy was my partner for many years when I worked for the Archdiocese of New York. Her husband, Bill, gave me a CD by John McDermott entitled *Remembrance*. It is a beautiful collection of songs, written during wartimes from the civil war to the Vietnam conflict, with tributes to those who lost their lives. Only a truly sentimental, maudlin person of Irish descent could appreciate such an album. He especially wanted me to listen to a song *One Small Star* because he felt it represented Kirby's spirit. The lines of this song have always resonated with me. He describes some memories as being comforting and consoling while others may feel jarring and painful. The lyrics also invite the listener to briefly visit the person who is gone. I have often used this song when I want to have a tearful connection to my daughter, knowing that she is somehow still with us.

For me, memories are just like that; some feel so comforting and I am filled with gratitude for her life, but sometimes those same memories or others might feel like a gut punch, reminding me she is gone and will never be here again. Especially in the early years, I had to carefully choose when I would listen to music that provoked strong emotions. Is this a day when I can cry freely or is this a day I need to be focused and inspired? Is this a day when I already feel tired, weak, lonely, disappointed, or angry? Can thinking about my firstborn today bring me joy or immobilize me in sorrow? Right now, do I want to feel sorrow to bring her closer or do I want to experience her spirit to spur me forward? Music can provoke powerful memories, as can pictures or even the kind of day or the place. Kirby was a blue sky, bright sunshine kind of person. She was also in love with the beauty of the world around her. So, fabulous days, mountains, oceans, brilliant stars, full moons, amazing storms—all these remind me of her. Sometimes, memories come unbidden and the emotional tenor of the day may dictate the first response I may experience. Then, I have to choose: collapse or shift focus. I have learned that living with grief is like that.

As I write this story, I often weep, and many times second guess the importance of this story. Can telling others about Kirby truly influence them to make more critical decisions about what they are seeking and who to believe or follow? Then I return to the reality that telling her story is for ME, regardless of to whom or how its impact is realized. I want the world to know HER, keep her alive, and provide a lasting legacy that she was unable to establish because her life was cut short. I need to feel that I have been responsible in alerting others to potential danger in the self-help world.

Yesterday, I found four postcards that Kirby had written to friends, but never mailed, wishing them a Merry Christmas and Happy New Year. I don't remember ever seeing these before, but they served as a message from beyond: Keep going. Live, love, enjoy life, be grateful, be happy.

In living today, I try to remind myself when I wake up that today will be a great day. Today will be the kind of day that is truly a choice. I don't always remember to choose to see and be the best in each day. Sometimes, I know I am too tired, too discouraged, too sad, too weak, and I allow myself to slip into the pit that is always nearby. I have learned that strength does not come from succumbing to weakness. My strength emerges by recognizing my times of weakness, gently caring for myself, praying, and getting back up and out. I know when I choose, I am more productive, more energized, and see opportunities that the emotional morass will never unveil. Maybe it is my desire to contribute, recognizing that I have a purpose beyond myself that helps me to re-balance. Life is a gift—the thank you note we write is living it well and making a difference.

I have always been basically happy with my life and myself. While I am sentimental and relish a good cry at sad movies, inspiring stories, or tales of heartbreaking loss, I was never more nostalgic for the past than excited to live in the present. It is only since Kirby's death that I sometimes long to go back, before October 8, 2009. I have had to stop thinking about what today would have been like if she were here.

With the passage of time, the intensity of this loss remains with me, but I feel it less frequently. By the second year, grief had taken a backseat as we dealt with the trial. The trial started in February 2011 and was concluded by November 2011, a full two years and one month after the tragedy in Sedona. By year three, 2012, I was not crying every day and I was chan-neling more time and energy into the creation of SEEK Safely. However, I realized it was not until October 8, 2014, FIVE years after Kirby's death, that I could envision our family as having a new shape. We have four children, but our family now consists of three grown adults, their spouses, and their children. I think, until that time, I was still waiting for time to magically reverse itself; I was still fighting simply accepting that her presence was now totally in spirit and not in the flesh. Really recognizing this amazed me. I am a rational person. Of course, I knew she was dead, but this new image, new definition of us, our family, was just another finality.

Now, when I introduce myself before I give a talk, I note my professional experience first and then my personal history, mentioning each of our children:

> George and I have raised four children: Kirby, our eldest, a victim of a homicide a few years ago; Kate, who lives in the Dominican Republic with two gorgeous, towheaded, bilingual, Scottish lads, named Angus and McCloy [this usually provokes a chuckle]; our son, Bobby, in Connecticut with his beautiful wife, Kory and three very active children, Lyle Angela, George Hawksby, and Quinn Kirby. I often add that their home is a controlled chaos of constant activity. Finally, our youngest daughter lives in Canada with her husband, Mike, and two little ones, Linden, who is attending a French immersion grade school, and Machrie, who will soon challenge the authority of his older sister. So despite our devastating loss, we have been truly blessed by these wonderful grandchildren, four who were born after the death of their amazing Aunt Kirby.

So, yes, I acknowledge that I am a grieving mother, along with being a wife, a professional, a mother to adult children, a grandmother, a friend, and a seeker who desires growth, faith, wisdom. All of these are pieces of me.

In writing this story, I have had to stop many times. I knew reviewing those first few weeks would be painful, but I was unprepared for how overwhelming it would feel to revisit those "days of discovery." Reviewing phone conversations, reliving the rarefied time of wake and funeral, the confusing public media attention, the trial and, finally, the stark reality of Kirby truly being dead, brought me to the edge of a pit that has threatened to swallow me up many times in this journey of grief.

That pit, which stalked me every day for two years, resurfaces. I had made a tentative peace with its threats as I focused on all the other areas of my life: my children, grandchildren, family, friends, professional work and, finally, a cause to bring some positive meaning to these otherwise meaningless deaths. Yes, creating a cause and attempting to make something good happen as a result of something bad is a way to cope with grief, and ease the pain.

I wonder about how each person responds to their own losses. While there is no "right way" to grieve, as a mental health professional I know there can be reactions that lead to unhealthy results, like constant isolation, aggression toward others, martyrdom, addictions to substances, or behaviors that cause pain to the self or others.

My mother once wisely said, "You better be who you want to become by the time you are fifty, because after that you will only intensify. Change gets harder the older you are."

I heard that insight as a warning to make sure my "default personality" was well-formed by middle age. My personal "default" are my beliefs which are largely unquestioned, having served me well over time and my basic attitude about life that has come to make sense to me. Defaults operate without conscious decisions. If you want to change the default on an electronic device, you have to actually choose another option. I like to think that as I get older, my immediate personality default has been to understand before making a judgment, to choose love over hate, beauty over ugliness, people over things, joy over sorrow, purpose over pleasure, optimism over pessimism, faith over egocentrism. It is for this reason that I sought out counseling and spiritual guidance a few times while grieving. I found myself struggling to be the "me" I want to be. Talking to another person with proper training can be a way to dispel troubling emotions, untangle confusion, and choose responses, not reactions. It is a way to reboot my "default" to the setting I want it to be. This pain may teach me, but ultimately it will not alter my essential self. I am still me.

I am also reminded that, in the game of life, any hand one is dealt can be a winning one depending on how it is played. When people ask me, "Ginny, why you?" I say, "Why not? No one is immune from the painful challenges of life." But I can decide how to play the hand dealt. I guess that is what I was trying to tell my children when I advised them not to let anger and sadness run their lives. Because that would allow another victim, create another death in our family.

Chapter 6

❝ I am ready within for the creation process to start over and over again after each and every enlightenment. ❞

—Kirby's Vision Quest Journal

Jean

*T*hese are the things I took from Kirby's home (from Kirby's life, I guess):

- *Emerald-cut aquamarine ring (made in Thailand);*
- *Original Elisabeth Rosefield oil painting of white Datura;*
- *Necklace from Noche Azul, Croatia;*
- *Wormwood apothecary cabinet (handmade in Mexico);*
- *Diploma from Blue Elephant cooking school, Bangkok;*
- *Beaded crystal strings made by Kirby;*
- *Faux fur bolero jacket;*
- *Ten-inch wooden Buddha statue from Thailand;*
- *Floral silk scarf.*

I couldn't bring the painting and the cabinet with me on the plane home to Canada from the Cabo memorial, but I did bring the other things, tucked carefully into a suitcase that was also Kirby's. Leaving Mexico was not an issue. But I had to collect all my luggage when I connected through Houston. As per the rigorous security procedures in the US, I had to go through customs and security again, though I'd already done this in Mexico, and I was not staying in the US. Of course, the customs line was huge, snaking through switchbacks of roped off rows. I had about forty minutes to get to my next flight and I knew I'd be in that line for nearly that length of time. Finally, I saw a maroon-vested airport employee.

"Excuse me," I said, leaning in her direction because I didn't want to relinquish my spot. "Is there any way I can get ahead? My next flight leaves in thirty-five minutes."

While I spoke, her eyes rolled in a slow blink as she pursed her lips together.

"Nooope," she drawled. "Y'all have to wait like everyone else."

The same thing happened when a different airport employee passed. So I stood on that line for a long while and watched the clock on the wall beneath the huge "George Bush Intercontinental Airport" sign count me down to my departing flight. When I got through, I had about five minutes to get to my next gate. I stood in another line to check my bags through security. The man working this line was making jokes and chatting, clearly trying to manage the grumpy moods of the many passengers who were missing connections. He was great.

I was carrying a backpack and an extra suitcase full of Kirby's stuff. All of the things I carried of Kirby's—they were beautiful things. But they were mine now because she wasn't alive to own them anymore and I just didn't want them at that point. When this nice guy told me I couldn't carry on these extra bags (though I had on my previous flight) and I'd have to check them (at a different desk), and pay more, and I'd definitely miss my flight, I broke. I held back my sob story and that effort seemed to bring me right to rage.

"This is BULLSHIT!" I stomped, then punctuated my complaint by skittering under a rope, knocking the stand over with the bag on my back, and not returning to right it.

To his credit, the guy made some joke and I heard a number of the people who'd been behind me laughing.

I feel so embarrassed when I think back on that exchange now.

That extra bag just felt so heavy. It was excess baggage before I even got to the airport. To have it literally hold me back as I tried to carry it all the way home was an extra charge in unfairness.

I missed my original flight and, as a result, had to make an extra connection in Chicago, but I did carry all those things home.

Emerald-cut Aquamarine Ring (made in Thailand)

There's a strange thing that happens after a family member or someone very close to you dies. As you come to accept this reality, you become very aware that this is a defining aspect of who you are now. There's an urge to include this fact any time you meet someone new.

"Hi, my name is Jean. I have two kids. My sister died."

But that's awkward, so you probably don't do that.

After Kirby died, we tried to become a part of our new town. Mike started playing on the local men's soccer team, I became an assistant coach to a girls' team. We became regulars at the farmer's market and the little pub down the street from our house, the Blueberry Hill Bistro. But I felt like I was keeping a secret from everyone I'd meet. We'd talk about where we were from, what we did for work, what sorts of things we liked to do for fun. But what I was always thinking was "if you really want to know who I am, you need to understand this very awful thing that just happened to me."

Once in a while, it would slip out, if I somehow found a way to talk about it—an invitation embedded in the small talk. At that time after Kirby died and my internship at Health Canada ended, I was working at my in-laws' jewelry store in Lancaster, Ontario, about forty-five minutes from Vankleek Hill. One quiet afternoon, a customer walked in. She was the only one in the store, so we started chatting as she looked at the jewelry in the displays. We talked about travelling, about yoga and massage, and other things I knew Kirby was interested in, too. She reminded me of Kirby in many ways, I thought, as I pulled out amber pieces for her to admire.

And then, as though to prove my instinct right, she noticed my ring. Kirby's ring. The aquamarine I'd worn on my wedding day as my somethings blue and borrowed. It is noticeable—an emerald-cut hunk of ocean blue stone standing out of a silver setting.

"It was my sister's," I responded to her compliment.

A pause.

"Was? I'm so sorry. Did you lose your sister?"

"Yes—a few months ago, actually."

"Oh my goodness, but you're so young! She must have been very young, too. Was it cancer?"

I explained what had happened; she'd heard something about it. She shifted back and forth, the 150-year-old floorboards sighing beneath her feet, with curious and empathetic blue eyes fixed on me.

I never saw this woman again and yet letting her in on my "secret" was like offering her a shimmery, silver string attached to my soul. In a moment like that, I'd feel closer to a stranger than I would to the people I lived next door to, who never knew about Kirby.

This still happens—the revealing of my sad secret. It's especially awkward when I've known someone for a while but never had an opportunity to discuss it. And then, for whatever reason—mentioning our non-profit organization, discussing a media interview I did, or even just discussing family—it comes out.

At this point I've developed a certain voice, a countenance that goes along with the scripted telling of the story. I imagine it's serene, with a small smile perhaps to reassure the person I'm telling that I'm not going to suddenly start crying on his or her shoulder. Who knows if it actually looks that way? But I explain what happened, offer my own platitudes to fill the gaps where they don't know what to say.

"Yeah, so, it was pretty crazy...." It's still awkward.

Maybe this is why I started to think of grief like a mean little friend. It's isolating. But it's also something you hold onto, or that holds onto you, and in that mutual clinging there's some sort of comfort, because it's your connection to the person who died. You can't call them. You can't visit them. You can't like their post on Facebook. They're not there anymore, but the grief is.

And now, many years on, has that grip loosened? Perhaps. But it's always there. And, sometimes, when I can't find the connection to her that I crave, I still retreat into that little meeting place deep inside where the grief waits.

Original Elizabeth Rosefield oil painting of white datura

Elizabeth Rosefield is a painter who lives on Gringo Hill in Baja. She is well-known in the West Coast art world and her paintings fetch a decent amount of money. Most of her work is floral portraiture—intimate, up-close views of the flowers and plants that surround her lush little home in Mexico.

Kirby knew her well as a friend, neighbor, yoga partner. Kirby also did some faux painting work in Lizzie's home in exchange for some of Lizzie's work.

She had two such bartered paintings. I took home a white datura. It materializes out of this red-tinged purple background, with silky folds of white petals that look like you could rub them against your skin. A yellow light glows out of the center of the flower where the petals and stamen converge, as though it holds the origins of life itself there.

When I got this painting, we hung it above my dresser in our small bedroom, facing our bed. Our home, the one we'd moved into just days before Kirby's death, was a sweet little brick Victorian from the 1850s that was typical in Ontario at that time. Not a grand, ostentatious Queen Anne-type Victorian, but a modest four-square, with a summer kitchen tacked onto the back that extended into a dilapidated earthen-floor shed we affectionately referred to as the "murder room."

Despite the creepy room on the back, the house had a warm, loving vibe. A wooden step that led down to the kitchen was sunken in the middle, worn down to a buttery soft parabola made by 150 years' worth of footsteps.

The bedrooms were tiny. The tin roof sloped above the second floor, so we tucked our headboard underneath the vault of the ceiling in our room. There was only space for the bed, one dresser, and two nightstands—cozy but minimalist. The datura painting was the focal point of the room.

When we first moved in, I knew that Kirby would come at some point and paint in our house. We had a condo in Montréal that she'd visited, but this felt like our first real home, our married home. I couldn't wait for her to come.

Mike and I met when we were in Thailand in 2003—me for a semester abroad in college, him for volunteer work after graduating. The night that we met, there was phosphorescent plankton glittering in the sand and I knew I was going to marry him. Getting to that point took many years and required the hard decision of me moving to Canada. My parents were upset about us living together before getting married and I had to work to convince them that this relationship was serious, though we weren't even engaged yet.

Kirby was the first one in our family whom I told that I thought Mike and I would get married. She and I were visiting our nana in New Jersey together. It was the fall of 2006. I had spent the summer in Montréal with Mike but had to come back to the US when my visitor's visa expired. I was living with my parents in Westtown for a few months and working at a nearby farm. Nana was in a nursing home near our aunt and uncle's house in southern New Jersey, about a three-hour drive.

I was nervous to tell Kirby about Mike. I was twenty-three years old. I knew that she believed in getting married older. Having been close to marriage a few times herself, she was more experienced in serious relationships than I was. I thought she might try to dissuade

*me and encourage me to wait longer. We were in the car before vis-
iting Nana, turning into a Walgreen's parking lot to pick up some of
Nana's favorite Pepperidge Farm cookies.*

"So," I started. "I wanted to tell you something."

Kirby turned to me after putting the car in park.

*"I have a feeling that I'm going to marry Mike. We haven't made
any plans yet, but we've talked about it a little bit, since I'm making
the move up there." I held my breath, looking down at the console in
our mom's Ford Taurus.*

"Oh, baby, that's amazing!"

"Oh my God, you think it's good? I was afraid to tell you!"

*"No, no!" Kirby laughed. "I'm glad you did! I think you guys are
wonderful for each other. He totally gets you—you guys seem very
happy."*

*I was so relieved to have her approval and I trusted her opinion.
This conversation was one of the first I had with Kirby in which I
felt like a real grown-up. With a twelve-year age gap, for so much
of the time I had with her I was just a kid—the little sister who ran
around barking like a puppy whenever she brought friends home
from school. Connecting on a more meaningful level set us as equals
rather than just big sister–little sister.*

*I'm happy at least that she was there for our wedding. But then
what? There's supposed to be so much more. When I remember that
beautiful datura hanging on the wall in the bedroom of our first
house, it makes me sad about the fact that she was never able to visit
us there. Not to mention see the store we opened when we moved to
Toronto, read the blog I started, meet our children! She's supposed to
be a part of all of these things in my life, but she's not here.*

*Right after Kirby died, I quickly seized on something about grief
that sounds obvious but is hard to get a handle on until you experience
it. We hear about the "stages of grief," as if it's a state or process you
pass through. But I don't believe that. Grief never goes away. You don't
"get through it." It is always there and becomes a part of who you are.*

Every good or bad thing that happens in your life after loss will be tainted by this grief. That I lost my sister is as much a part of me as my gender or my nationality or the fact that I'm a mom. It shapes how I respond to people and situations. Who am I? A mother. Sister. Daughter. Woman. Expat. Writer. Griever.

Necklace from Noche Azul, Croatia

After witnessing the death of my grandparents and Kirby, I've learned that the deceased person's stuff is like an anchor to the pain of the loss. The process of going through that stuff takes a long time.

Kirby had a lot of jewelry. It was kind of her thing. She loved jewelry, especially pieces that were handmade, vintage, or one-of-a-kind. When Mike and I went on our honeymoon to Croatia, we tracked down Kirby's friend, Manu, on the island of Hvar where she had a shop filled with her handmade jewelry. Noche Azul ("Blue Night" in Spanish) is the shop's name—tucked into a winding alley in the whitewashed seaport resort town. We wanted to buy Kirby a thank you gift, because she had paid for the amazing band at our wedding.

We picked out a wire choker—dramatic with black and white stones, all obsidian shine and milky pearlescence. We never gave it to her. When Kirby dropped us off at the airport the morning after our wedding, that was the last time Mike saw her. I saw her back in New York for Kate's wedding in August, but Mike couldn't come with me and we had wanted to be together when we gave her the gift.

I put it on Kirby during the wake and that was the only time she ever wore it. Then, it went into her jewelry collection, which we had to go through multiple times over the next couple of years.

The first time we looked through the trove was at the memorial in Cabo. Kate had taken all of it—the bulk of it encased in three large wooden jewelry boxes, some tucked into a number of little boxes, and some stuffed into travel jewelry pouches—to her house, where she kept it in a corner of her walk-in closet. I helped her pull out the bags and boxes and we spread it out across Kate's king-sized bed.

There were a few pieces I set aside for myself—a simple sterling silver chain, a few pairs of earrings. But then I saw the Noche Azul necklace, still in its mesh pouch, perfumed with the scent of Manu's shop. Kate and my mom agreed I should take it.

"I'm not ready for this one yet. Maybe later," I said, placing it back into a drawer in one of the jewelry boxes.

The jewelry collection eventually travelled to my parents' house in Westtown. It is a cruelty of losing a child that their stuff seems to become the parents' responsibility. It's usually the other way around, right? The children are supposed to manage the parents' things after they pass. These items become a burden—a constant reminder the perversity of losing a child. At least that's what it seems to me.

In the few years after Kirby died, almost every time we visited as a family, my mom would look at me gravely during the visit and say something like, "Maybe at some point over the weekend we can take a look through some of Kirby's things."

The first summer after Kirby died, we had a family vacation at Lake George, New York. My parents rented a little house along the road between Lake George and Lake Luzerne. They said they wanted us to get together for a vacation every summer, especially since we are scattered—Mike and I in Canada, Kate with her family in the Dominican Republic where she and her husband had moved for business opportunities, Bobby with his family in Connecticut. And there, again, we reviewed all of the jewelry—me, Mom, Kate, and our sister-in-law, Kory. We were in the enclosed porch at the front of the cabin, framed by the brown-painted siding typical in the Adirondacks.

Light coming in through the windows, filtered by the screens and cobwebs, glittered off of the jewels and chains as we held them up for inspection. We helped each other clasp necklaces around our necks to see how these pieces felt on us—if the weight was light enough to bear.

The little footsteps of Bobby's two kids would thump gently on the cabin floorboards, a welcome interruption to our reluctant appraisals.

This particular memory is a sweet one, now. And I did appreciate the opportunity to go through Kirby's things—it would be worse to have all of the things just be gone without any chance to look.

"It's okay if you don't want any of it, but I didn't want to just throw things away," my mom would say.

But mostly I dreaded these reviews, clothing or jewelry spread out on the floor or the guest room bed—things I'd already looked through multiple times. It's always been a joke in our family that Mom loves watching sappy movies because she loves crying. She shows her emotions easily, healthily. But this grieving of Kirby— there's something about watching my mom break down that is too much sometimes. Going through the things always extended an invitation to cry and it felt like my mom was compelling us to show more emotion than we typically would—to feel with her.

One of the difficulties of losing a sibling is that it's one of the very few times as a child that you can't lean on your parents. They can't be an objective comforter, because they're in it too. The heft of their own parental grief is additional weight on the remaining children—or it has been for me, even when I know my parents are very conscientious of us.

So all of these Kirby stuff reviews, I came to resent them. I resented this forced opening up—this return to the sadness. What is it? Maybe I couldn't handle that burden of comforting my mom. Maybe I didn't want to foist my own pain onto her. And then all of that holding back, all of that hesitation would coagulate into a gelatinous, weighty guilt.

The reviews have gotten less frequent over the years. Many of Kirby's things have gone to friends and family. We've also all become less attached, more ready to let go, less concerned about releasing Kirby as we release her things or accept them and appreciate them just for what they are rather than everything they may represent.

I finally took the Noche Azul necklace, when I started to write this book. I asked my mom to bring it up for me on their last visit, after I carefully shared these recollections about reviewing Kirby's jewelry. I put the necklace in the small jewelry box tufted with green fabric and beadwork that was also Kirby's, where I keep most of her other jewelry. When the thought of it is less of a brick, maybe I'll even wear it.

Wormwood apothecary cabinet
(handmade in Mexico)

In the first couple of years after Kirby died, I hesitated when I spoke about her, uncertain of what tense to use. In fact, when we were on Larry King Live, he asked me, "Just briefly, Jean, what was your sister like?"

I answered, "My sister, she's just an amazing person."

That wasn't an involuntary slip; it was a conscious decision to talk about her in the present tense. It felt like a violation to speak in the past tense. Perhaps this is an aspect of an unexpected death. When someone is and then suddenly isn't—the acceptance of that shift cannot be as abrupt as the fact of it.

One of my most favorite items from Kirby's home is a wormwood apothecary cabinet. I acquired it a few months after Kirby died, after our cousin, Geronimo, drove Kirby's 4Runner back to New York. My parents brought it up to our house in Vankleek Hill when they visited before Christmas.

It occupied a prominent position in the house—on a perfectly sized section of wall in the dining room between the doorway to the front foyer and the door down to the basement.

The cabinet itself is interesting. It's about four feet tall and two feet wide. Two columns of five drawers run down the front of it. Because the cabinet is handmade, the drawers are quirky: some get stuck if slid into the wrong opening. One drawer is noticeably a few inches shorter than the others. The cabinet pulls are about silver dollar size, with irregular flourishes in wrought iron, like lazy fleurs-de-lis. Most striking is the wood itself—the little nooks and wormholes mar the earthy red surface, making it particularly difficult to dust, the cloth always snagging in the tiny tunnels.

Because the drawers are small, it's not the most utilitarian piece, taking up much more space than it offers as storage. It is easy for it to become a chest of junk drawers and this was pretty much what it was when it came to us, still full of Kirby's things: matchbooks from Manhattan restaurants, incense she'd purchased in Malaysia with me, four pairs of sunglasses (with cases), two film cameras, a pair of binoculars, beaded wine glass tags she'd never gotten to use.

I consolidated the Kirby things in bottom drawers and took over the upper drawers with our own stuff. This arrangement stayed for the two years we lived in our house in Vankleek Hill.

Then we moved to Toronto in November 2011. The cabinet came with us and took up a new home in our junior one-bedroom apartment, a few blocks from the store we opened. As the landing point in our home, we filled it with more of our things—the dog's leash and waste bags for walks, storage for mail and keys. I tried the sunglasses for myself, but they didn't work. We put one pair in the car to keep for driving.

When we moved to a bigger space in Toronto before our first child was born, again we put the apothecary cabinet in the foyer. That move was in September 2012, three years after Kirby died.

Having kids makes us feel like unwitting hoarders. We try to let go of their things regularly, plead with relatives to curb the gift-giving, and relinquish our own things, but still the amount of stuff feels suffocating at times.

A few times in the earlier years after Kirby died, I would peer into the drawers with a mind to empty them. But though the things inside were items I had no use for, I couldn't just throw them away.

They were hers. For a long while, those scraps meant something to me—the debris of her daily life, a connection.

Over time, I have opened those irregular drawers and gradually let go of the outdated cameras and a couple of the pairs of sunglasses that I never wear. I threw away or passed along the items that were disconnected from their use or context. The incense has stayed—the scent puffs out into the air whenever I open that drawer. I've used up the matches from Stanton Social. The binoculars went into our camping gear.

Now, it's our own "junk drawer" of sorts—I keep Christmas cards (the ones with photos of the senders), a drawer with sunblock for applying before our fair kids run out the door, candles, my own sunglasses. It's a landing zone at the front door; I reach for things there every day. It'll always be "Kirby's cabinet," but it's also ours now.

This cabinet is the furniture item that will have us renting a storage unit if we ever move abroad for a spell as we hope to; I won't ever get rid of it. But the process of shifting it over to our own use has been gradual, like the shift of the tenses I use to discuss Kirby. Until now, I hadn't even realized that we've totally filled it with our own things: ownership, claim, acknowledgement, acceptance. Grief doesn't follow a schedule; it just happens.

Diploma from Blue Elephant cooking school, Bangkok

The raw grief of the early years after a loved one dies tends to come less frequently and it opens up a space for softer thoughts: happy memories, tender feelings and, sometimes, signs that just maybe something of our loved one lasts beyond their physical lifetime and stays with us.

I've had a number of these happen since Kirby's death—perhaps even more often now or maybe I'm more open to them. Maybe it's a phenomenon that comes with acceptance.

One of the hardest things about losing Kirby is the fact that she'll never know my children. When I was pregnant with my first in early 2012, James Ray's criminal trial had just wrapped up. The "normal" grieving hadn't even happened yet; the trial had put that on hold. I hesitated to think about Kirby in conjunction with this new journey of motherhood. Maybe my brain had to keep these two aspects of my life separated in a sort of self-preservation, like a painter's pallet, containing colors in their own little cups so that they won't blend.

But once I was pregnant with my second, it seemed that I was ready to put those two colors together, and they mixed and slid through one another to form something completely different.

In that newness, I saw signs, little sparkles of light that suggested to me maybe Kirby is here with us somehow. The first was my due date: October 8, the anniversary of Kirby's death. When the midwife gave me that date, I had to just shrug at first.

"Oh," I said. "Well, that's interesting."

Further along in my pregnancy, we were discussing names. Mike and I had come up with a name for a girl, but we were having a lot of trouble choosing a name for a boy. I wrote in to a baby name column on an online gossip blog. The "name guru," Duana, considers preferences, other children's names, heritage, and any other factors that are important to the expectant parents and offers a selection of name suggestions. I typed out what I thought was an interesting letter, documenting my love of Scandinavian influences, but also my desire to nod to our shared Scottish heritage and our search for a name that was unique but not completely out there.

My letter made it through to Duana's column and one of the names she offered me was Kirby. She also suggested the names "Angus" and "Lyle," Bobby and Katie's oldest kids. I felt like this was Kirby saying, "Yup, this is me, just in case you weren't sure!" It was almost too crazy a coincidence to believe; it sounds made up.

I've come to call these little signs "postcards." Kirby loved sending postcards when she travelled. She'd send them even from her *home, which I suppose made sense, too, because her home was often somewhere far away. Every now and then, I open up a book or a box or an envelope tucked into a file and I find one of these postcards, a hidden treasure.*

My efforts to send postcards when travelling have always been tripped up by the compulsion to pen a detailed message about what I've been doing, where I've been, what I've seen and eaten and felt. Too much effort—I rarely send them.

But I've realized the trick that enabled Kirby to send so many. Her messages were always succinct. Simple. "Sending love from ___!" "This made me think of you!" etc. Kirby understood that the postcard is meant to do all the talking; the message is understood and the magic is in the simple experience of receiving this 3×5 note from somewhere, anywhere, with her distinctive signature at the end.

Another "postcard" I got from Kirby recently was when I was cooking. I'd written a freelance piece reviewing Thai cookbooks, which gave me a craving for a good Thai fried rice. When I opened up a colorful, photo-rich Thai cookbook that had sat on my book-shelf for many years, out slipped a letter from Kirby. She'd bought the book for me after I'd returned from my first trip to Thailand. The curly-cues in the corners, the distinctive loop in the "K" of her name—it was a Kirby classic.

I pulled out Kirby's certificate from the Blue Elephant cooking school in Bangkok. The Blue Elephant is a restaurant in a posh sec-tion of downtown Bangkok. They serve "Royal Thai Cuisine," the historical, traditional Thai that is elevated above the street-food stalls and market fare (that is still life-changingly delicious). The butter yellow, three-story colonial building stands out among the taller towers surrounding it. It had originally been built as a depart-ment store and was then taken over by the Japanese as a command center during WWII.

I had always wanted to go there and, when Kirby visited me during my second stay in Bangkok in 2005, when I was there after university teaching English, we went for a meal and then signed up for a cooking class. They awarded us with these fancy diplomas after the class. I found Kirby's when we went through her apartment in Cabo and I took it, thinking it would be a cute decor piece framed in the fancy kitchen I hope to have one day.

When I collect all of the little signs together, it occurs to me that Kirby is still sending postcards from whatever adventure she's on now. The trick is staying open to receiving them.

Beaded Crystal Strings made by Kirby

Among the many little wedding gifts that Kirby gave us were two beaded crystal strings that Kirby and her business partner Nancy had created. About two-and-a-half feet long, these typically included flat glass beads, pearls, smaller crystals, and then, usually, a large crystal ball at the bottom to weigh it down so that it would hang in a smooth strand. They work well in a window, where the crystal ball casts the sun's light in little rainbows at certain times of the day.

With their keen eye for color, Kirby and Nancy beaded each crystal strand with a unique composition—patterns and gradients to fit the finished piece into the spaces they painted or to match the occasion of the one who received the crystal as a gift. In my case, one of the crystal strands is grassy green and pale yellow, the colors of our wedding. The other strand is pearly white and silver, evoking traditional wedding whites.

I'd first hung these in windows in our living rooms, both in Vankleek Hill and our first Toronto apartment, wanting to see and enjoy them every day. In Vankleek Hill, I'd get rainbows reflecting across the living room floor as I did yoga in the morning.

When I was setting up the nursery for our first child, I hung the crystals in the south-facing window, where they would catch the morning light. Although at that time thinking of Kirby in conjunction with my daughter was painful, it was a way that I could keep

Kirby in that space passively. I call these the "Kirby crystals" and I could explain that Aunt Kirby had made them.

They're a way to bring Kirby into the lives of my kids, a way to talk about her. I tell them stories and show them pictures. It's still abstract for them—they're little—but they will grow up having always heard about her. Every time I see the rainbows dancing around their bedroom, on the floors, the walls, their bed and dresser, I like to think that this is my invitation to Kirby, to come in and be with them, and for them to see her, to feel her, to know her.

Parenting is hard. People say it's the hardest job you'll ever do and I don't believe that's an exaggeration.

One of the most unexpected and challenging aspects of parenting for me has been the anger. People acknowledge that kids can be a pain in the ass. But rarely do they acknowledge the waves of rage you experience in a day, directed at these helpless little beings.

Whether it's a baby who refuses to nap despite her obvious exhaustion or the toddler who will not put his shoes on when you're running late, your children bring out anger that you've likely never experienced. It's the seeing red, head-splitting sort of feeling that pounds through your brain and erupts in a shout or a jar of honey thrown out the window. Afterwards, when you're suffering the anger hangover, flooded with guilt and shame, the reason for the anger seems ridiculous. And the fact that you get so mad at the people you love so dearly is just incomprehensible.

I began to worry about this. Having never been a mom before, I started to wonder if this was normal. I did worry if this was a sign that maybe I wasn't grieving "right." Had I suppressed my feelings about Kirby's death? Were these the buried feelings coming up and erupting in these challenging moments with my kids? One of the greatest fears as a parent is that you will screw up your kids. I was beginning to think that my anger was reflecting more than just the feelings of the moment and that I was in fact going to scar my children with my wounds that hadn't healed.

I hadn't seen a therapist right after Kirby died, but after I had my second baby I decided it was time—seven and a half years after Kirby's death. In one of the first sessions with my therapist, I expressed to her these concerns. She had me start writing in a journal and the first question was about the anger—how I felt about it, what I think it meant.

I came to the realization that it sort of made sense. The love I've experienced with my kids is unlike any love I've ever had for anyone. People do talk about that. So then, isn't it possible that the other emotions we have in relation to our kids are also deeper and stronger than we've ever experienced? People don't talk about that. But it seems very likely to me. The capacity to feel expands and, as we know, feelings aren't always happy, positive ones. Seeing this gave me more self-compassion, which made it easier to manage these emotions more effectively.

In therapy, I spent most of my time talking about parenting, less about grief. Discussing these relationships and how constant the effort is to understand the partner in the relationship relates to grief too. I have a relationship with this loss and, like all other relationships, it takes constant work and reevaluation—how I allow it to impact me and other aspects of my life, how I will allow it to fit in without filling me up.

Sometimes, I go into my kids' bedroom and spin the large prism at the bottom of the strand of crystals Kirby made. I watch the rainbows fly around the room, whirling blurs of color—sometimes intense, sometimes washed out and airy, always different. We often think of peace as a stillness, but it is possible to find peace in movement, in flux and shift and whirls. I think maybe it just takes a bit more effort.

Faux Fur Bolero Jacket

When I was growing up, Kirby would often buy clothing for me. She would send something in the mail with a note or bring a piece to *me when she'd be home for a visit. She'd say something like, "I saw this, and I immediately thought of you—I just had to buy it."*

I remember a flowy summer dress in that faux silk polyester material that was everywhere in the nineties. It had a halter top and a loud blue and green floral print. It never quite fit; I think I only wore it once.

Another one was a slinky, knee-length A-line dress with an empire waist and cap sleeves. The upper part had gold and black stripes. The seam at the waist marked the shift over to solid black in the same sinuous knit. I wore this one once, for a chorus concert.

These gifts were always a source of guilt for me—the generosity and enthusiasm I appreciated, but the style didn't fit in with my own self-image. The little worn items would get squirreled into the back of a drawer or the far end of the closet. Sometimes I'd try one on out of a sense of obligation and ultimately take it off again—it just didn't feel quite right.

Kirby had gone away to college when I was in kindergarten. We didn't spend a lot of time together growing up and our twelve-year age difference meant that we never existed in the same phase of life together. We never just hung out at the mall, so Kirby wouldn't have seen what I'd try on in a store. She didn't even get to observe what I wore on a regular basis. All of her picks, I guess, were based off of an image she held of me—one that was perhaps more daring or adventurous or sparkly than I ever saw myself.

When we saw Kirby's closet in her home during the memorial, I thought back to the spring break visit I'd made to Baja in 2003. At that time, Kirby was living with her fiancé, Ross. In their room, she had a walk-in closet, just off the master bathroom. In-laid river rocks dotted the floor, offering a massage if you walked in without slippers. Kirby's vibrant clothing contrasted with the earthy colors of the floor and walls. Liquid turquoise, dreamy French blues, leafy greens, punches of neon, saturated reds, gold, pinks, purples, all in rich materials like silk and velvet. Kirby's sense of style was as adventurous as her lifestyle.

We'd gone into the closet with the hopes of finding something I could wear out for a night of dancing. I picked up a low-cut halter top and complained about my small chest (a physical trait we shared) and my inability to "fill out" a top.

"No way!" Kirby said. "It's so sexy!"

Then, she told me a story about when she and Ross had been out to dinner.

"Around here, you see so many fake boobs everywhere. So we were at the restaurant, and there was this one woman at the table next to us who was flat, like us. But she was wearing this really, really low-cut top. I mean, super low." Kirby looked at me conspiratorially and ran her index finger down to just above her navel.

"Ross leaned over and was like, 'Man, she looks gorgeous!' It was so refreshing and elegant to see a real body and not the enhanced cleavage we get around here. You can do that sort of thing—show so much skin and still look so elegant."

Big sister advice—Kirby was a confident person and I often felt her trying to build that in me, too.

Kirby wasn't a stunning, otherworldly beauty. But this confidence was so attractive. She commanded what she put out to people and that drew people to her, I think more than any physical attribute. I also think this tended to cause her trouble in relationships.

One time when she was East for a visit, we were out together and she declared to me, "I'm taking a break from relationships for a while. If I call you up in a few months and start talking about some guy, remind me I'm done for now!"

As she explained to me, she would be in a relationship she assumed was casual, but then while she thought they were just having fun, the guy was suddenly declaring his love for her or maybe even proposing. She'd been engaged to three different men. This was certainly part of her motivation in going to Spiritual Warrior—to challenge herself and let go of whatever it was that led her into relationships she ultimately recognized (before making a lifetime commitment) weren't right for her. Finding the right partner was an elusive goal she was ready to realize.

As we unpacked Kirby's things and divvied them up, I wasn't interested in her clothing. I already knew our styles were different. But I did take one item—a cream colored faux fur bolero jacket. When I saw it hanging in her closet, I thought, "Yes, I can pull this one off"—an accent piece.

I've tried to wear it a few times, out to dinner or to parties. But I find the cropped length awkward, the three-quarter length sleeves impractical in Canadian winters, and the interior of the faux fur a bit scratchy. It, like many of the things I'd gotten from Kirby over the years, migrated through my closet to the end of the row.

It has finally found a home with my daughter, Linden. After we got home from a particularly contentious playdate involving an Elsa costume both she and her friend wanted to wear, I brought Linden into my room and opened my closet.

I took out the jacket. She tried it on and turned to my full-length mirror. On her, the three-quarter length sleeves stopped perfectly at her wrists. The cropped style lent just enough extra space for a princess dress to fit underneath. While on me it was always awkward, on my four-year-old it was the regal cloak of a Snow Queen. The bolero jacket lives in the dress-up box now.

It's funny—Kirby's picks for my own wardrobe would probably suit my daughter well. I do wonder what sorts of things she'd pick out for me now: how we've changed, how we would know each other better today, how maybe we would have accepted things about ourselves that the other always knew, even when we didn't.

When I remember the black and gold dress Kirby had gotten for me, I believe I'd love it today—the neutral color scheme fitting my attempts at a minimalist, grown-up sort of wardrobe. Perhaps Kirby's gifts reflected things she saw in me that I never saw in myself. They weren't necessarily mistakes—they were aspirational. More adventure. More confidence. More elegance. Sisterhood is a sort of magic, isn't it?

Ten-inch Wooden Buddha Statue from Thailand

The example of how Kirby lived her life is really the greatest gift she left me and everyone who knew her—possibly even those who didn't know her (that's my hope, anyway, and one the reasons I'm writing this).

Kirby left a blueprint for living a meaningful life. One spring, about a year and a half after Kirby died, I started to feel like I was waking up. I was ready to be less sad and it became safer to think about her. In those reflections, I found little gems as brilliant and sparkly as my aquamarine ring.

In January of 2011, I set two goals for myself for the New Year: I wanted to do yoga every day and I wanted to write in a journal. These small movements in my life were the little quake of a flower bulb as it begins to awaken from the winter and start spreading upwards toward the light. It felt like emerging from hibernation.

I made good on the yoga and started practicing nearly every morning with Kirby's Buddha statue I'd brought back with me from her house watching over me. I didn't keep up my journaling, but instead I created a blog, which was even more significant—a tendril reaching out to the world rather than just curling inside of myself.

The hook behind my blog was the trend I sense of women of my generation wanting to find more flexible careers, outside of the nine to five model, that allow for raising a family and pursuing creative aspirations. Kirby was a perfect example of this.

She lived where she wanted and moved easily, never getting trapped in a specific life. She'd had many jobs: restaurant server, limo driver, horse farm manager, pottery studio manager. She created her most consistent career in San Jose del Cabo as a decorative faux painter but, even then, she and her business partner were constantly evolving, and Kirby also added new pieces to her life and career.

*What I really admired about Kirby's lifestyle was how delib-
erately she'd constructed it to suit what she wanted out of life. She
found a way to live in paradise. She arranged her schedule so that
she would work intensely for about seven months out of the year, but
then travel to new places or visit friends and family on her extensive
"off time". I thought about this a lot and I shared the elements of her
approach that made this all possible on my blog:*

- **Hard work:** *Kirby lived in a lot of different places—New York,
  Mexico, St. Croix, Lake Tahoe, etc. Wherever she was, though,
  she found gainful employment. She often had multiple jobs, too,
  and rapidly progressed to other opportunities by impressing
  employers with her work ethic.*
- **Living within means:** *Kirby was a purveyor of fine things
  but knew how to wait or work a little harder or creatively to
  reach her goals. These skills maximized the value of her hard
  work, even in lower-paying jobs.*
- **Prioritizing needs and wants:** *This makes living within
  your means possible. Kirby decided what was important to her.
  She wanted those four or five months to travel and visit loved
  ones. So she worked her ass off in the preceding months and
  gave up other luxuries to get the time she wanted.*
- **Recognizing other value in opportunities:** *Kirby frequently made alternative payment arrangements with her
  employers. In managing the horse farm, the pottery studio, and
  at times when faux painting, Kirby negotiated a place to live as
  part of her payment. She also bartered for things she needed or
  wanted, such as a vehicle or gemstones. She defined the value of
  her work and, by looking beyond money, she was often able to
  fill basic needs or acquire the pretty things that brought a little
  richness to her life.*
- **Courage:** *Stepping off the tried and true path is scary. Yet she
  did it over and over again.*

Around this time in 2011, Steve Jobs, the founder of Apple, died. His epic commencement speech to the 2005 Stanford University graduating class began making the rounds and that's when I first came across it. Jobs was a Buddhist and his encouragement to relinquish attachment to the suffering the world can manifest is straight out of the Four Noble Truths. These words struck me:

All external expectations, all pride, all fear of embarrassment or failure—these things just fall away in the face of death, leaving only what is truly important. Remembering that you are going to die is the best way I know to avoid the trap of thinking you have something to lose.

When we face death, especially harsh, unexpected death, the sense of mortality becomes much more tangible. Of course, intellectually, we all know we're going to die one day. But we always expect it's far off. When Kirby died—vigorous, full-of-life Kirby, only thirty-eight years old—the realization that I could die at any moment became a lot less cliché. I can see how a fear of death can make a person go one way—the knowledge of an unpredictable but inevitable death turning them into a shut-in. The other way is the fearlessness that Jobs talked about, because in the finality of death there is no ego, self-doubt, or pride. Whether you believe in an afterlife or not, all of those worldly concerns are obliterated in the end.

If there is one positive thing I can take away from Kirby's death, it's that one—the intimate way I now know death transformed that knowledge of mortality from a merely philosophical understanding to something I can grasp, internalize, and use to propel me forward. And that Kirby seemed to live fearlessly before she ever faced death is sort of remarkable.

One of the great tragedies of Kirby's death is that someone exploited and abused her intense and beautiful self-motivation and set it against her. When I began to reflect on her example, I was starting to reclaim her for myself, to derive inspiration from the life that she lived, rather than dwell on the death.

The process of writing my blog was an important step in integrating her example. It helped me move forward. I was taking the last words I'd heard from Kirby, her encouragement as I finished my master's thesis, putting them into something for myself that could move me beyond the place of sadness in grief. It was also a sign of a newfound courage. For many years, I had been afraid to even try to write in a professional, public way, even though it was probably the most important thing I had ever wanted to do. I attached too much value to the outcomes and was too afraid to even try. Instead, I gave myself distractions and other goals to chase. But faced with death, it became a little easier to let go of that fear. It was time to just go for it.

During the early days of grieving, the grief feels like a part of your identity. Eventually, it shifts away from this active thing. Acceptance is one of the stages of grief that I can understand better now. I've filled those drawers in the apothecary cabinet with my own things, finally, after years of thinking I needed to hold onto Kirby's junk.

But though the weight of the grief dissipates over time, there is always this fact of who you are. I am a member of the "Prematurely Dead's Siblings Club." My parents are in the "Dead Child Club." I feel an instant kinship with someone I meet when I learn they also lost a sibling. And when I hear about a friend losing a sibling, I feel a responsibility to reach out to them, to explain a few things about how it's going to be now, to describe the rules of this shitty club to which nobody seeks membership, but whose card you can never relinquish.

I reach out to these friends because I know what's about to happen to them—that isolation—and I want them to know that they're not as alone as it can feel. And that it won't feel exactly the way it feels now.

Thinking about what would have been—the loss of the future with Kirby—is where the real hurt will always still be. The grief that *lasts is not about losing the person who was before he or she died; it's about losing the person that should have been now. The grief that lasts is about the relationship you don't get to have.*

Somehow, you have to find a way to let that relationship continue to exist. You have to look for the signs that they're still with you or find ways to carry them with you. Kirby's things have allowed my relationship with her to continue to evolve.

This relationship will be riddled with falsehoods. It will rest on assumptions that may not be true, like the unworn clothing Kirby would buy for me. But that doesn't actually matter. It's a soliloquy that exists just for me, for what I need in the moment—something for me to hold onto.

The intangible things we keep with us also offer a way of keeping a departed loved one alive. Their life doesn't have to remain stagnant within the confines of their physical life on earth. In some ways, I feel like I've assimilated what Kirby was to me, what she meant to me, in my own life.

The memories I have of her change and grow along with me. She changes as I change. This can happen for anyone who holds memories of Kirby close to them, anyone she touched and impacted. Through all of us, there are all of these versions of Kirby out in the world even now. Immortality, I think, is this process of infinite metamorphosis—living, mutable memory.

Floral Silk Scarf

Kirby enchanted her living spaces. Whether it was her dorm room at Geneseo or when she lived at home after college and took over the attic, or in any of the apartments or homes she occupied, she always managed to transform the space into a sanctuary. There were a few items that she'd had for as long as I can remember.

One of these was this floral silk scarf. It's a peachy, floral silk, with a fringe that lends it a gypsy aesthetic. I remember it more as a decor item than a piece of clothing. She often draped it over the top of a lamp shade, so that the background of the floral motif filtered the light into amber. The little sequins that dotted the scarf would catch the light in sparkles. Sometimes, she spread it across an end table, the painterly flowers energizing the tabletop.

When we went through her house in Cabo during the memorial, I saw this scarf in her closet and it transported me to all of those cool, bohemian rooms, right along with the crystal ball in its polished stump stand and the smell of Nag Champa incense—cozy, shadowy, just hippie enough to me that, as a kid, it was all pure magic.

I love that she had kept this scarf for so long, a little piece of her identity that stayed with her through so many different lives, it seemed. When I packed up my things after the Cabo memorial, I used the scarf to wrap up some more delicate items. At home, I tucked it into a box with all of my own scarves.

The early years of grief were muddled by the trial of James Ray. While the raw sadness fogged every view and the effort to keep moving staggered under the weight of this loss, the trial was a looming unknown, completely outside of our control.

Toward the end of the trial, we were given an opportunity to give a victim impact statement. I couldn't go to Arizona for that part of the trial—spending a couple of thousand dollars on that trip when we were just opening our store wasn't an option—so I sent in a video which they played in the courtroom.

As I looked over the victim services representative's advice regarding the victim impact statement, I struggled with what to say. It was an opportunity to address how the crime had impacted us personally—financially, emotionally. It was also an opportunity to make comments on the accused in the crime.

In the video, I sit at my desk in front of my computer. Behind me is the office room in our Vankleek Hill house—the intricate plaster crown molding that sold me on the house when we bought it, our piano with the stodgy jacquard paneling, a picture of Mike and me in Thailand.

215

I recorded the statement when I was home alone. Even though our house was on the main street through town, there was little traffic outside the window I faced from my seat. It was quiet. I tried not to be.

Dealing with the death of my sister has been hard enough. But in addition, watching James Ray carry on as if nothing happened has just added another layer to the painful process of accepting this into my life. I have followed James Ray online. On his Facebook page and his Twitter feed, he has just about ignored the events of October 8, 2009. He made no mention of it or the people who died on the 2010 anniversary. He has continued to try to influence people, sell his services, and has often made insensitive comments given what has happened. For example, on the day he left California to travel down to Arizona to stand trial for three counts of manslaughter, he tweeted 'It's a beautiful day for a road trip.'

Experiencing that kind of callousness in response to Kirby's death—I can't describe the feeling that that evokes. Losing her is hard enough but seeing the person who caused her death act as if nothing happened breeds an anger that goes beyond what is normal in the grieving process.

There were many gaps left in the trial proceedings. With my impact statement, I wanted to fill those gaps, express the deficiencies of James Ray's character: that he knew his "sweat lodge" was dangerous, because people had been hurt previously; that he had shown little remorse or genuine concern for the victims and other participants of the sweat lodge; that he hadn't cooperated with the police to help them piece together what had gone so wrong that three people died; and how grieving the loss of my sister was so much harder when the person who was responsible was so unaffected.
I could see that Ray wanted to forget about Kirby, move on as though she had never really lived. He'd been trying to rewrite the

facts of what had happened from the start with the words of the "channelers" and assurances to other participants, trying to spin her death as a choice she'd made to move on from this world. But I knew she hadn't made that choice. She hadn't had any choice. She would be very much alive today if she'd had a choice.

I struggled to capture all of this in what I said. But capturing Kirby in what I wore was easy. I pulled out her silk scarf right away. She'd kept it with her for so long. She'd used this scarf as a way to illuminate her spaces with her own energy, so much so that it feels infused with her energy now. This was how it functioned as I read my statement—it was my way to bring Kirby's energy into that space. While I read, I needed to have Kirby visibly there with me. I needed the watercolor petals and leaves to flash, the amber to pulse like an aura, the fringe to stir in my breath as I spoke

Part III:
The Trial

This Sweet Life

Chapter 7

66 It's not about winning or losing... it's about how you
show up... how you play the game and what you
have learned. I died with great honor and integrity.
Discipline was my lesson. 99

*—from Kirby's journal reflection on
the Samurai Game*

Jean

*A*s if it's not enough to lose a family member, when the death is
criminal, you have to live through a trial.

*When James Ray's trial began in March 2011, I had just started
emerging from the initial fog of grief. I'd started writing my blog. We
had also really begun digging into the work of SEEK, trying to define
our mission and even just define the self-help industry in general.*

*In some ways, maybe a trial like this is a blessing. Death is rarely
just, no matter the circumstances, but if your loved one dies of illness,
age, or an accident, you don't get to question that death in a concrete
way. Many people find someone or something to question, like God.
But this is intangible, like throwing stones at water while expecting
something solid to shatter. When the death involves a crime, you
get to hold it—and the accused—to account for how fucked up and
devastating it is. There's some perverse comfort in that.*

*After a year and a half of just being sad, the trial was an oppor-
tunity to confront all of it: Kirby's death, the place where it happened,
the man who orchestrated it, and what it would mean to move for-*

ward, regardless of what happened to him.

It was surreal, though. March was still winter in Ontario, while this unknowable thing was taking shape out in the desert thousands of miles away. I followed along with the events through news articles, email updates from the Yavapai County Victims' Services office, and the news coming from family and friends who were attending the trial. All of these connections to what was happening were a rope thrown across the continent to me.

Mike and I would discuss what was happening, tentatively. After the opening statements, we were down at the Blueberry Hill Bistro one night. I wondered if the people at the table adjacent could hear our conversation, if their ears pricked up on words like "trial," "manslaughter," "death."

After the server had cleared our pork vindaloo and beef curry, we lingered while finishing our pints. Mike looked at me seriously.

"Do you feel certain that he's going to be convicted?" he asked.

I stared at the foam ringing the meniscus of the beer left in my glass. "Yes. Well, I don't know. ...Maybe not," I finally said.

"I guess, I mean, it's just important that you are prepared for that. That you're not counting on a conviction."

Mike is direct. I appreciate that about him.

"No. I don't think I am. It would definitely be frustrating and disappointing. But on the other hand, as it is I feel like he should be on trial for murder! So my expectations for it are already... limited."

And that was it. Even from the beginning, I believed that what had happened was so convoluted and fucked up that there was no way it was all going to fit into a court trial. It was just too crazy. From all the information we had at that point, it seemed clear that Ray had to know how reckless he was being. And knowing the breadth of that recklessness but continuing anyway—that felt like murder. The important pieces of information, though, such as the belief that he'd used "mind control" type tactics that ultimately made it impossible for his participants to make rational decisions about their own safety, would be too much for a courtroom trial, I knew.

But despite my low expectations, was I counting on this trial to put James Ray away? Yes, probably.

Ginny

February 16, 2011: The TRIAL BEGINS

As jury selection began on February 16, I wrote in my journal:

Lord, guide this process. May the right persons be chosen for this jury… people who can hear, understand, and fairly judge the evidence, appreciate the danger and manipulation employed.

Guide the prosecutor, her judgment, wisdom, understanding and experience. Help us have faith in her, understanding that this is her case….

Help me relax and be patient as this process unfolds. I know there will be times when what we hear or see will be upsetting, infuriating, feel unfair, etc. Through it all I want to be the "warrior princess" my daughter loved and respected. I don't want to disappoint her, but represent her with dignity and grace, being her voice to seek and speak the truth.

When I think about 2011, the year of the trial, I see a box of primary colored crayons. The whole year felt like those stark, vivid, loud, definite colors, no pastels or subtle shading, just red rocks and a landscape that assaults one's senses—blue sky that seems to expand into forever, and the relentless yellow sun, drenching the landscape, intensifying everything, along with the black and white of lies, truth and omissions. Much of that year is painted in my memory with these blaring pigments, felt in the deafening emotions of anger, despair, fear. And yet there was also hope and gratitude.

As the trial was about to begin, George and I discussed when we should attend. I would need to arrange my work schedule to accommodate trips to Arizona. We wanted to be there for the beginning and possibly for the verdict.

When I was ten or eleven, my parents joined a local swimming club that had a huge pool. The measure of pre-adolescent maturity was the ability to dive off the twelve-foot diving board into the deep end of the pool. I could swim fairly well but was never really comfortable with heights. Climbing up that ladder was a statement of bravery. Looking down into the pool was quite another matter. I remember climbing down at least once, trembling with fear, overcome with the shame of not jumping in. Finally, on that diving board, I resolved, I won't dive but will jump, holding my nose, fearful of water going up my nose or crashing my head into the bottom of the pool. Letting go was both terrifying and exhilarating and it felt good to have faced my panic. Eventually, with many trips to the board, I confronted my trepidation and even learned to dive. There have been many times in my life when I have pushed past fear. Going to the trial in Arizona is on the top of that list.

Questions about what to expect, what we would hear, what to say, how to respond, who we would see, filled me with dread and yet I knew this was something we had to do. Kirby was dead, along with Liz Neuman and James Shore. We all needed answers and culpability had to be determined. I had to "jump in." Maybe I would learn to dive. By the end of 2011, I would feel a little braver, my resolve to be Kirby's voice would be strengthened, and I would also have received some incredible gifts through this horrific experience.

George felt a strong sense of responsibility to ensure a continual presence in court to represent the victims, letting the jury know that the dead had family and friends who were forever altered because of this man's reckless incompetence. Mika and Bobby brought their RV from Moab and camped out a good portion of that year in order to attend the trial. Deborah Goldstein traveled to Camp Verde four times to represent Kirby. My brother, Bill, his wife Jerelyn, George's sister, Kay, her husband, Al, our nephew, Jimmy Kelly, friends, Vinnie and Kathy Brennan, my dear friend, Liz Holst, and her daughter, Sarah, all changed plans, appointments, work obligations to sit in that courtroom. Other friends traveled for the sentencing in November: Lisa Brusseau, Bill Dahly, Deborah Goldstein, Mika Cutler, Bob Magnanini. Liz Neuman's cousin, Lily Clark, who lived in Tempe, Arizona, was there throughout the trial to represent the Neuman family. Andrea, Liz's daughter, also traveled to Camp Verde. Jane Gripp, James Shore's mother, his brother Chris, sister Virginia, and his wife, Alyssa, the mother of his three children, made sure James was remembered. A group of Native Americans, led by Ivan Lewis, outraged at the bastardization of their sacred sweat lodge ceremony, sat in the last row of seats every day in both protest and support.

We tried to plan when we would go to the trial. We were both working—George in his counseling practice and me at the Dispute Resolution Center running the Strengthening Families Program with probation officers for the teens on probation and their families. I was also teaching anger management to parolees and a parenting program to adults whose children had been removed due to abuse and neglect. I had limited windows of time for extended absences. That year, George started to wind down his private practice as he approached retirement. We decided that we would need to be present at the beginning and end of the trial and possibly another time in the middle, depending on how long it lasted. He coordinated the "trial watch," a continual presence for the jury to see the people in

Kirby's life who had been impacted by this crime. George managed all the arrangements for us, booking flights, car rentals, and hotels. In the course of that year, he would make and cancel, and then reschedule these plans at least a dozen times as trial dates were canceled due to motions for mistrial or legal wrangling designed to delay the proceedings.

On February 28, we boarded a plane for Phoenix, Arizona. The trial of James Arthur Ray for the death of three people in his sweat lodge on October 8, 2009, was about to begin. Picking up a car at the airport, we drove north to Cottonwood where we stayed in a small motel for a few days. I was immediately aware that the sun and the landscape felt radically different from the northeast in the winter. As campers, we have always loved the stark beauty of the Southwest. The dramatic, rugged mountains and the harsh, barren countryside have always held a rather strange fascination for me—different, other-worldly, exciting but oddly unsettling at the same time. We had entered foreign territory. This physical place shouts out: The way is unmarked, unknown, possibly hostile, maybe even dangerous. We live in the northeast, in a rural section of New York State just below the Catskills, where the mountains are sculptured in a gentle, comfortable way. Every shade of green soothes the senses; even the sun warms and embraces. The roads meander and lead to lovely tranquil vistas. As we drove north, closer to Camp Verde, this alien landscape further jangled my nerves. We were a long way from home. We lost cell reception in these mountains.

The courthouse in Camp Verde is in the middle of nowhere. Driving up to this beautiful modern building of stone and glass with our son, Bobby, and Bob Magnanini to hear the opening arguments, we were assaulted by the sight of reporters and cameras littering the entire walkway into the building. I tried to keep my eyes lowered, not wanting to draw any attention to myself, not wanting to speak to anyone, fearful of saying anything that would negatively impact the proceedings.

I fumbled through my bag to find my cell phone and put it in the dish to go through the metal detector. Jarred by the blaring beep of the security alarm, I was reminded to take off my shoes. My stomach roiled as we walked up the stairs, not knowing what to expect.

Entering the hallway on the second floor, we were immediately greeted by Pam Moreton of Yavapai Victim Services. She introduced herself, extending a reassuring hand. Her open face and warm smile helped to dissolve some of my nervousness. She shepherded us into "our room," a private space set aside throughout the proceedings for the victims of the trial. Bottles of water, tissues, candy, and some simple snacks were set out on a small table. Eight chairs were placed along the walls of this small, intimate room. Pam was our "Yavapai Mom," making sure we were taken care of throughout the trial. The comfort of a place to sit, to cry, to regroup, and hydrate was a huge relief—a small oasis in this strange and foreign territory.

We were ushered into the courtroom. It was small—so small for such a big story. Ray sat only a few feet away from us at a long table in front of the judge with his lawyers. The jury was to our left in two graduated rows. We sat on a bench behind a railing that separated us from the lawyers, prosecutor, and the jury. During the trial, before the judge and jury appeared in the court, every day, the bailiff would read a list of warnings: we were not to show any emotion during the proceedings—no gasping, no hand raised to cover our mouth, no whispering, no reaction of any kind to any testimony, or we would be removed from the court. How was I going to refrain from weeping? This emotional numbing lecture greeted us each time we entered that court. Conditions we had to accept to simply witness this trial.

The energy it took to refrain from answering the questions asked of witnesses or from screaming in rage as Ray's lawyers cleverly twisted the traumatized witnesses' words was exhausting. After being admonished by the bailiff when a response automatically emerged from my lips, I started to write in a journal to keep my head down and thoughts focused. As each witness took the stand, I was horrified. The testimony was robotic, showing no real emotion. Did no one care that Kirby, James, and Liz were dead?

In that first week, three participants recounted more and more facts about how Ray had conducted the weeklong retreat. The "syntax" as they referred to the schedule, was as follows:

- Saturday, 10.3.09: 4:00 pm arrival, registration, introduction and head shaving
- Sunday: Lectures, meditation, breath work, more head shaving
- Monday: Lectures, journaling, Holotropic Breathwork
- Tuesday: Lectures, code of silence, Samurai game, preparation for Vision Quest
- Wednesday: Vision Quest, starting at 12 am and going into the next day
- Thursday: Return from Vision Quest, sweat lodge

We learned that the head shaving was strongly encouraged shortly after people arrived on Saturday night to bear witness to their commitment to play "full on." Many details that I had discovered from the few participants I had spoken to after Kirby's death were now laid out in a clearer timeline. The Sunday evening session set the stage for the week, the push to participate fully, risk fearlessly in order to maximize each person's investment of time and money. Monday and Tuesday started with early morning yoga sessions, meditation, and hours of Holotropic breathing exercises intended to create an altered state. These activities were interspersed with lectures, video clips of *The Last Samurai* and personal reflection time. Participants were told to stay up all night writing in their journals, concentrating on their individual histories, and not conversing with others. We heard that Ray had said that sleep was overrated and would waste what precious time they had. "Many great opportunities and experiences can be stolen by sleep," he said in one of the recordings played in the courtroom.

After a full day, on Tuesday night, participants played the "Samurai game." Everyone was challenged to live with integrity and told not to fear death. Dream team volunteers dressed in black were the "angels of death" who struck down individuals who did not adhere to the confusing rules created by Ray, who was arrayed in white garb—God. To protect your team members, anyone declared dead had to remain immobile on the ground or a teammate would also die. The rationale behind this game was to challenge the fear of death, concentrating on living impeccably with honor. The rules of the game and the participants' understanding of the purpose seemed murky as we listened to their testimony.

Immediately after that exercise, everyone was put under a "code of silence" and taken to separate, secluded, private spots in the dessert. They would remain alone for the next thirty-six hours, from late Tuesday night, all day Wednesday into early Thursday morning, without food or water. Once brought back to their lodging, participants gathered for a brunch and then an open session to share their experience before the culminating activity, a sweat lodge.

After witnesses testified about the events of the week, they shared their experience of the two and a half hour sweat lodge ceremony. Ray conducted the lodge as a test of endurance rather than the cleansing ceremony performed by Native Americans.

"You will feel like you're going to die. I guarantee it," he said before they entered the lodge.

Throughout the trial, the defense was constantly creating confusion and doubt about the testimony of the participants. Discrepancies were found in the testimony that was taken on the evening of October 8 from traumatized participants gathered in the Crystal Hall, still in shock, and the testimony given by the same participants a few days later. There were unending challenges to the District Attorney's right to prosecute. It felt like every week they motioned for a mistrial or brought up some other procedural issue. The judge stopped testimony, honoring an objection, referencing a witness's testimony as being "prejudicial to the defendant." Prejudicial? These statements might make him look bad? Three people are dead! Numerous people were harmed for life!

At one point, we heard that Kirby was delirious, rocking and chanting "We can do this, we can do this." Participants told her to shut up. I wept. Were these the last words she heard? Shut up? Why did no one recognize this behavior as a sign of developing heat stroke?

A preliminary hearing of motions had been held the previous November to set the rules for testimony. Prior dangerous acts were deemed inadmissible. Unethical business practices were out. While the events of the week could be revealed, guilt would be determined and limited to Ray's actions in the sweat lodge ceremony. Those two and a half hours alone. References to his character, past situations where he had knowingly placed others in danger, or his behaviors throughout the week, also out. I was outraged and confused. How can a prosecutor prove the charge of the grand jury—manslaughter—without revealing prior knowledge of danger? Sheila Polk cleverly used defense questioning to "open the door" to explore past situations, but this was clearly limited. It was obvious to us that this would be a David versus Goliath trial. Ray's lawyers were Munger, Tolles, & Olson, described by *The American Lawyer* as "an army of trial lawyers capable of waging war... a litigation power-house" with 170 attorneys and 450 employees in three major cities, Los Angeles, San Francisco, and Washington D.C.

Sheila Polk was the Yavapai County prosecutor who had one assistant, Bill Hughes, and a law secretary. Ray's lawyers cranked out motion after motion for perceived violations and repeated requests for a mistrial. They buried the prosecution who had to defend their right to prosecute.

Unforgettable were the hours of legal argument about playing the recording of Kirby's voice to indicate her resolve to "play full on." All the sessions during the week had been recorded: Ray's teaching, his instructions, and the words of any participant who spoke during the open mic period. I was curious, fearful, and excited once we discovered that Kirby had spoken right before going into the sweat lodge. It was argued that playing the recording of her voice was actually "hearsay" because she was no longer present to confirm that what was recorded was what she really meant. I was incredulous. "She cannot corroborate because she is dead!"

Sheila Polk wanted to show Ray's clear knowledge of her state of mind going into his final and ultimate challenge. I just wanted to hear her sweet voice. When the recording was finally played, we heard Kirby describe being dead during the Samurai game. She was freezing and in pain, laying immobile on the floor, but was adamantly determined to live and die with honor, not moving in order to protect her teammates. She described her vision quest and the awareness that "our loved ones that have passed are with us." I was no longer in that courtroom. Listening, as tears rolled down my face, her voice caressed me like a blessing, a message of her assured presence from beyond.

After the recording debacle, my hopes that justice might be served in this trial began to diminish and darken with each legal argument. One day, I walked out of the courtroom into the glass walled hallway, awash with light, looked out the window at the austere beauty of the spectacular landscape in Camp Verde, and thought, "Breathe and see this beauty." Breathe, because there is so little air in that courtroom. See these solid rocks in the midst of this complete unreality.

This was a totally surreal experience and yet the fact that Kirby was dead was all too real.

Once, while sitting in a cafe in Sedona, I was struck by an odd sensation. The red jagged cliffs set against the brilliant blue sky appeared to be two-dimensional, like a huge poster board or movie set facade—no shrubbery in the foreground, no outlines of mountains in the background to create a sense of depth. Every once in a while, those optical illusions and resulting sensations of odd unreality play on our senses, like the vehicle moving next to you when stationary that causes you to startle, thinking your car has moved. Throughout the trial I felt that two-dimensional sensation, like something was amiss—a third dimension to provide depth was overlooked.

The jury would not be privy to information we had. They would not hear about past incidents at other Ray events: broken hands at an event in Hawaii; people hallucinating or unconscious after other sweat lodge ceremonies; Ray walking away, never following up on participants' injuries. Nor would they hear about the staff cover-up of Colleen Conaway's suicide at the San Diego Absolute Wealth event in July 2009. They would not hear about Ray's lack of preparedness and inadequate response in previous situations. The prosecutor would not be able to explore the impact of sensory deprivation and mind control tactics designed to impair rational decision-making. The rules of law would prevent any education about the effects of trauma on the witnesses. The third dimension to create depth and real understanding would not be revealed. The trial would be a two-dimensional, inadequate reality. In this court of "law," where highly paid, clever lawyers were determined to create any kind of "reasonable doubt," any depth to produce understanding and reveal truth would be eliminated.

During breaks, Pam and others who worked for victim services were wonderful, protecting us from the media invasion, making sure we had water, sandwiches, etc. We had been warned against speaking to the media, lest comments be misconstrued and inhibit the prosecution. Eventually, we figured out how to leave the court complex to lunch at some local eateries. Being with members of the Shore and Neuman families, I knew we would be forever connected through this tragedy. We were all numb. We were good people, bleeding and damaged together.

Lily Clark, Liz Neuman's cousin, talked about Liz, who was sole caretaker of her elderly, ill mother. At her own travel expense, Liz had worked as a "dream team" volunteer for Ray's events for seven years. When Lily talked about Liz and I saw pictures of her vibrant smile, I wished I had had the opportunity to meet this strong woman who was so focused on her personal growth, integrity, and her devotion to her family and young adult children.

Jane Gripp, James Shore's mother, was present during some of that time and I felt we bonded as mothers, wounded and stunned at the circumstances of our children's deaths. The lunch break became the time to express our outrage over the defense tactics and our frustration at the limitations imposed on Sheila Polk, the prosecutor. It was also the time to share everyday information about our families, past experiences of travel, and things we had in common, connecting us forever in a friendship that would live beyond this moment. I heard

Jane's love and concern for James' wife, Alyssa, and their children, who at the time of their father's death were eleven, nine, and seven. George, a consummate storyteller, would break the tension with funny accounts of our forays into the Southwest, camping misadventures, and interesting people we had met on various vacations.

I believe physical beauty, laughter, and good people can provide the balm needed for healing. I kept thinking, "Breathe, open your eyes. See the beauty of these people and this place."

Hearing repeated descriptions of the weeklong activities and the sweat lodge itself made Kirby's death vivid and intense. When a person dies, a family member might have to identify the body in the morgue. But when that death is part of a criminal trial, that identification, the careful examining of your loved one, being told how she died, viewing the damage, happens day after day—for months. The continual revisiting of the morgue was emotionally draining and exhausting.

The first few witnesses described the conditions creating "sensory deprivation" foisted on the group throughout the week: encouragement to forego sleep, breathing exercises amid loud banging noises designed to alter brain waves, limited protein intake, and then no food or water for the thirty-six-hour vision quest activity. These conditions were certain to impede rational decision-making by day five. Group pressure designed to create "group think" encouraged compliance. Isolation prevented collaborative processing among the group. The participants testified to their clear intentions and resolve to play "full on." Many mentioned that Ray stated repeatedly that he was "in charge," insisting on the strict following of his rules to bring everyone to a "breakthrough" in order to realize their hearts' desires. Participants testified to their confidence in his knowledge and experience, clearly trusting his directions, and their fear of challenging him in any way. Listening to them helped me understand Kirby's commitment to participate fully for the entire week and eventually to stay in the sweat lodge.

The two and a half hour sweat lodge ceremony was described in great detail by at least seven witnesses. There were accounts of Dennis screaming outside the tent, thinking he was having a heart attack; people being dragged out of the tent disoriented, some unconscious; Lou sustaining serious burns from falling into the pit of steaming rocks. The participants reported general chaos during the ceremony. I screamed in silence, "Why didn't you stop this?" The defense lawyers hounded the witnesses, "You didn't think anyone was dying, did you?" The implication that the paying customers had a responsibility to help others was infuriating. The defense continually implied that only if you have absolute knowledge that someone was dying would any sane person help another. The participants not saving the victims absolved Ray from his inaction.

Once, when on a flight to Arizona for the trial, a young man seated across from us fainted in the aisle of the plane. Immediately, attendants converged around him, bringing cold cloths and water. Assured that he was breathing, they began discussing the possibility of notifying the tower that an emergency landing would be necessary to secure proper medical attention. A whole planeload of people would be derailed to save one person who had fainted! Within a few minutes, the young man recovered and was helped to his seat. He was given water and food, and the crisis was averted as he responded to the quick intervention by the flight crew. I could not help contrasting their care with the fatal carelessness encountered by my daughter when she passed out in that tent.

At the trial, each witness testified to fighting for their own life, going deep within to endure the intense heat, being disoriented, yet focused on completing this abusive test of endurance. We knew about these details, about the chaos at the end of the ceremony. But hearing it firsthand from the witnesses was appalling. Ray did nothing to help. He did not call 911; however, after the police arrived, he was able to call his lawyers (his probation report revealed that he became upset when he was informed that this was a homicide investigation). His attorneys advised him to leave the scene immediately. And, he did, in the middle of the night. He denied that he was in charge to police. He claimed that the fire tender, Ted Mercer, was running the event. Each retelling felt like another gut punch and confirmation of Ray's callousness. People repeatedly testified to being fearful of challenging Ray in any way, choosing instead to believe in his knowledge and experience. I heard it said more than once, "He was my teacher. I believed he knew better and would keep us safe." He had successfully convinced many of these participants that he was God, just like the role he played in the Samurai game. One gentleman said, "I was only aware of me and my wife; it was his [Ray's] call. He was running the show."

Then there was the argument that James Ray International held responsibility, not James Ray, the individual, who was the spokesperson for the corporation—another "fine point of law" that would be debated by the attorneys. People often say, "common sense is not very common." We began to describe the defense strategy as "baffle them with bullshit."

After the first few days, we met Mike Murphy, our lawyer in Prescott who suggested we stay at his home over the weekend because he and his wife would be away, ensuring us some privacy. I had spoken to Mike on the phone during the settlement, but I was delighted to meet him in person: a tall, athletic, commanding yet gentle man. Lucia, his lovely, diminutive wife, a talented seamstress, avid gardener, and dedicated teacher, opened her home and heart to us. They insisted that we should be in a comfortable environment, rather than a sterile hotel during this difficult time. Their generous gift was like a warm, toasty blanket on a dark, stormy night.

Mike and Lucia's home is nestled in the mountains of Prescott, a mile-high city in Arizona that is an escape from the relentless heat of Phoenix. About five minutes outside town, up a steep winding road, the Murphy's home overlooks the valley and allows for fabulous sunset views. Surrounded by gardens of beautiful desert vegetation, decks overhang the sloping hillside. A hot tub sat on a patio, offering us relaxing respite. With our own key, we entered their home and immediately felt the soothing balm of a loving, comfortable space. Walking through the house, I noticed the bookshelves were filled with familiar titles and authors: books on theology, philosophy, sociology, even the fiction was authored by people I had read. I found a book I had wanted to read, and it allowed me a fabulous mental escape for the entire weekend. The following week we shared this lovely home with Mike and Lucia, allowing us to come home from a day at the trial to conversation and emotional support. Sitting in the living room, having coffee in the morning as Mike read the daily paper, lent a reassuring sense of "normalcy." Talking about Kirby and our other children, conversations about the trial, our lives, grandchildren, careers, places we had traveled, created a bond of belonging. I know their gracious hospitality enabled us to feel less like the outlanders while in Arizona. They hosted a dinner gathering for the group who was in the courtroom, some of our friends and family, at the famous Murphy's restaurant in Prescott and invited the group to their home on a few occasions. Such thoughtful generosity kept us afloat through this storm.

We wanted to stay through the second week so that we could support Beverley when she was called to testify. Beverley's testimony was compelling. It was emotional. In precise detail, she recounted the week, each round of the sweat lodge ceremony, and the traumatic aftermath. She described the conference call made on October 14, when a dream team member assured the group that the channeler reported Kirby and James chose their deaths. Ray suggested that anyone having difficulties should speak to his "like-minded" person who would provide counseling. A licensed psychologist or social worker would simply not understand the situation. Unfortunately, we had to leave before she was finished on the stand and the pull of our other life in New York angrily beckoned us homeward. I wanted to go home, but I also wanted to hear every detail, every testimony, like the child who fights to stay up and watch the horror movie, peeking behind tightly entwined fingers to view the carnage.

Once home in New York, Pam Moreton, from victim services, sent us daily updates about testimony. I spoke to Lily Clark, Sidney Spencer, Beverley Bunn, Alyssa Shore, Jane Gripp, and others frequently as the trial proceeded. Friends and family who traveled to Arizona as part of the "trial watch" sent updates. Others reported on what they were seeing on Court TV. I could not watch the televised proceedings and stay focused on work, our life, everyday responsibilities. During March, April, and May, I was constantly rearranging my work schedule, trying to plan programs around times when we would be in Arizona for the trial. Just concentrating on going through the necessary motions of life, I sensed the trauma that awaited me—the trauma of being in the courtroom with Ray and his lawyers, hearing arguments intended to confuse rather than enlighten the jury, being instructed to deaden all emotions by the bailiff. I felt gagged: what could, or could I not say publicly? I was terrified that I might do or say something that would negatively affect the trial.

Still, life happens. On May 2, my twenty-nine-year-old nephew, Logan, was fatally injured while working with my brother, Joe. My younger brother by two and a half years is a man of strong faith, dedicated to family, overseeing the care of our parents in their last years, and helping his three boys and step-children while building a successful landscaping business on the South Fork of Long Island. Logan was trying to bleed the hydraulics of a bucket loader, but the safety was not secured, and the stabilizing arm fell on Logan, severing his spinal cord. He was declared dead at the scene and was revived in the ambulance that sped him to the Stony Brook Trauma Center. He was on life support machines, but the doctors declared him "brain dead", and now his wife of nine months and the family had a terrible decision to make. We spent three weekends traveling to Stony Brook to be with my brother and his family as they absorbed this devastating loss—three hours of driving each way to Long Island while crying. I felt so helpless watching my brother, his wife Tina, and Logan's mother, Karen, suffer the indescribable pain of the loss of their son.

Logan, Joe's son, was a twin who had an infectious laugh and an irrepressible zest for life. Suddenly, he was dead. Another senseless loss scarred us, our family, forever. I shared with Joe our experience: Kirby's death—the anger, depression, hopelessness, and gut-wrenching pain that overshadowed every other emotion and event. I knew Logan, like Kirby, would want everyone to continue to live and love life. But how do we when our hearts are suddenly broken? There was nothing I could say. This grief just needs supportive presence. I was torn, wanting to be with them, needing to work, and having already planned to return to Arizona with our daughter Jean on May 10. Joe said that watching us mourn Kirby helped him face his loss. Grief reverberates through time and relationships. Life is unfair. I wanted to take away his pain. But we cannot allow ourselves to be buried along with our dead. We have a responsibility to live well the gift of life we are given.

Jean

*I was never questioned as a witness at this trial—there was no
legal reason for that—but I did need to witness it. I went out to
Arizona twice, once with my mother and once with my father.*

*The first trip was with my mom in May. At that point I'd already
heard stories of some of the people and places I would meet. I'd been
well-primed by my dad on the javelina—the invasive, boar-like crea-
tures that roam in packs and are surprisingly destructive (sometimes
even aggressive) despite their resemblance to hairy, rat-like pigs. I
watched for them in backyards and dried up riverbeds as we drove
to the Murphy's house. It was a winding road of driveways hidden
behind switchbacks and scrubby pines ascending into the Arizona
mountains.*

*They had dinner for us when we arrived. This was the first time
I'd eaten one of those pre-roasted chickens you can get in the grocery
store. It was delicious. Whenever I grab a chicken on a night I need a
quick dinner, I think of the Murphys and their hospitality.*

*The first morning we left their house to go to the trial, there was
snow on the ground—just under an inch. The feathery, cool wisps of
snow were a surprise, knowing the deadly heat that waited below.*

*James Ray's criminal trial was held in the Yavapai County
Superior Courthouse in Camp Verde, Arizona. The officials had
decided to hold the trial here, anticipating large numbers and media
presence, rather than in the usual Yavapai County Courthouse in
Prescott. That building has a classic look, with Grecian columns
and historic symbols in relief on the upper pediment. It oversees
the Prescott village square, surrounded by mature trees and cozy
restaurants.*

*The superior courthouse, in contrast, is outside of the town,
isolated. The building itself is linear and modern, with big glass*

panels set in concrete slabs and a thick roof overhanging the front entrance. As many things do in the desert, the courthouse appears out of nowhere, set abruptly in the ground, with little more than shrubbery surrounding it and huge vistas and mountains behind it. It's exposed but dignified.

My experience with courtrooms to that point was limited to watching my high school friends in "mock trial" in the county courthouse back home. I'd never even dealt with a traffic ticket, let alone sat through a proceeding that felt so close to me personally. While it was satisfying to see James Ray in the defendant's seat, the whole experience was disembodying, as though with each person who testified there was some piece of my own self spliced off, displayed with him or her in the witness stand. This was my sister's life, filed in motions, objections, and rulings. I was expecting tedious and impersonal before I arrived, but the full surreality of it was something I guess I couldn't have prepared for.

During these days in May, the prosecution reviewed the science of how the victims had died. First, we heard the cross-examination of the coroners and medical examiners who'd written the death reports. This period drew a stark contrast between the professions of medicine and law. Doctors deal in facts; lawyers reinterpret facts. The defense lawyers left these coroners looking so confused, uncertain. Ray's lawyers drafted their alternative theory—that maybe the victims died of organophosphate poisoning; that somehow, insecticides in the ground used to eradicate pests like ants and weeds had been present in sufficient quantities to poison the select three victims of Ray's event and that somehow this deflected any blame from Ray himself. It was just a terrible, horrible accident. Not his fault.

The medical examiners who looked at Kirby's, James', and Liz's bodies had determined that all three victims had died of heat stroke. Given how hot the tent was and how long they were in there, this was obvious. The defense attorneys were "doing their job" by twisting and questioning endlessly the possibility of this—after all, Ray really had no true defense for his actions. But the constant placing of mistruths—I had to continuously take deep breaths and release my shoulders down and back away from my ears to diffuse the tension of my anger.

I knew what had happened to Kirby. The Spiritual Warrior retreat was five days of being thrown off balance, being told to follow Ray, being deprived of water, food, and sleep to the point where she and the rest of the participants were unable to think clearly and independently. And then they were put into a poorly constructed sweat lodge, led by a man who was not qualified to lead a sweat lodge.

It felt like the jury and everyone watching the trial was being put through a similar regime of bewilderment—like this trial was another iteration of Spiritual Warrior that would break all concrete reality into pieces so that we were unable reconstruct the reality in front of us, the once obvious truth of James Ray's part in these three people's deaths.

By the time Dr. Matthew Dickson took the stand as a witness for the prosecution, I was wound up by this constant beating down of an essential fact that was so clear. Dr. Dickson was the hero we needed at that point. In 2011, he was an emergency doctor in Yuma, Arizona, and as an expert in heat-related illnesses (in a place where extreme heat is a constant in the environment) he gave training to first responders.

He was clean-cut and neat, but not slick like Ray's lawyers. I think that worked well for him—he appeared affable and honest. He had just a hint of a country drawl, clipping the "g" off "-ing" words—just enough that he seemed trustworthy, but not to the detriment of his intelligence.

To that point, so much of the testimony felt confusing, unclear, flat, or simply sad, but not always indicative of criminality. Dr. Dickson's testimony was authoritative and direct. His experience as an instructor was obvious; he spoke directly to jurors and broke down any technical information into everyday language. When *asked to describe a medical term, he'd turn to the jury and say things like, "You guys ready? Okay." He described how heat injuries fall on a continuum, and how the symptoms a person experiences are like markers on a path to the ultimate destination—death—unless the person is removed from the heat and properly treated.*

"[People] talk about heat illness as heat exhaustion and heat stroke like they're two separate things. And they're really not. They're a continuum. If you're heading down that path of heat exhaustion, if you don't correct what you're doing, you're going to become heat stroke, guaranteed. And if you still don't correct it, you're going to die...."

The things that had happened to Kirby and other victims in the sweat lodge that had been covered in previous testimonies—disorientation, nausea and vomiting, labored breathing and gasping, altered mental state, loss of consciousness—clearly lined up with the continuum of heat stroke that Dr. Dickson described.

He also explained how dangerous it is to have a group of people all exposed to the same levels of heat, because they will all start to experience mental status changes. Once that happens, "They're not going to recognize it among each other that something is not right, and they can progress to death."

This lined up with what earlier participants had noted. One of the earlier witnesses was Melissa Phillips. Sheila Polk, the prosecutor, asked Mrs. Phillips if she was aware of changes in her ability to perceive things while in the sweat lodge. "Afterwards, I wondered if I had been as with it as I thought I had been. I wasn't sure.... I was very emotional, shaken up, overheated, not feeling well. I had a headache. I was nauseous. And I didn't know what to trust in my ability to perceive or do anything. I was shaky."

Dr. Dickson was also able to describe, with his rare first-hand knowledge of organophosphates, why he did not attribute the deaths to organophosphates, the alternative theory of death-by-pesticide-poisoning that the defense kept pushing. He was informative in his initial testimony with the prosecution lawyer, but it was really in his cross-examination that we were silently cheering for him. On cross-examination was Truc Do, a young lawyer who'd been dealing with the medical examiners throughout the trial. Do was a recent hire of Munger, Tolles & Olson. Previously, she'd been a prosecutor with the Los Angeles district attorney's office and had an impressive 100% conviction rate for the murder trials she'd overseen, including the trial of music producer Phil Spector. If not for the context in which I got to know Truc Do, I would have had a lot of respect for her.

She'd been irritatingly successful at creating a lot of confusion about the medical examiners' conclusions of heat stroke as the cause of death. But Dr. Dickson took Truc Do down. In response to her relentless questioning of his knowledge, he remained unflappable while still friendly and polite. She was trying to paint a picture (literally, she'd drawn a hypothetical chart on a poster board) of Dr. Dickson as an outlier among the medical professionals in the case, because he had expressed clear certainty of heat stroke as the cause of death. The line of questioning was absurd, because the other medical examiners had in fact concluded that heat stroke was the cause of death, while allowing that there is always a chance of an unknown factor (as any person of science would allow). The "mic drop" moment was when Do blasted Dickson with another line of absurd questions:

Do: So Can you concede the possibility that perhaps one doctor against four, that one doctor is wrong?
Dickson: I still don't see how it's one versus four.
Do: Hypothetically.
Dickson: Hypothetically. Hypothetically what?
Do: Hypothetically you're the only one with this conclusion that is different from Dr. Cutshall, Lyon, and Mosley?
Dickson: Hypothetically pigs can fly, but I'm not going to concede that.

When she persisted, he asked with exasperation, "Are we going to do this all day?" The questions stopped then.

245

I made eye contact with Dr. Dickson when he was finally leaving the stand. I smiled a bit, trying to convey how grateful I was for his testimony. He probably did not know how I was connected to the trial, but I hope he felt the gratitude anyway.

While the trial was ongoing, I knew there were a few bloggers following the case, commenting and providing context and analysis, and lots of conversation on Twitter. I felt like I should have been following all of it, even while I was there, and especially when I wasn't. But I couldn't. When I attended the trial, during recesses and breaks, anyone there from "our team" of family and friends—we'd rehash everything that happened, and sometimes it felt like the entire trial might be resting on a single sentence a witness had spoken on the stand. I can see now why I didn't follow along too closely with the commentary on the trial. It would have driven me mad.

The witness testimony was hard to hear. The trauma that these people endured was evident. My parents, the therapists, could comment professionally on this. I knew it without any professional background. They had experienced something huge. And though it may have been positive for many of them, that others died would only confuse their full understanding of what they had survived.

Throughout the months since Kirby had died, I had heard so many details about what had transpired in that tent. My dad had even laid out the dimensions of the tent in our backyard. After his first time in Arizona at the beginning of the trial, he was frustrated by Ray's lawyers commenting that the tent was so spacious Ray couldn't have heard people in distress. In reality, the tent was about twenty feet in diameter—not actually a great distance.

When he returned to Westtown, he took wooden stakes and his wooden fold-out measuring tool down to the back field. In the spot where my wedding reception had been set up nearly two years earlier, he measured a rough outline of the tent's four corners—north, south, east, west. He took two more stakes and pushed them into the dirt to note where Ray sat and where Kirby sat. She'd been at about *two o'clock in the circle; he was between four and six o'clock. That would have put them about ten to twelve feet apart—certainly not the great distances Li and the other lawyers had demonstrated in their exaggerated explanations to jurors.*

My dad shared this information with Sheila Polk and Bill Hughes. At some point in the proceedings, they did attempt to correct the impressions that Ray's lawyers had put in the juror's minds about the size of the tent. I just wish they could have seen my dad pounding wooden stakes into our back field with a mallet.

As a bystander to any legal proceedings, there's so little over which you have any control, and that is maddening. I had to curb my desire to email or call the prosecution team with my own "ideas." And when chunks of what felt like absolutely pertinent information were deemed inadmissible in court, there was nothing I could do about it other than hope that the prosecution's objections would be upheld.

But regardless of what the jurors heard or didn't hear, or maybe couldn't understand, I saw it clearly—our own discussions with participants, my late-night research about real sweat lodges, my dad's stakes in the ground, and then Dr. Dickson's testimony, which rounded out the science of what had happened to her body, why her cells were so shriveled that her body puffed grotesquely with embalming fluid. I now understood it all in a more complete way. Hearing all of this and the words of other participants, one after another, it put me in that tent, too.

The tent is dark. Small. Like a cave. The grandfathers, the stones, have been baking in an open fire outside. Now they are in a pit in the center of the tent, the heat of that inferno radiating like angry memory. We are listening, have been listening all week. We shaved our hair. We stayed alone. In the desert, without food or water. We relinquish our grasp on ourselves so that we might discover the new self that will bring us beyond whatever keeps us back. We want this. We are ready.

The heat is intense. The steam envelops. The dark cloaks our sense of self—where the boundaries of our own flesh end and those of the people around us begin. We hear James, the leader, the architect. The God who told us who lived, who died.

Kirby died. She lay on the floor so long. She didn't move. She was listening.

The heat reaches inside. It becomes our inside. It reaches into our cells. We sweat. And then we don't. It is so dark.

We grasp at any coolness. The breath that comes from outside when Ray opens the flap of the tent. The light reminds us that we are still alive. But then it is dark again. We cannot turn on the light. That is sacrilege. We listen.

We can do this. We can do this. We can do this. We must push past the feeling that we can't. That is what we have been told. We are listening.

It is the hottest hot we have ever known. We dig our fingers into the dirt. To feel the coolness that existed before. We lean down to breathe the memory of cool. The mud swells under our fingernails, stretches the connection between keratin and skin. It aches.

Why are we here? Who are we? Some of us are vomiting. Some of us urinate. Some of us are screaming. We are supposed to be here, wherever here is.

We hear noises. We hear struggle. We are all struggling. We ask for help. We are told to wait. To be quiet. We listen. We cannot do anything else.

We hear gurgles. They sound strange. Also, familiar. They are us. They are what we feel. The gurgles are where we all end.

We are told to wait. We cannot worry about that. Her. Who?

Kirby, someone says.

We worry about ourselves. When is this over? Have we learned? Are we reborn?

My sister's death was horrible. She was cooked. It was torture.

But I knew this. I had known this from the beginning. We can't die, too. She died. We had to keep going, to do what she would have done if she'd lived. It's a hard charge; she lived So Big.

We keep going.

Ginny

Jean and I traveled to Arizona on May 9, leaving the airport in Newburgh, transferring in Philadelphia, and finally arriving in Phoenix. Once again, the Murphys invited us to stay with them. As I anticipated returning to the courtroom, I felt "beaten up" by everything that had transpired in the past few months and was grateful that Jean was with me for this trip. My youngest daughter is a quietly formidable person: sweet, gentle, smart, and strong. I felt braver being with her. At Mike's suggestion, we traveled through Sedona to view the beautiful red rocks one day after the trial, the last place Kirby had been. It was sadly beautiful and somehow fitting, dazzling. Being with Jean was pure gift, a special time to talk, share, commiserate, and vent. In my trial journal, there are scribbled notes, silent conversations between Jean and myself: comments on testimony, outrage over a ruling, jokes about a defense lawyer. It reads like the notebook of two grammar school kids, best friends, exchanging comments on the teacher. Her presence was empowering and comforting.

May 10 began with a pre-argument before the judge concerning the testimony from a medical doctor who had attended Spiritual Warrior in 2008. He had warned that people were suffering from heat exhaustion and predicted that if this activity continued someone would die of heat stroke—surely, a spike in Ray's coffin. But then came the ruling: his testimony was inadmissible. The defense argued that the court had already ruled that prior events were not relevant to this trial. Manslaughter requires the proof of prior knowledge of recklessness. Was this not proof? Why can't the jury hear the truth of Ray's reckless disregard for his clients' safety? Why?

We heard more details of the sweat lodge ceremony from other participants. The constant reliving of Kirby's final hours felt like the relentless scorching of the Arizona sun, an intensifying of the inhumane manner in which she died. The various coroners testified, and their testimony introduced doubt concerning inconsistent language on the three death certificates. Confusion about reports explaining symptoms and injuries from area doctors who treated victims following the sweat lodge was advanced. One coroner changed his mind numerous times and finally decided that secondary processes might have or could have contributed; therefore, "heatstroke" as the cause of death was inconclusive. Massive organ failure was listed as the cause of Liz's death, but somehow the reason for why her organs failed, namely "heat stroke," was omitted from the death certificate. Some local doctors who examined those taken to area hospitals were confounded and confused about the cause of the symptoms victims were presenting. Defense attorneys used the lack of absolute clarity to suggest that something else besides the heat could have caused the deaths. Confusion and doubt—that was the defense. In the Crystal Hall, late on the evening of October 8, there was a two-second recording of an unidentified EMT saying, in response to participants asking what had happened, that "maybe 'organophosphates' or carbon monoxide were involved." The defense used the tape to sow doubt. There was no proof that organophosphates or any poisonous materials were in the soil, air, on the covering of the lodge, or found in the wood heating the rocks. But, time and again, the theory was pushed as the cause of death, not the extreme heat. "Reasonable doubt," they argued.

I could hardly breathe as I listened to this bizarre legal wrangling. In my dreams, I struggled throughout the trial to "get out of that tent." Months of testimony from countless witnesses seemed as limitless as the sky. I tried to absorb this strange story.

I was an alien in this place, an outlander. The court testimony, carried by Court TV, which numerous friends were watching every day, was a persistent, never-ending assault.

Finally, on May 10 and 11, Dr. Dickson put the matter to rest: Kirby, James, and Liz had clearly died of heat stroke. For the first time, the jury was hearing truthful testimony. I felt a flicker of hope that justice might be served.

Thursday morning, May 12, began with the prosecutor petitioning that I be permitted to testify. However, the defense argued that a family member's statements could not be admissible. I think she wanted me to explain the condition of Kirby's body when she arrived in New York to help clarify the cause of death as heat exhaustion—severe dehydration leading ultimately to heat stroke. The defense won the argument—another defeat. We were drowning in omissions and confusing contradictions.

Later, that same day, Sarah, the daughter of the fire tenders Ted and Debbie Mercer, testified. On the day of the sweat lodge, she was seventeen years old. She helped her parents during the ceremony, providing water or fruit to participants exiting the tent. She reported that Ray definitely encouraged people to stay in the tent. "He would just kind of stress the point that this is what you're here for and you should be in here and staying in the sweat lodge. I remember him saying that you are... you are more than your body. You are your mind...." When told people were unconscious, he said, "...something about that being a good thing. And they asked if we should do something or take them out. And he said, no. There was one more round left. They'll be okay."

During defense attorney Thomas Kelly's redirect of Sara's testimony, he asked about people being able to leave:

Kelly: You would agree with me that whenever a person wanted to leave the sweat lodge, he or she would leave the sweat lodge; correct?

Mercer: Correct.

Kelly: And you'd also—

Mercer: If they were able to

Kelly: Pardon me?

Mercer: If they were able to.

Kelly: If they were able to?

Mercer: Like, on their own.

Kelly immediately changed the line of questioning, but Sara later clarified with Sheila Polk: "If they were physically able to. Like, some people were trying to leave, but they couldn't and had to be drug [sic] out and... the people who were unconscious, obviously they would have left if they had the ability to."

She was confused, unable to do anything other than cool off the people who were desperately crawling out or being dragged out of the lodge. There was total chaos outside the tent, especially at the end when Ray emerged and gave a victory sign. Fifteen minutes later, she looked into the tent and saw three bodies inside. She and her mother asked Ray if they could open the back of the tent to pull them out. Ray said that "it would be sacrilegious." Sarah and her mother did it anyway. They pulled Kirby, James, and another person out of the tent. She had to walk away when her dad started performing CPR on the three people who were "unconscious with their faces all funny colors."

The defense grilled her about the testimony she provided at 8:00 pm the night of the ceremony. They pointed to possible discrepancies in statements she made the next morning. I wanted to scream, "Leave her alone! She saved people! She dragged James and Kirby out while your man did nothing. She saved another person's life. What did Ray do?"

If Kirby had been noticed earlier, if she had been dragged out or discovered immediately, maybe she would be alive. My heart broke for this young woman, another traumatized victim of this tragedy. She talked about being afraid, getting sick when she learned people had died, crying all night, not wanting to go back to school and, ultimately, leaving Angel Valley where she had lived with her parents for a year. I cried for Sarah.

Delays, accusations of prosecutorial misconduct, and motions for mistrial peppered the trial for months. Initially, the proceedings were carried by Court TV, but after months of tedious, boring wrangling, they lost interest. I'm sure that was a deliberate tactic by the defense.

On June 4, a memorial was held for my nephew Logan, two weeks after he was severed from life support. Jean traveled from Canada for the service on Long Island to stand with her cousins in loving support, knowing this kind of loss only too well.

George wanted to return to Arizona for the conclusion of the trial. After rearranging plane tickets three times due to delays, he was scheduled to fly June 13, the Monday after the memorial. I was torn. Work obligations piled up. Jean and I decided he shouldn't go alone, so she volunteered to accompany him— another trip to Arizona. We thought the defense would end its closing arguments on Thursday and the jury would begin deliberations on Friday, but Luis Li, the defense lawyer, spoke for eight and a half hours, repeating himself, insulting the state, the investigation, reiterating endlessly their unsubstantiated "organophosphate" defense. I was enraged as I watched at home with my friend Terri. Then, I went to the airport to pick up George at midnight.

Jean

*A*s hard as confronting all of these details was, it was necessary—a compulsion, almost. When the unexpected chance to
go again with my dad in June came up, I wanted to go. I had been
visiting my family in New York, following the death of my cousin Logan. His memorial service brought me back to Long Island,
where we'd had Kirby's East Coast memorial and dropped her ashes into the bay. Although we said I was going so my dad wasn't
by himself, it was for me, too. I don't think my brain had enough
energy to fully reckon with the death of my cousin and perhaps
somewhere in my heart was the knowing that I didn't want to leave
my dad yet either.

Sedona—there is something about that place, a magnetism. The
whole self-helpy, crystal-wielding mysticism industry that exists in
Sedona is an obvious outcrop in this landscape of geologic formations
and Mars-like mountains, so red the color bleeds out beyond the
lines of the rock, tinting the air around it. There's a vibration to the
beauty. People claim that vortexes are hidden in the rocks, and it's
not hard to imagine getting sucked into a place like this and depos-
ited in some alternate reality.

The power of that landscape was grounding—something I could
connect to, a reminder that we can still appreciate something beautiful and wonderful, even when we are very sad. I don't think I knew
it at the time, but now I realize I drew some strength from that. I
wanted to be there again.

I felt like I had an important job when I attended the trial. God,
obviously it was serious. It was a mission. What happened to Kirby
was sad. It could leave a person broken and weak. But I wanted to
project power and strength. I wanted James Ray to see and feel that
he had fucked with the wrong people. And I wanted everyone else to

see not just grief in the family of Kirby Brown, but determination. Maybe I wanted them to see Kirby in us.

So, as a start, I wanted to look good, put together. But because this Arizona trip was not planned for me, I had no appropriate clothing. The day before the flight, my mom and I ran around Middletown, NY, looking for a "courthouse wardrobe." TJ Maxx and Kohl's were a letdown; naturally, Target delivered. I remember exactly what I got: one Diane von Furstenberg-style, black and white shirtdress (but $35 Mossimo); a pair of ankle-length white slacks and a shimmery fawn-colored short-sleeved long cardigan sweater; a pair of nude peep-toe pumps that worked with both. Despite downsizing my wardrobe, I can't seem to give these pieces up. They were like a security blanket at such a strange time in my life. They helped me feel tall. I was self-conscious when I attended the trial. I knew James Ray and his lawyers knew who I was and I wanted them to see me—cool, in control, maybe even a bit intimidating.

My mom had warned me ahead of time that my dad would probably want to eat at the same restaurants he'd already been to on previous trips. My dad has always had an excellent sense of direction and memory for routes, but it did feel weird that he had familiar places in this unfamiliar town—the last place Kirby had existed.

He took me to the Red Planet Diner. Playing on the red rocks theme, it was all aliens and outer space kitsch. But man, the huge plate of refried black beans over rice I ordered was really good. This meal is now on our regular rotation in my home, with sliced avocado and sour cream on the side.

This time, my dad and I stayed in a suite in a Travelodge. While we were there, I helped plan a trip to Scotland. It had been a dream of Kirby's, shared by my parents, that we would all take a trip to Scotland to experience our ancestral heritage together. The full family reunion would have to wait a few years due to the birth of new grandchildren, but Mike and I were excited for this trip with my parents, and some other family and friends they'd recruited to fill the extra rooms in our rental house.

With all of the trial mayhem, though, booking their flights had been put off, so on one of our first nights, after we'd gotten back to the hotel for the night, I opened up my computer and helped my dad solidify the details of the trip: flights, train schedules, membership to the National Trust of Scotland for discount entrance to historic sites. I love travelling. My fingers flit across the keyboard and, in the clicking of the keystrokes, I hear my feet on the cobblestones of a Scottish close. It was a welcome diversion. With the synthetic carpet of the hotel suite under foot and the frustrations of this trial twisting in my gut, I imagined crumbling castles and Highland mists.

But in the daytimes, it was back to the trial. We were close to the end. No more witness testimony, just James Ray's defense team nit-picking the instructions that would be given to jurors before they heard the closing arguments. I kept grinding my heel into the courtroom floor, listening to this exhausting list of demands which felt like the defense contriving to delay the closing arguments as much as possible.

Even Judge Darrow seemed exhausted as he dismissed us during one of the periods of these endless arguments. I went out into the hall. In what felt like the most appropriately strange detail, the courthouse's neighbor is the Out of Africa Wildlife Park. Lions roam around in their cages just a few hundred yards beyond the huge picture windows outside the courtroom. I imagine people who work at the courthouse must hear every possible joke about throwing convicted criminals to the lions.

That little zoo was a natural focal point during breaks in the proceedings. I was standing there, looking out to the sandy ground and low brush, when Luis Li came and stood next to me. In the weird and windy desert, a miniature cyclone picked up dust and twisted briefly in between the courthouse parking lot and the lion grounds.

I hardly registered it, though, for the rage pulsing through me while standing next to the guy defending such a callous criminal—

the guy whose incessant arguments seemed to be grinding us all into some sort of apathetic pulp. So when Li turned to me and exclaimed, "Did you see that?" I didn't have more than a stare for him in response. What a dick.

Chapter 8

**❝ Where there is light, there is dark. The sun is setting
into the mountain. Thank you for your warmth today.
Thank you for the glistening of nature....
Oh sweet sun, have a safe journey. We shall be
together again tomorrow. ❞**

—Kirby's Vision Quest Journal

Jean

*When the closing arguments finally began, we got to hear Sheila
Polk deliver the prosecution's statements. Under the burden
of proof and the defense team's prickliness, Polk and the other prosecutors seemed to tiptoe a lot. I don't blame them. They couldn't display the same fire I was feeling while listening to it all. But I worried
that amid the sometimes-over-the-top exclamations of the defense
lawyers, the prosecutors' bland deliveries of important information
would be lost. Like the desert itself, there was so much detail tucked
into the hidden dips and cracks in the flatness. I feared that the jurors
wouldn't be able to see all of that.*

*Polk's closing arguments were an antidote to this worry for
me. She aggregated all of the information about what had actually
happened to the victims, all the reasons why the defense's alternative theories were ridiculous when looking at the "big picture,"
the statements made by participants about how they'd been intim-
idated and conditioned to listen to Ray. Without too much drama,
but with enough confidence, she pulled all of these threads together.*

I had to hope that the jurors would see it all as clearly as I did.

Nevertheless, it was all very satisfying; and, yet, startling. Recordings of Kirby had been played earlier in the trial and were a recurring source of irritation to the defense. They'd been arguing about the admissibility of her "testimony" all along, given that they couldn't cross-examine her. It had been allowed with some caveats to the listening jurors. I had heard these recordings before, but not like this—her picture projected up above the witness stand, her voice echoing through the large courtroom.

I squeezed my hands together in between my legs, pressing my knuckles into the varnished oak benches. My skin prickled and I looked up to the ceiling, trying not to show too much emotion. To hear her voice, her ironic laugh, laughing at herself. Her own incredulity, the touch of West Coast lightness that had been hers even before she'd followed her particular manifest destiny to California and Baja. And then the way she lulls you in with gentle openness before delivering the thing she really wants you to hear.

She was talking about her experiences during the Samurai game and then on her vision quest in the desert, the last event before they had entered the sweat lodge. She talked about what she felt and learned.

"The dead are with us…," she said. "Our loved ones that have passed are with us."

Then, she described how she had a vision of our Great-Uncle Bob, a Christian Brother who'd given her this advice before, advice she'd carried with her like a mantra but needed to hear again:"Keep things simple."

I kept absolutely still. I didn't blink, but the tears collected on the rims of my eyes and fell down my cheeks anyway.

We did hear a bit of the closing arguments by Li (we did not hear all of it because he dragged on for over eight hours). It was clear that Ray's lawyers were nervous about a few things when facing a jury of regular people from Arizona. Ray was an out-of-towner—a flashy, rich guy who'd exploited the pull of their hometown and damaged its reputation with his weird, borderline-cult, woo-woo "retreat." And his lawyers were no better—Los Angeles big shots trying to defend all of it. So they took the libertarian American values tack—that the government was trying to blame a good man for the free will of other people, the choices they had made which unfortunately got them killed. James Ray has parroted this defense of himself in the years since the trial.

Evidently, it didn't really hold up with the jurors of Yavapai County. They found him guilty of the lesser charge of negligent homicide, rather than the higher charge of reckless manslaughter. The essential difference between these charges is the question of whether or not Ray knew he was putting people in danger. Had the prosecution been able (or allowed) to show that Ray knew he was endangering people's lives but moved forward anyway, he would have been convicted of the higher charge of manslaughter. The lesser charge of negligent homicide indicated that he was guilty of failing to see the obvious risks he had put before his customers.

I was happy that the jurors had found Ray guilty of something. But I did wonder how they would feel when they heard about facts that had been excluded from the case—facts that would have made Ray's prior understanding of the risk obvious, like the fact that participants of previous years' sweat lodges had been injured. And, sure enough, some of the jurors did speak out after the trial. As it turns out, eight of the twelve jurors wanted to convict him on the higher charger, while four did not feel that Ray was fully aware of the risks to the participants. Needing a unanimous decision, they settled on a conviction for the lesser charge.

One juror noted in an interview after the trial that they should have been told about people who had been harmed in previous Ray sweat lodges and the death of Colleen Conaway at a Ray even just months before the 2009 Spiritual Warrior. That information likely would have led to a unanimous decision by the jury on the higher charge. It was frustrating, so frustrating, to hear this, but not unexpected—I already knew how hard it was to get one's head around everything that had happened at that retreat, even with all the information. I'd been grappling with it for nearly two years at that point.

I cannot remember exactly where I was or how I heard the news when the conviction came through. I do remember waiting for the jury to decide and suddenly realizing in my waiting how much I was, in fact, counting on their decision. I felt quite uncertain at that point. So the conviction, even on a lesser charge, was definitely a relief. I watched video of the conviction. They read the charges related to Kirby's death first. As I saw Ray's face tighten on the guilty verdict, I thought about how the name "Kirby Brown" will probably haunt him for the rest of his life.

The conviction came on June 22, 2011. Throughout the trial, I had been writing consistently in my own blog—not about the trial itself, but just my own reflections. The process of writing that blog was an important lifeline. It helped me move forward. I was taking the last words I'd heard from Kirby, her encouragement as I finished my master's thesis, putting them into something for myself that could move me beyond the place of sadness in grief.

The other step forward, or away, was our trip to Scotland, the trip I'd helped my dad book. I had never been to Scotland or anywhere in the UK before. Mike and I took five days in London before meeting up with my parents in Scotland. Some of our friends also met us there.

I'd developed an early love of travel from family cross-country camping trips and especially after my first international trip to Italy in high school. Travelling is often a deeply reflective experience for me. Seeing a new place, encountering different food and climates and voices always helps me look back on my own home and wonder if it's where I'm really meant to be.

While we were in Scotland, my dad's cousin Robbin, our native host, had rented a Sprinter van to take us into the Highlands. Another cousin of my dad's, Stuart, our family bagpiper, played an album of pipe music in the van for us while we twisted around stark highland hills and the lochs that pool in the perfect u-shaped valleys between them. When the moving notes of *Highland Cathedral* played, I got choked up. A single bagpipe starts the song, sliding across the mournful but uplifting melody with a string accompaniment behind it, and the full emotion finally breaks in as an entire company of pipers and orchestra take it up toward the end of the song. Stuart had played *Highland Cathedral* at my wedding, and I thought back to that bright day and how much fun we had all had—together and complete.

We traveled up as high up as Mallaig. While there's more of Scotland north of this town tucked into the West Coast, the twisty, cozy fishing village felt like it was perched on the top of the world, a lone finger reaching out into the gray Atlantic. Sometimes places like this can feel lonely and cold. But in that place, I felt energy—as if from there I could jump off, fly over the mists, and glide out to all the rest of everything.

The trial brought me back into the tent and I could have stayed there, with her. If Kirby had lived, though, she would not have stayed in the tent forever. She would have broken out. Like Beverley, she would have spoken out about what she had endured and why nobody should have died. She would have been a force. God, to think about what Kirby would have been on the witness stand! I honestly think the outcome of the trial could have been different with testimony from Kirby.

And what would she have done after? She would have faced life with renewed energy, if a person could have even more excitement for life than she already did. Sometimes I connect to that energy, like she's trying to feed it to me, to remind me to get out of the tent even when she didn't. I felt it there in Mallaig.

Ginny

My stomach was in knots after listening on TV to much of Sheila's final statements. How would the jury vote? How long would they deliberate? Around 6:00 pm on June 22, as I was finishing my Anger Management class, my phone blew up. The verdict was in. I dismissed my class and hungrily reached for the phone. With shaking hands, I read "Manslaughter: NOT guilty. Negligent Homicide: GUILTY. Three counts."

By the time I arrived at home, the local TV station had just left; Bob Magnanini was there along with Ed and Liz. We had press statements ready for either outcome which had already been released as the various outlets called for our reaction. I couldn't sleep that night, feeling happy and relieved that this was finally over, yet very angry and upset that Kirby, James, and Liz's deaths were being treated like a drunk driving case. Unable to sleep, George and I talked and cried from 3:00 am until we rose at 5:30 am.

But the trial was not finished. It was not over. Before sentencing, there would be aggravation and mitigation hearings. These hearings, conducted under the rules of evidence, were designed to protect the accused.

On June 28, I was back in Arizona to testify at the aggravation hearing. Prior to the trip, I spoke with Sheila Polk. What could I say in my testimony? Facts only—not my take on Ray's fraudulent behavior, his ignoring repeated warnings that Kirby needed help, his not answering requests for help; not his lying about training, experience, credentials; not his encouraging followers to believe Kirby and James chose their deaths. FACTS. There were many that certainly screamed manslaughter in my eyes. She explained the rules: if the jury found for two out of three aggravating factors (impact on victims, personal financial gain, the participants being in a unique position of trust) they could then recommend to the judge to sentence above the presumptive sentence of two and a half years per count. We talked for two hours on June 24, discussing the emotional impact on our family; the emotional impact of the trial; Kirby's trust in Ray; how we heard of her death; my calls to others to find out what had happened; our experience of Ray; my attendance at Harmonic Wealth with Kirby in March, 2009, and George attending the same event in San Diego with her in May; Kirby's fiercely independent personality; and Ray's phone call on October 13. I could not report anything that was told to me by another person. I could not say I knew he was not cooperating with the police or share what I was told he and his staff did following the sweat lodge ceremony. I could not share what I believed happened, what I would like the jury to do, or my personal psychological analysis of Ray as a narcissistic psychopath.

I could not believe I was on a plane again, headed for this legal debacle. I was confident I could state the case clearly, articulately. I was determined to do my best. I had repeated and rehearsed possible answers for days while driving to and from work.

From 9:00 am until noon, the defense lawyers engaged in oral arguments debunking the very definitions of the aggravators. How to prove trust? Financial gain must be proven to be a direct cause of the crime. Instructions to the jury were debated amidst admittedly vague and unclear definitions. I left the courtroom, my head spinning, unclear as to what could be proven, said, asked, or testified to. We were instructed to return at 1:20 pm.

Andrea, Liz Neuman's daughter, was called to the stand first and she explained the impact of her mother's death on her whole family; her grandmother was left without a caretaker, her younger brothers were angry and lost. She, newly married, was left without her mother to witness the birth of grandchildren.

Alyssa, James Shore's wife, had not been present for any of the testimony. I'd spoken with Alyssa often during the trial. I knew she felt conflicted, not wanting to leave her traumatized children to travel to the trial from Minnesota. However, she was now here to explain the devastation to herself and her children caused by her husband's death. Being with Jane, Lily, Andrea, and Alyssa, I felt that the pure clarity of our painful losses was in stark contrast with the convoluted malevolence and the relentless confusing, complex legal wrangling of the trial.

I expected Sheila to call Alyssa first, so when my name was called before hers, I suddenly didn't know what to do with my glasses and shawl. Fumbling, hands clammy and body shaking, I struggled to walk up to the witness stand. When I was asked about our children, I blanked, suddenly unsure and trying desperately to accurately remember their ages. She asked me about Kirby. I began to relax a bit. I explained our exposure to Ray through the Harmonic Wealth two-day seminar I had attended with Kirby in March 2009. I described the effects of her death on her siblings and the nieces and nephews who would never know their Aunt Kirby. I shared how we were informed of her death by a state trooper.

I began to explain my desperate search to find out what actually happened and the phone calls I made. The defense screamed "Objection!" Rattled, I lost my train of thought, feeling lost and all jumbled. Then, I tried to explain how difficult it had been to constantly rearrange work obligations, to attend the trial, and the frustrations of enduring the whole court process. Again, "Objection!" The defense claimed that my statement was impugning Ray's right to a fair trial. "Mistrial" was what I heard next. The defense wanted a mistrial because of my testimony.

The lawyers continued to argue. I was simply dismissed, unable to say anything else. I was done—gagged again! I wanted to show how Ray had manipulated Kirby into trusting and believing in him. How he put her in a compromised state. How he had not responded to requests for help. Why couldn't I state the truth? Be her voice? Instead, I was dismissed, silenced. Had I blown my chance? I would dream about that exchange, replay it in my head a million times, and scream in my car until I was hoarse. I left the courtroom, ran into the room set aside by victim services for our personal use, threw my journal book against the wall and screamed, "The fucking bastard! Why can't the jury hear what happened? Why can't I explain? What the fuck?!" My frustration and rage overpowered me.

Pam Moreton, our victim advocate, hugged me and calmed me down. "Ginny, this is his game. He's just doing his job."

The jury was deadlocked on the aggravators. They came back into the court looking for more direction, better definitions, clarification, additional instructions. What a mess! The defense and the judge had created so much confusion and doubt, it was maddening. Finally, after hours, the outcome of their deliberations determined the maximum sentence Ray could receive was six years, the minimum was one year or probation. After the jury left the room, the defense lawyer from Arizona continued to accuse the prosecution of misconduct, lying, manipulation, petitioning for mistrial.

Exiting the courtroom, with heads down, not one juror looked at us. The foreman, however, wished to speak with us in another room. I thanked him for the sacrifice they had made to sit for months listening to the defense's arcane arguments—I think I said "bullshit"—day after day. The foreman was tearful and apologetic. He explained that they were deadlocked at eight to four for manslaughter. The only way to end the deliberations was to convict on the negligent homicide charges. They did their best within the constraints of the law, wanting a better outcome, but needing to apply the standards of the law to make decisions.

I was reminded of Bob Magnanini's statement: "This is a court of law, not justice."

Mika, Bob, and Deborah gave interviews for the press outside the courthouse. I was too drained to even think.

On the plane returning home, I realized my life would never be the same. What's next? What is this death calling me to address? Am I to expose new age bullshit spirituality that is polluted with irresponsible self-proclaimed gurus? I don't want to preach danger or be totally negative. Kirby gave her head, her heart, her trust, and her savings to improve her life, professionally, personally, spiritually. But she was manipulated and deceived. Can her death save others' lives? Can her life and the way she lived inspire others? That seemed ironic: to urge others to seek, take risks, grow, even though Kirby had lost her life doing just that. If Kirby had survived, would she have seen the difference between honestly seeking to improve your life and being manipulated and deceived? I believe so. I think she would have been outraged at Ray's false, exaggerated claims of training and experience to lead his events.

Within two weeks, I was again on a plane, this time leaving for Los Cabos to be with Kate after she delivered her second son, McCloy. She is a wonderful mother. I watched her with Angus, two and a half, and this beautiful newborn. I was proud of her, but in my new reality, pride and happiness were mixed with feeling devastated, sad, powerless, while wanting to be supportive. So jumbled, so many conflicting feelings and memories—I tried to focus on simply being with Kate, watching Angus, changing diapers, fixing meals, being with my daughter because her big sister could not be there.

I wondered when the tears would stop. As I sat on the return flight home to work, I started writing a victim impact statement. I thought about how life seemed so totally bizarre.

George and I planned a family trip to Scotland for the summer of 2011. The prosecutor assured us that we would not have to reschedule our vacation as the trial droned on endlessly. While this was to be an entire Brown family vacation to introduce our children to their heritage, other forces were at work. Our son's wife, Kory, was pregnant, unable to travel, and our daughter couldn't travel with her newborn from Mexico. Needing to escape, we decided to invite other family and friends to fill the flat we had rented in Ayr on the west coast of Scotland.

And so the summer began with a verdict, the birth of McCloy, and an amazing trip to Scotland with Jean, her husband, some of their friends who were traveling in Europe, as well as our good friends Ed and Liz, my brother Bill and his wife, George's sister Kay and her husband—all who had traveled to Arizona as part of the trial watch. George's cousin Sheila and her husband, Roy, also joined our adventure. Before there would be a sentencing, another child, Quinn Kirby, was born on September 6 in Connecticut. Miracles encircling heartbreak, joy amidst sorrow, love encompassing loss—the bookends of the days with which we are gifted: life and death.

During that summer, we remained on alert, waiting for when we would have to return to Arizona. In preparation for our next trip to Arizona for Ray's sentencing, I would write, rewrite, talk out, scream (in the car) everything I wanted to say in my victim impact statement. I had dreams and wrote countless drafts, trying to properly state my outrage and heartbreak.

We were informed by the prosecution that there would be a "mitigation" hearing to advise the judge on his sentencing decisions in late September, after which there would be victim impact statements and the final sentencing. The purpose of this rarely used mitigation hearing was to provide character witnesses for Ray to seek leniency. I was to testify again. The September dates were canceled, rescheduled for October, which were then canceled again. We were finally on a plane to Arizona on November 7, 2011. Maybe this nightmare would soon be over!

The prosecution was entitled to present witnesses to discourage a light sentence, although the trial itself and the aggravation hearing had already set the stage for a very mild consequence for Ray's recklessness.

I wanted to be focused and strong, despite feeling beaten and battered, frustrated and furious. I practiced speaking. I wrote down my thoughts, ideas, arguments, explanations that might impact the judge's decisions. If Kirby was here what would she be saying? Ray was dangerous. What happened could have been prevented. He knew what he was doing. He was reckless. I think he was convinced that these extreme experiences would bring him adulation.

The first testimony for the hearing was of a witness called by the prosecution: an expert from Outward Bound stressing the importance of risk management, responsible leadership, and proper training when engaging in "experiential education," i.e., teachings using physical challenges.

A past JRI employee was called to give witness to the lack of staff training and confusion after past disasters where people had been harmed. She described the staff environment as extremely competitive, with Ray often putting someone on the "chopping block," who would then be doomed to failure. But, on cross-examination, she declared, "Everything happens for a reason. There is always good and bad." It sounded to me that she was saying, "What happens just needs to be accepted."

Then, lead detective Ross Diskin testified to all the areas where Ray was not properly trained. These statements brought forth angry objections from the defense. I never thought that facts could be construed as "hearsay."

My turn. This time, I was more prepared when called to the stand. The prosecutor established some background. I described Kirby's embalmed body which showed severe dehydration.

Then, Mr. Kelly, the Arizona defense lawyer who had objected to my statements at the aggravation hearing, started his grilling, after making a few placating comments.

"Didn't you receive a settlement, proving Mr. Ray's remorse?" he asked me.

"No, actually I received money from Mr. Ray's underinsured insurance policies. This was not a sign of remorse. There were seventeen people on the suit to share that settlement."

I was about to add, "His money is paying you," but he quickly asked: "Didn't you take your lawyer's advice when the settlement was decided?"

"Yes."

"Well, since you took your lawyer's advice, don't you think Mr. Ray had a responsibility to take his lawyer's advice to leave the scene on October 8?"

"No, I think Mr. Ray had a responsibility to his participants who paid and trusted him, and whom he abandoned."

These are the two answers I remember because I sensed him stumbling after my responses. I felt a small perverse thrill, a tiny victory, a sense of satisfaction that he had not cowed me as he had tried to do to so many other witnesses.

The defense then began a parade of people who claimed Ray had changed their lives by his teachings. I have always adhered to the dictum that, "When the student is ready, the teacher shows up." I have no doubt that Ray has positively impacted some people who were ready to change their lives. He is a persuasive, authoritative, charismatic speaker. That, however, does not preclude that he (and others like him in the self-help industry) administer advice for which they are not properly trained; that dangerous, unsafe behaviors which can be harmful or even fatal to participants are encouraged. A brilliant charlatan can still be inspiring and motivating.

It was torture to sit through those testimonials. I am sure there are people who admire and have been helped by Ray, but this trial was about three people who are dead. And when Luis Li summarized, pointing out to the judge that Ray had helped thousands and only a few had been harmed, I wanted to scream, "So, to you these three lives are statistically insignificant!"

That night, about fifteen of us—friends and family members of the Browns, the Shores, the Neumans—went to a Mexican restaurant not far from the Camp Verde Courthouse. This tragedy had brought us all together and we ate and drank, toasting new connections and our hopes for justice. Sitting in the restaurant, I felt optimistic and encouraged that all who were gathered would survive this tragedy. Despite being hurt and dented—as George liked to describe our condition when someone asked, "How are you doing?"—we would survive.

We were staying in a hotel in Prescott to be near the courthouse where the final sentencing would be declared. The night before the actual sentencing, I struggled to write the victim impact statement I had been practicing for two years. I wanted to create the right tone, not just that of a reactive, crazed mother, but the attitude of a rational thoughtful woman, grieving, but determined to bring something positive from this horrific injustice. Liz Holst traveled to Arizona with us. I read my statement to her on Thursday night.

She said, "Ginny, you don't even sound angry."

I had been working so hard to maintain my "public face" and was trying so hard to control my emotions that my statement hardly reflected any. With her help, I rewrote some of my statement to more appropriately reflect my anger. It is ironic that the televised clips of my statement only show me looking somewhat deranged, screaming at Ray, "That lodge was just too damn hot!"

I read Bobby and Kate's statements and they showed Jean's video comments. Their sadness and anger magnified my own heartbreak.

After everyone read their statements, Ray responded tearfully that he was so sorry this had happened, that he may have made mistakes in judgment. Luis Li apologized for making Kirby's death sound statistically insignificant but wanted the judge to appreciate that this was an unintended "accident."

Those comments were to be expected, but for me, the final indignity was Judge Darrow apologizing for giving Ray any time in prison. He explained that given the incredible impact of these deaths on the victims, he had to sentence him to two years for each victim. At the time he made the pronouncement, there was confusion about whether Ray had to serve the term concurrently or consecutively: six years or two. We left the room thinking it was six, only to discover it would be two years. I must admit, I felt some relief that it wasn't just a probation sentence.

When we left the courthouse, reporters and cameras greeted us, awaiting our reaction to the sentence. I remember responding that some time in prison certainly was some measure of accountability. We also thanked the Native American community for their support during the trial and cautioned against any backlash on the proper traditional sweat lodge ceremony that Ray had misused and corrupted. After our remarks, Ivan Lewis, who had been in the courtroom almost every day during the trial, presented us with a beautiful dream catcher that had been made for us in honor of Kirby. He explained that a prayer ceremony had been offered for her spirit. I was filled with an incredible sense of wonder and profound thankfulness for the people that Kirby was now bringing into our lives.

We all gathered for a final luncheon at a local restaurant in Prescott. It was a lovely warm room and the glass of wine felt luxurious. As the light streamed across the table, I could feel the relief, exhaustion, and tears. We all were so grateful to Sheila and her team who, despite all odds, had won the case. Earlier, Sheila, Bill Hughes, and Ross Diskin had presented George and me with small, silver gift bags for our family, containing Kirby's last words—the CD recording of what had been played during the trial. I was overwhelmed by such thoughtfulness. This was the woman and the Yavapai county team who had valiantly fought for us, for over a year of their lives, to bring some measure of justice to our loss.

Jean

*O*ur Scotland trip was the event that inspired us to leave Vankleek
Hill and move to Toronto. Our explorations invigorated us. They
reminded us of our love of travel and the dreams we'd always had
for ourselves. We loved our house and the town it was in, but it was
all tarnished by the events that had happened just days after we'd
moved there. It had served as a safe haven, but then it was time to
move on. So we did.

We made plans to open a jewelry store in Toronto. I had experience managing my in-laws' store and they were a family connection
to the stock. We made a few trips to Toronto to find a location and
find a place to live.

Vankleek Hill's housing market is a slow one, but somewhat
miraculously, it seemed, we sold our little house to the woman who
lost out to us when we'd bought it two years before. We packed our
whole house into a U-Haul. Mike drove the truck, I drove our car
with things like the Datura painting, our wedding china carefully
packed in the back seat, a ten-inch wooden Buddha carving that I
had taken from Kirby's apartment. After taking just a few steps, this
was a huge leap.

It was a new beginning, a chance to start again after living
through something soul crushing, an important leap away from comfort, quiet, and a stillness that threatened stagnancy. Our store did
fail, ultimately. The rent was high and the timing, just emerging from
recession, wasn't kind. But the move was, overall, a very positive one.

In Toronto, we rented a small apartment eight hundred meters
down the street from our new store, on a prominent midtown commercial stretch. The property manager laughed when our huge truck
pulled up to the busy sidewalk in front of our new home—an apartment building with our fourth floor junior one-bedroom apartment,

the cheapest place we could find within walking distance of our shop location. During that first month, November 2011, we were so busy: buying displays, patching and painting walls, setting up our computer system, and everything else that went into setting up a retail operation.

We did a lot of the work ourselves, but on some jobs, we had to hire professionals. On November 18, the day James Ray was convicted, the electricians were there installing the new track lighting we'd bought. Luckily, the Internet was already up and running and I was able to follow the sentence hearing streaming on Court TV.

I had my computer propped up on a white, foil-finish pillar we'd purchased from a store that had just closed next to us. I plugged in my earphones so I could listen amid the zips of the electricians' drills. The cord of the headphones kept me attached, so that I could not run away with disbelief or incredulity or disgust. It was a line that pulled me back to the ground when the surreality of the experience set my head afloat.

Zip, zip. "How does this look? You wanted two lines down this side, right?" the electrician asked me. He was a handsome guy with short, ginger hair—a young entrepreneur, like us.

"Yes, exactly," I said. I turned back to the screen.

At that point, we'd feared that Ray might get probation. One of the witnesses who had testified on his behalf during the sentencing phase was herself a probation officer who claimed he'd be a "perfect candidate" for probation.

But three people were dead. How would that be justice?

Maybe I'd known he would be convicted of something, because hearing the conviction didn't make me feel as tense as waiting for the sentence.

But there it was. Judge Darrow did determine that James Ray would go to jail. I looked up from my screen, looked around at the electricians, like they would be able to share my relief with me. They continued drilling and measuring.

Concurrent sentences, though. He would only go to jail for less than two years. Three lives. Two years.

Later, I heard an interview that my brother did with Fox News following the sentencing: "In terms of the sentencing, like a lot of things with this whole ridiculous ordeal, it's a little bit bittersweet. You know, we find a little bit of comfort in the fact that James Ray is going to be held accountable on some level and he is going to see the inside of a jail cell today, but at the same time, you know, we've been serving a two-year sentence already just to, just to get to this point."

James Ray would get two years. Kirby, James Shore, and Liz Neuman got life. Is that justice?

Part IV:
Aftermath

.

Chapter 9

" I know my true self.
I know my true power.
I am a Spiritual Warrior! "

—Kirby's Vision Quest Journal

Ginny

Leaving Arizona in November 2011, I felt relief. Ray is in prison, people will be spared his recklessness, his deceit, his hubris. I now felt I could turn my attention to the organization we had created in 2010, SEEK: Self-Empowerment through Education and Knowledge, a 501(c)(3) not-for-profit organization.

The decision to start SEEK Safely Inc. was made by all of us, as a family. However, I recognize that I am the spokesperson. I do more of the "talking." In granting numerous interviews for TV and printed articles, while I am struggling to sound like a rational person, my strong, talented, insightful husband is often emotionally overwhelmed, unable to speak when asked to talk about what happened.

We had frequent conference calls as a family following the tragedy and throughout 2010. Initially, they were a kind of an extension of George's check-ins, helping us to share how we were feeling, information about the investigation and upcoming trial, and eventually—with input from a few select friends—the purpose and goals of this organization. In discussing what had happened, we kept returning to what we had learned about the self-help industry. We wanted to warn people about potential harm because we now realize that there were no licenses, certifications, laws, policies, procedures, or regulations for the operation of this type of self-help event. One cannot go to an expensive retreat and assume that there is a risk management plan or medical support in the event of an accident. So SEEK was created with a threefold mission:

- **Educate the public** about the self-help industry
- **Empower consumers** to be safe when seeking to improve their lives
- **Promote ethics and safety** in this unregulated industry.

By the end of 2012, I left my fulltime job and was focusing on SEEK: researching, writing for the website, seeksafely.org, and trying to connect with others concerned about the self-help industry. From those researching or working within this industry, we have learned that people are scammed, shamed, and harmed emotionally, financially and physically, without proper recourse for their losses. Victims do not come forward due to embarrassment, guilt, and shame. We have heard that when some victims complain, they are silenced and told this was their personal failure or are "paid off" if legal action is threatened. Sedona was not an anomaly, not an isolated incident.

We created a promise for self-help providers to sign—a public statement of intent to practice in an ethical and safe manner. However, it is always up to the individual to assess their experience, so we created red flags to enable consumers to educate and heighten awareness. We are pursuing consumer protection legislation in New York State. As stories emerge of scams with outrageous claims of instant change or of self-help programs turning into abusive cults, SEEK responds, encouraging people to pay attention, to be aware and wary.

Many would write about what happened in Sedona on October 8, 2009. Shawna Bowen, a witness to the tragedy, wrote, *Never Again: The True Story of Tragedy, Betrayal & Healing within the Self Help Industry* in 2011 from the perspective of a student and a teacher in the personal growth field. The Hamiltons' book, *Transformation at Angel Valley: A Journey of Integrating the Sedona Sweat Lodge Tragedy* was published in 2012, giving voice to the life-altering experience that took place on their ranch.

The first book I read about Sedona was published in 2010. Connie Joy authored *Tragedy in Sedona: My Life in James Ray's Inner Circle*. Connie and her husband, Richard, attended twenty-seven James Ray seminars and events over a two-year period and spent close to $200,000 on his teaching, guidance, wisdom. Her book details what she learned at his events and also the disturbing changes they observed as Ray became more popular after appearing on Oprah and *Larry King Live*. She wrote her account to expose the dilemma of separating the message from the messenger. They had become disillusioned by his growing recklessness and aggressive behavior.

Her account of her own personal growth gives testimony to Ray's charisma. However, she knew in 2007 that the sweat lodge activity was too extreme. She wrote, "After experiencing a James Ray sweat lodge two years earlier, I knew his version of this ancient ritual was an accident waiting to happen." She voiced her concerns to JRI in an email in October of 2007.

I do not know how I received the book, but I read it before the trial in 2011. In the chapter that dealt with the tragedy in Sedona, the details of the two and a half hour "ceremony" were incredibly distressing, but it did prepare me for the testimony I would hear during the trial.

As I read her book, I kept thinking, "You knew. You knew this was dangerous. If we had had that information, would Kirby have gone or stayed in the lodge?" When I saw Connie

Joy at the trial, I was angry and realized I could not speak to her when she approached me, thinking, "You knew. You knew, you spoke too late!"

After the trial, I read the book again and realized she had tried to warn others. Writing that book was a courageous act to explain how James Ray had corrupted himself and his basic teachings. It helped to explain how something so awful and bizarre could happen to strong intelligent people. Connie and I have since become friends, and she and her husband hosted a SEEK Safely summit in San Diego in 2015. She gave me books to sell, donating all the proceeds to SEEK Safely. This sad, horrible story will connect us forever. I think of Connie in my determination to warn seekers to be aware, knowing what we now know about the industry.

CNN Documentary: *Enlighten Us*, 2016

In April 2016, the CNN documentary *Enlighten Us: The Rise and Fall of James Arthur Ray* aired at the Tribeca Film Festival in New York City.

George and I decided that we should go to the opening. I tried, unsuccessfully, to get tickets to the opening and called the director who I had met in May 2015, to see if she would be able to help me. When I never heard from her, I purchased tickets for the next day's viewing. Knowing three of the women who were featured in the film were going to attend the opening, I made plans to meet with them on Saturday. I was excited and anxious to see how this story was going to be told.

Fortunately, we were sent the reviewer's link for the film ahead of the screening. I am so grateful that we had warning about the content. Sitting in my home office, we watched in disbelief as the film concentrated on Ray, his pain, humiliation, suffering, and resurrection back into the self-help arena. There was little mention of the victims of this tragedy and no mention of SEEK. From our perspective, it served as an infomercial for Ray's comeback.

Kirby's friend Deborah Goldstein offered us her apartment in the city, and we arrived there on the afternoon of April 15 for the opening night. Sitting in a corner coffee shop, we sipped coffee and shared a piece of cheesecake, unable to stomach real food, before standing in front of the theater. Resolved to distribute a simple handout, directing people to read the "whole story" on our website, my heels clicked the pavement as we approached the theater. Standing alone on the sidewalk, I cautiously approached people milling about in front of the theater, feeling overwhelmed at our exclusion from this story which had changed our lives. Summoning every ounce of strength and swallowing my pride, I took all my energy and walked up to strangers with information that made my private pain public. I again had that feeling of total unreality. How did we get here? I wanted to be heard and respected, not seen as some crazed, grieving mother.

Ray's social media seemed to indicate that he was going to New York City to see "his" documentary. Our son, Bobby, originally planned to be present to provide some support. However, after he called the director's office and was assured that Ray would not be there, he decided not to come. I did not see Ray arrive at the theater but learned later that his picture was taken on the red carpet that night and he was present at the opening night party following the premiere. While I spoke to festivalgoers at the main doors of the theater, George was watching from the curb. He would not leave me alone in front of the theater, but with Parkinson's, moving through the crowd, speaking, controlling his tremors relegated him to the sidelines. Both of us were locked out of the inner circle of this event.

On Saturday, we met with Brandie Amstel, Julie Minn—

Kirby's roommate who had stayed with her things—and Laura Tucker, the three women featured in the film who had attended the opening viewing. They were relieved that the film portrayed them as intelligent seekers of personal and professional development, instead of cult members. However, they expected the film to reveal more about their personal growth after surviving the tragedy in Sedona. I think they had anticipated that their current professional ventures might have received some promotion rather than the film's sole concentration on Ray's reinvention of himself. Over lunch, there were tears, some shared memories of the trial, and expressions of sympathy for our loss.

After lunch, we headed to the Bow Tie Cinema for the 3:45 pm viewing. Sitting in the theater, watching the documentary, we saw the man responsible for our daughter's death giving a presentation on screen and crying on stage about losing his good friends.

I wanted to vomit. Listening to him say, "Sedona had to happen so that I could teach others how to overcome adversity" caused an internal explosion of rage. I knew I had to say something publicly at the end of the film when Jenny Carchman, the director and the producer, did a Q&A. I felt betrayed by the director, angered at the sympathetic treatment of Ray, and outraged that the victims were barely mentioned. Nervously, I stood up and identified myself and my husband. I can hardly remember exactly what I said, but I know I tried to convey the message that, though technically well done, the documentary left out copious, relevant, important pieces of information. I explained our organization and invited viewers to get the whole story on our website.

As people approached us after the viewing, I was so emotional that George started to usher me out of the theater. I felt a paralyzing exhaustion. With astonishing clarity, I knew the story of Sedona would never really release me. There will be books, re-enactments, interviews, coverage of this tragedy, because it never should have happened. I knew SEEK needed to exist to bring some balance to the revisionist version of the events of that week in October 2009. This documentary gave Ray a forum to explain what HE had learned from this tragedy—specifically, that HE can rise above adversity, unfairness, and victimization. We have learned that this problem is much bigger than James Ray. And the solution is much bigger than us. We have learned that while our grief over the loss of Kirby is always with us, it seems the circumstances of her death will also shadow us forever.

Motion to Set Aside his Conviction of Guilt, 2017

In January 2017, James Ray entered a motion in Yavapai County Court to set aside his conviction of guilt. All the victims were invited to the hearing to explain our position on Ray's request.

The public nature of this tragedy carries its own hurt and trauma. We knew from the beginning that this story needed to be made as public as possible. We also knew that the other two families were not anxious to speak publicly of their pain and outrage. James Shore's wife needed to protect her family and would not release any pictures of the three children who were now fatherless. For James' mother, Jane, a beautiful person and forever friend, this was her second son that had suffered an unexpected, traumatic death. She testified at the motion hearing that, unlike her first son's death, James' death was not an accident. It was preventable and actually facilitated by the actions of the man leading the retreat. James Shore had tried to get out of going to Sedona but was threatened by JRI that the no refund policy prevented any return of his monies and he might as well go to Arizona, despite his hesitancy.

Liz Neuman's children were young adults, starting their adult lives. Liz's daughter Andrea did some amazing interviews when the story broke. Andrea's statement of protest to this motion was read and written into the record of the proceedings.

When we learned that Jane and her daughter Virginia would be at the hearing, we planned to stay at the same hotel in Prescott and travel together to the courthouse in Camp Verde. Amrita, Alyssa's second daughter, called into the judge to explain how her father's death had affected their family. It was heartbreaking listening to her tearful testimony. I know Jane felt so proud of the bravery of her granddaughter.

All of us had met at various times during the trial, sharing our bewilderment at the bizarre nature of Ray's defense, knowing so much relevant information was being withheld from the jury. That sense of impotence was visceral. To sit in that courtroom or watch the proceedings on Court TV was maddening. We all felt physically restrained, our voices silenced.

Now, at this hearing, those old sensations of rage and disgust washed over me as I remembered all the motions for mistrial and the lawyers' attempts to blame the compromised and eventually traumatized victims of Sedona for not taking action to save the lives of Kirby, James, and Liz. We were here once again to watch the court struggle with the conflict of law versus justice, manipulation versus truth.

Now, five years later, James Ray wanted the court to set aside his conviction of guilt to facilitate the international expansion of his business—the business he is rebuilding by rewriting his personal history.

I was back on the plains, my voice disappearing, and that same sense of futility threatened to swallow me up in that courtroom. "Listen!" I screamed internally. "His narrative is *false*!"

We cannot allow him to publicly declare himself innocent of his actions, which caused the death of three people. He was the victim? No. He was the *architect* who made death inevitable due to his actions and inactions. Was he deliberately deceitful or simply delusional? Sociopathic or so blinded by his own declaration of omnipotence that he cannot see the reality of his own behaviors? Either way, he refuses to recognize his role in the deaths of three of his customers and that makes him dangerous. The judge restored Ray's civil right to vote but denied the motion to wipe out his record of guilt.

We shared a collective sigh of relief after the hearing over lunch with Sheila Polk and Ross Diskin, as well as news of life and family, reigniting forever connections. These are good people who upheld us through the trial nightmare and worked so hard to provide justice. That evening, we shared a tapas meal with Jane and Virginia in Prescott. I know our children Kirby and James have brought us together—a great blessing, a balm to help soothe our sorrow.

Both families have supported SEEK and have been grateful for our efforts to bring a positive purpose to these three deaths. We have tried to be sensitive and protective of their privacy.

Thirty-six hours later, as we returned to Phoenix, the sun was lighting the sky once again as it rose. The mountains were awash in pink and peach, reminding me that the sun always follows the dark of night. We have prevailed; the motion to set aside guilt was not granted, this time, leaving us to battle another day.

Public Death

The publicity from *Dateline*'s "Deadly Retreat," the *20/20* coverage with Dan Harris, and the Investigation Discovery Network show *Deadly Devotion*, which was filmed at our home in January 2013, has given our story international legs. Though our impact seems small, I have received emails from people from as far away as Calcutta, Brazil, Germany, and Australia.

In telling Kirby's story, our hope is that her life will inspire others to seek growth and adventure and her death will warn people to seek with open eyes as well as open hearts. I believe it is our human condition to desire growth and people will always seek personal, spiritual, and professional guidance to become more or to solve problematic challenges. While there are many wonderful, inspirational teachers, charismatic charlatans are also dispensing advice without proper training or knowledge.

The "metaphysical" explanation for Sedona, and life in general, has always been challenging for me. I do not condemn those who take a metaphysical, new-age approach to understanding what happened in Sedona, but I do not agree with their conclusions.

The Hamiltons' book, *Transformation at Angel Valley*, highlights our profound differences surrounding the events in Sedona. While I do not agree with all their beliefs or approach, I believe they are truly well-intentioned, good, gentle, peace-seeking people. The differences revolve around our understanding of divine intervention and the refusal to say the word "blame," because they believe whatever happens was meant to happen. All are players, instruments in the inevitable, being given an experience to encourage personal growth.

Cynthia Williams, the channeler the Hamiltons invited to Angel Valley on Friday October 9, was to provide comfort and healing for those still at the ranch. In their book, some of the messages provided through the Archangel Michael explain Kirby and James' deaths:

It is a week of transformation. The two blessed souls that passed did so as part of their earthly journey because it was their gate time to exit the planet. They had a choice always…. They had completed this leg of their mission here on earth and they chose to go. …They [Kirby and James] were looking to transform to the next level. The exiting provided their next level of growth… once they were free and realized that what had happened with all the commotion, they very much enjoyed the freedom of being without the body. (pp.51–56)

In their account, the channeler explained that whatever happens in our lives provides us with an opportunity to learn. Archangel Michael spoke and said:

Some lessons come a little more painfully than others. Nevertheless, these are lessons. Do pray for them [all those affected by this event]! Hold them within your heart! Love them! But understand that there is a bigger picture that is served. The lessons that have been learned through this are multilevel. No victims here, only choices on how to learn one's lessons. (p.53)

The full message from the Archangel Michael takes twelve pages in the Hamiltons' book. This is a different perspective on the process of dying. In helping the survivors, it is intended to explain and encourage dealing with this trauma with love and compassion for ourselves and others. Our actions and our spiritual beliefs should help direct our reactions to a loving outcome. However, I believe that, in Sedona, deaths occurred because one person had become corrupted in his own pursuit of money, fame, power. He may have helped others, he may have a gift for intuiting the needs of others, but in this situation, he was arrogant and reckless. He acted cowardly and was, in fact, "harmonically bankrupt" (to use his own phrase for personal integration).

This may be semantics; however, I become concerned when language is used to twist facts. The Sedona tragedy could have been prevented. I have never consulted a "channeler," but I cannot accept that Kirby and James Shore "chose" not to return to their bodies. Does that mean they chose to die or that Ray created an environment that caused their bodies to stop functioning, so their spirits were outside this physical world and could not return? If those seeking a metaphysical reason find the latter explanation more palatable, then I contend it is still "manslaughter."

Looking at these events as an "inevitable" part of a "cosmic design," "a challenge from beyond for everyone's spiritual growth," minimizes and demeans a catastrophic loss that defies description. We are left without the persons who illuminated and enriched countless lives.

When tragedy strikes, when illness or unexpected death appear in our lives, we are challenged to respond in a manner that will facilitate learning and growth. I have seen it stated as, "We can become bitter or better." I do not believe pain and challenges are sent by God or the universe, but that spiritual forces walk with us through the difficulties we encounter in life.

I am wary of "spiritual experiences" that do not impact behavior. I have had many experiences that I would regard as "divine inspiration" or "revelation"—a moment of profound clarity, an experience of overwhelming joy, a deep sense of peace and wellbeing, being enveloped in gratitude, an overwhelming sense of oneness with others. For me, the value of such experiences is that they teach me and challenge me to expand my sight, my heart, to be "more" in my life.

I know I need spiritual teachers, scripture, religious practice, times of quiet reflection, and mindfulness to have spirituality impact how I live my life. These external resources are a guide to my inner growth. We all seek and

find our "higher power" in many ways, using many philosophies and various paths. In today's world, many people have
found established religions or more conventional, time-tested
approaches to be personally disappointing or even hurtful. It
is understandable that many seekers look to alternatives as a
spiritual guide in their lives.

I understand "religion" to be a set of attitudes, beliefs,
and practices that are both privately and publicly proclaimed
with others to enrich the life of the believer, while encouraging behavior that will enhance the community. As a Catholic,
I cannot prove everything I chose to believe. My beliefs make
sense to me and, therefore, I sometimes choose to make a leap
of faith. How do you measure the effectiveness of something
based on faith? For me, my "proof" in the value of my belief
system comes from how it has enabled me to live my life. I
believe my Catholicism informs and supports my spiritual
growth. So I think our spiritual belief systems, whatever they
may be, should be evidenced in how we live our lives.

SEEK encourages everyone to ask: What are you looking
for? Who are you listening to? What are you choosing to believe?
Is this experience helping me to be a contributor in this world?
Is this helping me to live more richly, with greater compassion,
love, insight, and satisfaction?

It is our hope that this book can offer some perspective on a
very dramatic example of a possibly well-intentioned, self-proclaimed guru, who was corrupted by his own arrogant hubris.
It is a confusing story of seeking growth and taking risks, while
trusting in the good will and protection of the leader. We have
learned that we have a responsibility to share Kirby's story with
others, to warn them of the dangers in this unregulated self-
help industry, while still encouraging personal and professional
growth. Seeking is good and must be done with an open heart
as well as open eyes.

FINAL WORDS

When we lived in Brooklyn and our children were nine, five, and three, I remember watching them play in our backyard one day. The morning light filtered through the large oak tree, covering the kids in dappled sunlight, their laughter and delight filling the air. I wanted that moment to last forever. That feeling of contentment, that all-consuming love for our children, our life, was so delicious. That moment and others like it are catalogued in my brain like sparkling pictures to be taken out and examined on rainy days. For the most part, I used to always feel grateful and basically satisfied with my life, despite ups and down, challenges and difficulties. Some days, since 2009, I wonder: Will I ever feel that kind of pleasureful satisfaction again? Is it possible to feel that when a huge part of my heart is shattered? A friend reminded me that maybe it is a different kind of contentment that I need to find.

In December of 2012, I read *The Shoemaker's Wife* by Adriana Trigiani. A particular quote captures my feelings. The main character, Ciro, says to Enza following the death of Enza's sister's, "You shouldn't blame yourself. ...Maybe you shouldn't blame anyone but accept that this is your sister's story and the ending belongs to her."

Enzo replies, "I never want to forget her" to which Ciro responds:

When you lose someone, they take a bigger place in your heart, not a smaller one. Every day it grows, because you don't stop loving them. You wish you could talk to them. You need their advice. But life doesn't always give us what we need, and it's difficult. It is for me, anyway.

After my father died in 2003, my mom struggled for five

years. The last few years, she needed someone living in the house with her and we arranged for 24/7 care. My siblings and I took turns spending weekends in Sag Harbor so her caregiver could have the weekend free. Whenever it was my turn, my mom would ask me to clean out a closet, a drawer, or organize pictures. She always seemed a bit frantic, looking for something. One day, it occurred to me that no matter how much cleaning, organizing, or purging we would do, she would still not find my father. I gently remarked that Dad was not lost, he was simply no longer here. He was gone, forever in our memory, but no longer physically present. As I said this, the tears slid quietly across her cheeks. In reflecting on my mom, it occurs to me that when a huge life-changing loss hits our life, our innermost spirit responds almost automatically. Just as I believe my mom was looking for Dad almost unconsciously, I feel consciously driven to bring Kirby into the world, because she is no longer here. And I am passionately striving to right a wrong, to bring something positive from such a searing negative. Maybe it is not all up to me. Maybe Kirby will make herself known in those "postcards from beyond", in the rich memories of those who loved her. Maybe, because this is her story, she knows how to have her presence felt. And maybe, just maybe, SEEK has done what I needed it to do. Maybe, I have to let a new contentment seep in, knowing I have done what I could and leaving the rest up to her.

Chapter 10

" In my heart I am overwhelmed with compassion... for the earth, for all people, all animals, every tree and rock and river.... In my heart I have the capacity and joy of forgiveness. Most importantly, I forgive myself. "

—Kirby's Vision Quest Journal

Jean

January 11, 2018

I was sitting in the Sunnybrook Hospital waiting room for family members of patients in surgery. My husband was having a delicate procedure to remove some decades-old scar tissue. It was to take about six hours. I sat in the molded plastic chair, my computer asleep in my bag on the floor at my feet, but rather than working, I was on my phone browsing Instagram. That's when I saw James Ray's post. He was holding yet another event: this one was a weekend in Las Vegas where participants would be working out with James himself—a special opportunity to get training from him. They would eat with him, gaining valuable nutrition information, and receive some of his sacred wisdom about overcoming adversity. That's his new shtick. And it always stabs me because I know the "adversity" he's talking about is that he killed my sister and didn't just get away with it.

He had tagged the photo's location with his participants at a gym. Do these people even know, I wondered, that he's not a trainer? He's not a nutritionist? And then I thought, does the gym know?

That some unqualified guy is charging people money to follow him and get fitness advice in their venue, putting the gym at risk for his irresponsibility?

So I called them. I called three of the gym locations in Las Vegas. I stepped out into the hallway. I held the phone to my head, my fingertips absorbing the heat of the adrenaline that always radiates from my cheeks when I'm doing something like this. I can't remember how I realized which was the right gym, but somehow, I did.

"Hi," I said to the employee who answered. "So, this is weird, but there's a guy using your gym this weekend with a group of people paying him for a seminar sort of event and I think you should be concerned about this happening at your establishment."

"Um, okay.... What is his name?" The employee sounded young or maybe he was just bewildered. I pictured him in his athletic uniform with a name tag stating his favorite fitness class.

I eventually asked to speak with a manager. I explained that I didn't really have a clear expectation for how they should act, but that I felt they needed to know this.

"Listen, I know about this man because my sister went to one of his events and she died there, along with two other people. Ray went to jail for it for two years. You can look it up. I just thought you should know that this was happening. I felt like I should tell you."

And that was it. I have no idea if they took any action or spoke with Ray. I looked for hints from his social media to see if there was any mention of being harassed by "those crazy sweat lodge people" as he'd once referred to us during a court deposition, but there was nothing. Perhaps he'd realized that personal attacks on the families of the victims were a losing strategy (he'd made a hurtful comment in a CNN interview around the time of the *Enlighten Us* premiere, suggesting that Kirby was estranged from her family—our family. I responded immediately with a video "letter" to Ray, asking him to leave my family alone). Or maybe the gym did nothing. But at least I had tried.

Aside from the endlessness of the legal aspect of our story—future motions to set aside his guilt, calling for yet another impact statement, or maybe even future trials after he hurts someone else—there's an endlessness to this pain because James Ray has continued to operate in the self-improvement, self-help world. He continues to hold days-long events, he continues to lead people in areas where he's not qualified, he continues to use questionable physical techniques at his events. He continues.

There is a part of me that wants to shut it out, just as I couldn't follow every detail of the trial. It's overwhelming and I have a life of my own, a family, and a responsibility to them and myself not to be mad all the time. On the other hand, I don't know that I'd forgive myself if another person got hurt and I knew that this dangerous person was continuing.

So then I wonder, what does this mean about forgiveness in the larger sense? Have I forgiven James Ray when I can't turn my back on his continuing? Having grown up Catholic, though I've fallen away from the Church in recent years, forgiveness holds much weight. It's pretty much the ultimate thing for Catholics. And, even aside from religious traditions, science-based understandings of our emotional health emphasize the importance of forgiving and releasing that hold on the negativity that comes with not forgiving.

So have I forgiven James Ray?

To be honest, I'm not completely sure and I allow myself to not fully answer that question. Forgiving someone who's wronged me in such a profound way may be an unrealistic expectation. But here's what I've come to at this point:

If forgiveness is simply a process of allowing that a person can continue to exist after the transgression, then I have forgiven James Ray. He served his time and I respect that. I don't wish him harm or a horrible existence. I am confident that if he is a feeling person, the burden of his actions will weigh on him forever, no matter what he says.

But if forgiveness is about never again feeling—never again feeling the anger, the hurt, even the rage that emerges about what happened to Kirby—then no. I am not there. And part of that, I know, is because James Ray continues and does not assume meaningful responsibility.

He claims to take responsibility. But I don't accept that while he continues working in the self-improvement field. If he had truly taken responsibility, he would recognize how profoundly he failed as a teacher—he was so profound a failure that his students died. Four of them! Obviously, he was doing something so wrong he should understand he is unqualified for this work. Instead, he continues, without bothering to learn more or gain more skills as a coach/teacher/guru/ speaker that would ensure he won't endanger the physical or emotional health of future customers. It would be easier to let James Ray be if he found a new line of work. Sales. Real estate, maybe.

And what's more is that rather than claiming this sort of meaningful responsibility, he instead claims the pain of these losses of life as his own. He claims the tragedy as something that happened to him, rather than something he orchestrated. When I think about that, I am angry, absolutely.

What I see now is that, like grief, forgiveness is not a one-time deal. It's not a transaction to conduct and complete, like buying a car and driving off the lot. It's a continual effort. Something we must confront again and again, every time the pain resurfaces. Every time I see James Ray holding another event, another speaking engagement, discussing a forthcoming book—every time, I have to face this question of forgiveness again.

But, for me, that is where I come back to Kirby. It's not about Ray, exactly. It's about accepting my own level of responsibility to hold James Ray accountable where he has not held himself accountable. If he will continue with this delusion of his "important work," that he must "guide and teach" people while disregarding their emotional and physical safety, I will continue to challenge that. Because Kirby would. And because I don't want another person like Kirby to die.

I am not an angry person. I am not obsessed with James Ray or his activities. But we are forever connected now and his actions tend to follow me. When I come across information about his activities in the self-help industry, it brings back feelings—maybe anger. I am okay with that, though, because even anger is an emotion that points to the need for something to be done. Something needs to change. It can't all just continue as it did before Kirby died.

Furthermore, the story of what happened to Kirby and the others is much larger than James Ray. The self-help industry (you may also come across names like "self-improvement" or "self-optimization," even "self-care", to describe the undefined industry) is huge. One figure has it at about a $10 billion per year industry in the US alone. While some people dismiss James Ray and the Spiritual Warrior deaths as part of some weird "new-agey" stuff, the fact is this industry is mainstream and it's all around us—in our entertainment, the books we read, podcasts, all over social media.

The problem that James Ray showed us is that there is no professional cohesion to this industry. There's no governing body setting industry standards and best practices or licensing professionals (and, conversely, revoking licenses when a professional acts dangerously or unprofessionally). This is why James Ray can make a comeback even after four of his customers died in his care.

How does a consumer make safe choices about a book to buy, a program to buy, or a seminar to attend? We make a lot of assumptions about professionality in our society. For example, have you ever asked a medical professional to see their license or credentials? Probably never. Most of us assume that the person with M.D. on the nameplate above the door is qualified. In the self-help realm, we assume that the speaker who gets vetted by the mainstream media, whose books are on the shelves in the bookstore, whose posts are being shared by our friends, deserves to be there. But that assumption is a dangerous one.

During one of our nightly check-ins in the first week after Kirby died, we discussed how we all wanted to honor Kirby—what we would do to commemorate her. It was just not okay to let her die and I suppose we all instinctively felt that we had to keep her influence in the world alive.

"What about a foundation to fund horse riding lessons for kids in Mexico?" my cousin Tommy had suggested. I loved this idea. It felt very Kirby; it felt so lovely.

But I think we all also felt that there was serious work to do. The injustice of Kirby's death was so plain even at that point, that we knew Kirby's legacy needed to be more aggressive. Lovely wasn't going to cut it. Death had changed Kirby and her legacy would have to reflect that. This was the genesis of SEEK—the week after she died.

This is why we created SEEK Safely. We believe that many of millions of people consuming this self-help material are like Kirby: driven and open-minded. Kirby was willing to look to novel and even sometimes "out there" means to find the next steps for herself in her life, a life that was, by choice, outside of the box. And yet, she was still a practical, discerning, and grounded person.

It's this combination of openness and practicality that makes me certain she would have been outraged and speaking out, like Beverley, about how negligent Ray was if she had survived the Spiritual Warrior week.

What we've learned about the self-help industry since her death feels too important to keep to ourselves. This story goes beyond our private grief. This is why we haven't simply moved on without sharing our experiences. This is why we don't simply let it go. So if it's calling a gym in Las Vegas, writing a blog post for SEEK, advocating for legislation to regulate the self-help industry, or writing this book, we do it.

Positivity and joy can be elusive when sadness grips your heart so tightly that your face must follow, and the tears squeeze out unbid-

den. But I do find this happens less when I can direct that energy into something purposeful. Kirby was a force. People like that don't just die without their loss reverberating. We share that echo, because we know it's too valuable to keep to ourselves. Her experience, her spirit, her words—we have to share them.

> **" Flow like this elegant river. Be liquid gently caressing the mighty boulders in the middle of this stream. As you flow over these great rocks and boulders, create a lovely, rhythmic music that is oh so pleasant for all to hear. Let your joy flow over and love.**
>
> **There is a reason for every boulder to go over or around. Do it gently and happily, be grateful, and give thanks....**
>
> **It all has a purpose. In that open space in the river, this is your time to be still and quiet but keep flowing slowly.**
>
> **Just around the bend there will be more boulders and it will be your time to sing again gently, elegantly caressing the rocks as you ramble on through. Enjoy these twists and turns. Ramble on, baby, ramble. "**
>
> —*Kirby's Vision Quest Journal*

Photos

Kirby and Kate, Christmas 1976

*Kirby on the top of Cadillac
Mountain greeting the sunrise, 1981*

*Kirby riding her horse,
Happy Dot, 1988*

Kirby swimming with a dolphin, 2003

Kirby, Ginny, and Kate, in Baja, 2003

Brown family at George's 60th birthday party at the Brown's house in Westtown, NY, 2004

Kirby, Bob, Kory, Jean, Kate, at Bobby and Kory's rehearsal dinner, 2005

Kirby and Jean on Koh Samui, Thailand, 2005

*George, Kate, Kirby, Ginny, and cousin Stuart, at the Hotel
California in Todos Santos, 2006*

*Kirby's riding club on Gringo
Hill, 2007*   *Kirby with her dog,
Tuffy, 2008*

Kate and Kirby at the Eagle's Nest on the Delaware River, summer 2009

Kirby and George at the Brown's house, March 2009

Brown Family at Jean's wedding, July 2009

Kirby dancing with cousin, Geremy, at Jean's wedding, July 2009

Kirby in her beloved Baja

Kirby working with her decorative painting partner, Nancy Brazil, in Cabo

The paddle out for Kirby's memorial in San Jose del Cabo, January 2010

Kirby's nieces and nephews at a family vacation on Long Island, NY, 2016

*The Brown family, celebrating George and Ginny's 50th Wedding
Anniversary, July 2019*

Acknowledgments

Family and Friends

Looking back over the last 10 years, this would not have been our story without the help and support of family and friends who immediately surrounded us with prayers, love, presence, food and flowers in those early days. We are blessed to have the love and support of an amazing family. Our gratitude to: Kay and Al, who showed up immediately to keep the household from collapsing; their lawyer son, Bob, who appeared on day one; Tommy McFeeley, my nephew who was instrumental in managing the media frenzy; and the rest of our incredible siblings and extended family of Browns and Kirbys (my maiden name) who have grieved their loss as well as ours and never lost faith in our mission to bring a positive purpose to Kirby's death: Mary, Anne and Gary, Bill and Jerelyn, Kay and Al, Joan, Joe and Tina, Tony and Gail, Frank and Belinda, Stuart, all our nieces and nephews who have mourned their "action figure cousin".

Our love as well to our many friends who have supplied us with unending support: Liz and Eddie Holst, who made phone calls and coordinated details for Kirby's funeral and reception; Debbie and Mike; Fran and Mark; Eileen and Bill; Gary and Carol; MaryEllen and Gary; Sue and Lou; Maria; and members of the Westtown Presbyterian, Holy Name, and Holy Cross Catholic Churches. A huge thank you and all-embracing hug to Beverly Bunn for her compassion and bravery.

Book Edits, Help

We would never have been able to write our story without the guidance and encouragement of my brother Frank, with whom we conferenced every Wednesday night for over a year as we wrote and revised. Friends who read our initial drafts provided invaluable suggestions. We are indebted to: Erin Carrington Smith (who was clearly an editor in a previous life), Bob and Barbara Driscoll, Sarah Hock, Deborah Goldstein, Jeanette Reid, Chelsea Kirkby, Sandra Pribanic, Rowenna Miller, and Helen Vozinidis.

Our first formal edit by Maeve O'Connell gave us a cleaner structure, a smoother read, and really helped bring Kirby's voice into the book. We also thank our publisher, Cheryl Benton of The Three Tomatoes, whose belief in us and encouragement has allowed us to share our story.

SEEK Board

Profound gratitude to our SEEK Safely Board members: Bernie Cassidy, who manages our finances; Bob Magninini whose firm, Stone & Magnanini, has provided legal advice and support; Tony Kirby, who has been working tenaciously to advance our legislative initiative in NYS; Deborah Goldstein, whose creative suggestions and great connections have advanced our mission; Dr. Glenn Doyle, whose prolific writing and insightful input has expanded our reach and enhanced our effectiveness. Thanks to friends who have helped our annual fundraiser, and our loyal supporters who have kept us operational.

During the Trial

For guiding us through the complicated maze of the trial, we thank: the prosecution and support team in Yavapai County–Sheila Polk, Bob Hughes, Ross Diskin, Pam Moreton and their staffs–who worked incredibly hard during the months of the trial but also showered us with loving compassion; our lawyer in Arizona, Mike Murphy and his wife Lucia, who offered us the generous hospitality of their home during the trial, making that trauma more bearable.

Thank you to the Native American people who were present daily during the trial to represent the nations who were also victimized by the appropriation of their sacred rituals, namely Ivan Lewis and Zhenya Rice.

We are also profoundly grateful to all our family and friends who were part of the "trial watch," traveling to Arizona to give witness to those affected by Kirby's death: Mika and Bobby Cutler, Billy Dahly, Lisa Brusseau, Deborah and Stan Goldstein, Michael Kohler, and many others.

And finally, thank you to Jane Gripp, Alyssa Shore, Virginia Shore and the rest of the Shore family; Andrea Puckett, Brian Neuman, Lilly Clark and the rest of the Neuman family; with whom we share this tragic loss and have become forever friends.

Immediate Family

To our amazing children, Kate, Bob and Jean, this is our story as a family losing your oldest sibling. You have conducted yourselves with dignity and grace throughout our shared grief and trauma. The loss of Kirby has affected each of your lives differently yet each of you have found ways to honor your sister and support Dad and me in our sorrow. Our grandchildren, three who met Kirby and four who will only know her through our stories, have given us the reason to continue to live with joy and gratitude.

In sickness and health, joy and sorrow, to my love, George

Brown who held me up in those first two years and has steadily supported me to be Kirby's voice–thank you.

—Virginia (Ginny) Brown

In addition to everyone mentioned above, I also want to thank my in-laws, the Allisons, for all of the ways they supported me through this difficult time in my life. Thanks to Linden and Machrie, for finding ways to do without Mama while I wrote and worked. And to my husband, Mike, thank you for your continued encouragement, careful concern, and love.

—Jean Brown

All proceeds from the book will benefit Seek Safely, Inc., a 501C3 non-profit. www.seeksafely.org

About the Authors

Virginia Brown, LCSW, is a wife and mother of 4, "Mema" to 7 grandchildren. She conducts a private mental health practice in Westtown, New York and has provided training and clinical support as a Family Life Educator in the Tri-State Area (NY, NJ, CT).

Following the death of her daughter at a self-help retreat in 2009, the family founded **SEEK Safely, Inc.**, a 501©3 charity to educate the public about self-help and promote safe and ethical practices in the industry. As a result of the international coverage of this tragedy, she has been featured in numerous interviews and media productions in the US and UK.

Jean Brown, MPPPA, is a writer and work-from-home-mom to two young children. She has bachelor's degrees in political science and writing from Loyola University Maryland, and a Master's in Public Policy and Public Administration from Concordia University in Montreal. She is active in creating content for SEEK's website, social media, brand outreach, and legislative effort. Jean lived in Thailand and has travelled extensively, including treasured memories of travelling with Kirby. She now lives in Toronto, Canada, with her family.

Made in the USA
Las Vegas, NV
10 April 2023

70422898R00198